Artful Leadership

"The focus on theoretical frameworks, evolving paradigms, and practical strategies within leadership literature often neglects the less tangible elements of humanity within the individual and community that serve as the foundation for leadership practice. *Artful Leadership: Retreat, Recenter, and Rewild* employs a holistic leadership approach by inviting leaders to consider the importance of art and creativity in their own lives and experiences. *Artful Leadership* effectively explores this topic through diverse perspectives and modalities of expression, inviting the reader to consider how creativity and the interconnectedness of our world might transform their lives and leadership. Challenging and inspiring, this work enhances the conversation surrounding what it means to be a leader."

Christopher B. Beard, PhD, Director – EdD in
Organizational Leadership, Abilene Christian University

"As the world we live in seems to be more chaotic and unpredictable by the day, we need a voice that calls us to a more beautiful way amid the ugliness. In *Artful Leadership*, Dr Alicia Crumpton has given us a diversity of voices which invite us, both in theory and practice, on a journey toward an imaginative, courageous, and holistic way of living and leading in a world that is not as it was intended to be. May we heed the call."

Mark Nelson, Executive Director,
Three Rivers Collaborative

"It is far too common for good leaders to become tired from endless activities, deadlines, and expectations, all at risk of losing themselves in the process. This book arrives as a lifeline weaving together artistic approaches, mindful practices, and ecological wisdom. Contributors share perspectives and practices not found in the traditional leadership literature on why and how leaders should and can take time to be still to reorient their souls. Practical exercises move beyond theory to immediate application, practices to help you develop presence, spark imagination, and rediscover joy in your leadership role. The book invites leaders to better understand and attend to their humanity, which as the authors demonstrate, is core to good leadership."

John R. Shoup, PhD, Professor, Leadership Studies,
Dr Robert K. Jabs School of Business, California Baptist University

"Alicia Crumpton always does thoughtful, unique work with credible scholarship. Her unfailing judgment has provided the field of leadership studies with valuable perspectives, especially at the confluence of spirituality and art. This volume gathers overdue voices on overdue themes, importing into the literature more of the humanities and the creative arts. Leadership is ultimately a performance and thus more of an art than science. Scholars will read in these pages more of what is possible as we study this phenomenon, and practitioners can reimagine their calling, lifting them from the quotidian into the truly visionary. And while they are at it, maybe both groups can recover a neglected sense of fun."

Nathan Harter, **Christopher Newport University (emeritus)**

"Artful Leadership: Retreat, Recenter, and Rewild is a breathtakingly original and deeply needed contribution to the field of leadership studies. Edited by scholar, creative, and entrepreneur Alicia D. Crumpton, this interdisciplinary volume invites readers into a transformative journey – one that is not merely intellectual, but spiritual, creative, and embodied. In a world weary from disconnection, crisis, and over-reliance on mechanistic models of leadership, this book offers a healing alternative rooted in imagination, wholeness, and interconnection.

Divided into three thematic movements – Retreat, Recenter, Rewild – the book offers a graceful unfolding of leadership as a sacred practice. 'Retreat' invites leaders to turn inward, to cultivate silence and solitude as necessary conditions for wisdom. 'Recenter' explores how identity, creativity, and values come into alignment, while 'Rewild' dares us to recover our place within the larger ecology of life. Each chapter is accompanied by somatic, creative, and reflective practices that help readers integrate insights into lived experience.

Crumpton has assembled a remarkable group of contributors – scholars, poets, artists, spiritual directors, and educators – each bringing a unique lens to the question of what it means to lead in these uncertain times. From Charlotte Hardie's exploration of equine relationality to Julian Norris's systems leadership lessons drawn from wolves, the essays speak not just to the mind, but to the soul. Brendan Ellis Williams' closing chapter, a philosophical and spiritual tour de force, reframes leadership as a metaphysical act of rewilding – one that calls us back to relationality, wonder, and the sacredness of all being.

This book is not leadership theory as usual. It challenges readers to move beyond linear thinking, transactional strategies, and individualistic paradigms. It dares us to approach leadership as art, as poetry, as spiritual practice. Leaders are encouraged to embrace creativity, silence, awe, improvisation, narrative ethics, and the ecological self – not as optional extras, but as essential dimensions of leading well.

What makes *Artful Leadership* truly remarkable is its capacity to hold both depth and accessibility. The tone is invitational, not dogmatic. The practices are adaptable, not prescriptive. And the language throughout is infused with poetic clarity and theological resonance. Crumpton has curated not only a book, but a space – a sanctuary for reflection and renewal.

In a time when many are asking what leadership can look like on the other side of exhaustion and disillusionment, *Artful Leadership* provides a compelling vision. It reminds us that leading artfully is not about perfection or control, but about presence, authenticity, and deep participation in the unfolding story of life.

I wholeheartedly commend this book to leaders, educators, spiritual guides, and culture-shapers of all kinds. It is a gift, a guide, and a gentle revolution. If you are ready to lead not just more effectively, but more soulfully, let this book be your companion. I highly recommend it."

Gary David Stratton, PhD, Author of *The Jesus Climb: Journeying from Student to Disciple*. University Professor of Spiritual Formation and Cultural Leadership, Dean of the School of Arts and Sciences, Johnson University

"*Artful Leadership: Retreat, Recenter, and Rewild* is a must for everyone who cares about how the world should work – and wants to know why it does not. Rightly positioning leadership as an art, the book's three parts revision leaders as authentic, wise, compassionate, collaborative, spiritual, ecological, integrative, and transformational. Above all, *Artful Leadership* means relinquishing the ego of Western modernity and recovering the arts of being and knowing through creativity and imagination. In a brilliant exposition, the artful leader retreats to quest for inner truthfulness, recenters collectively through collaboration and the sacred, and rewilds so that human beings can come home to nature. This book is a supremely practical 'how to' with a vivid and accessible 'why to.' It will guide readers and leaders into the art of engaged, mindful, creative life. *Artful Leadership* demonstrates that humans find joy through the art of visioning the world as it ought to be."

***Susan Rowland*, Professor at Pacifica Graduate Institute**

"The ensemble of thinkers, creators, and leaders featured in *Artful Leadership* reveal the surprising affinities between leadership, the arts and humanities, and creative expression. We are only surprised because our ideas (and experiences) of leadership so often center on hierarchies, unquestioned assumptions, competition, and control rather than on collaboration, curiosity, creativity, and spontaneity. Each essay in this book illuminates, in its own way, the oftentimes ignored, yet vital role of an 'aesthetic sensibility' or a 'sincere cultural attunement' for cultivating genuinely innovative, effective – and most importantly, moral leadership. In fact, the entire notion of 'leadership' is examined and shown to be related in many ways to acts of creative expression; at their best, both are *offerings*, acts of *service* that transform our world."

Mary Antonia Wood, PhD, Chair, MA Depth Psychology and Creativity Program at Pacifica Graduate Institute, Santa Barbara, CA. Author of *The Archetypal Artist: Reimagining Creativity and the Call to Create*

Artful Leadership: Retreat, Recenter, and Rewild

EDITED BY

ALICIA D. CRUMPTON
Kaleidoventure LLC, USA

emerald
PUBLISHING

United Kingdom – North America – Japan – India – Malaysia – China

Emerald Publishing Limited
Emerald Publishing, Floor 5, Northspring, 21-23 Wellington Street, Leeds LS1 4DL.

First edition 2026

Reprints and permissions service
Contact: www.copyright.com

British Library Cataloguing in Publication Data
A catalogue record for this book is available from the British Library

ISBN: 978-1-80592-500-2 (Print)
ISBN: 978-1-80592-497-5 (Online)
ISBN: 978-1-80592-499-9 (Epub)

Contents

Part 3   Rewild

About the Editor

Alicia D. Crumpton is an organizational and leadership consultant, PhD student research coach, researcher, and writer. She designed and founded the PhD in Leadership Studies Program at Johnson University, has been a member of the International Leadership Association since 2005, and is Co-founder of the Philosophy, Religion, and Worldview Learning Community. She holds a PhD in Leadership Studies from Gonzaga University, a Master's degree in Engaged Humanities and the Creative Life with an emphasis in Depth Psychology from Pacifica Graduate Institute, and an MS in Information Science from the University of Michigan. She co-authored *Architecture and Leadership: The Nature and Role of Space and Place in Organizational Culture*, which is included in the Leadership and Humanities Series (Routledge, 2024). For fun, she travels the world to take pictures of street art and graffiti. She serves as the lead editor for this volume.

About the Contributors

Sarah Andreas is a mixed-media oil artist whose artwork explores themes of transformation, healing, and empowerment, deeply resonating with women navigating life transitions. She has extensive experience in business operations, sales, and training and is a public speaker, leadership development consultant, and researcher. She holds a Bachelor's degree in Business and Marketing, an MBA, and a PhD in Leadership Studies from Johnson University. An emerging scholar, her research and writing explore transformation, leadership development, and career advancement. Recent publications include *Exploration of Women's Leadership Development Challenges and Transformational Learning* (*Advancing Women in Leadership Journal*/2021), *Exploring Leadership Development Experiences* (dissertation/2019), and *Effects of the Decline in Social Capital on College Graduates' Soft Skills* (Industry and Higher Education/2018).

Carol Burbank is a scholar, writing coach, researcher, and educator exploring the narratives and fundamental paradigms that shape our identities, experiences, expectations, performances, and roles. Her work examines art as activism and social movements, examining patterns of social change and evolution. She currently teaches in the MA in Engaged Humanities at Pacifica Graduate Institute. She has a PhD from Northwestern University's Performance Studies Department and an MA in Creative Writing/English from Boston University. She is also trained in traditional Hawaiian culture and healing practices and combines transformative talk story and community-based healing (ho'oponopono) in her creative coaching and workshops. Her writing includes *Shapeshifter Leadership: Responding Creatively to the Challenges of a Complex World* (Jossey-Bass, 2012); *Malala Yousafzai: The Power and Paradox of Global Celebrity* (Berret Koehler, 2014); and *Artists as Leaders for Social Justice* (BLB Series, Emerald, 2020).

Kevin D. Collins is an independent researcher. As an artist, actor, musician, and activist, he's performed megapuppetry in skits, parades, street theater, and community theater for over 20 years. He has been involved for many years in hunger and disaster relief, prison reform, houselessness, voting rights, racial integrity, environmental and immigration issues, and nuclear weapons disarmament. An emerging scholar, he holds a PhD in Leadership Studies from Johnson University where, using arts-based methods and autoethnography, his dissertation explored "When Megapuppets March: Making Meaning Through Performing Creative Nonviolence" (2023). Other pertinent scholarship includes: "Reflections on the

Madre Diaries: A Fiction-Based Autobiography of Mourning and Resistance," a chapter in *Women Embodied Leaders: Peacebuilding, Protest, and Professions* (2024), and "Living the Vita: Performative Education Through Collaborative Autoethnographic Megapuppetry" (special issue of the *Canadian Journal for the Study of Adult Education*, 2024).

Bradley D. Davidson is an executive coach, spiritual director, writer, and musician who explores ideas and solutions to personal and leadership challenges from diverse disciplines and perspectives. He is a member of the International Coaching Federation, where he earned a Professional Certified Coach credential. He is also a member of Spiritual Directors International. He holds a PhD in Leadership Studies from Johnson University, an MS in Industrial and Organizational Psychology from Kansas State University, a Graduate Certificate in Executive and Professional Coaching from The University of Texas at Dallas, and a Certificate in Spiritual Direction from Southern Methodist University. As an emerging scholar, his writing has focused on purpose, meaning, and spirituality. His PhD dissertation was entitled, "Finding Chazown: The Role of Coaching in the Discernment of Calling" (2019).

Catherine Etmanski is Professor of Leadership at Royal Roads University in Victoria, Canada. She is passionate about social and environmental justice and seeks to incorporate creative elements into her research, leadership, teaching, and administration. She holds an MA in Community and International Development from the University of British Columbia and a PhD in Leadership from the University of Victoria. She has edited and contributed to books related to: *Learning and Teaching Community-Based Research* (University of Toronto Press, 2014), *Food Leadership: Leadership and Adult Learning in Global Food Systems Transformation* (Springer/2017), *The Dance of Joyful Leadership* (BLB Series, Jossey-Bass, 2014). She also co-edited a Special Issue of the Engaged Scholar Journal on *Engagement through the Arts* (2019).

Tracy Ferron is Founder and Board President of Life On Art, a nonprofit that combines community artmaking, creative arts therapies, social action, and large-scale public art exhibitions. He developed a platform to create large-scale art installations through participatory and therapeutic community processes with populations facing systemic injustices. Through the symbology of winged hearts and cages, his artworks have illuminated incarcerated rights at San Quentin Rehabilitation Center (2020) and voting rights at the Sacramento Women's March (2020). Large-scale installations at the Museum of Sonoma County explored medical experimentation on children (2018), the murder of global activists (2019), and celebration of loved ones for Día de los Muertos (2021, 2023, 2024). He produced Unbound (2021–2022), an 80-foot sculpture of hundreds of paper mâché winged hearts flying free from a cage in partnership with one of California's largest psychiatric facilities. Unbound won a first place award for Arts for Innovation by the National Organization for Arts in Health in 2022. He co-produced Visions of Hope (2024), a multi-media installation featuring the art of nearly 225 men and women incarcerated in California state prisons for the Marin County Civic Center. He holds a master's in Engaged Humanities and the Creative Life from Pacifica Graduate Institute.

Kathryn Goldman Schuyler is Professor Emeritus of Organization Development, where she taught courses in ethics, leadership, consulting for systems change, and sustainability. She has published widely on leadership and is the author of Inner *Peace – Global Impact* (IAP, 2012) and the lead editor of *Leading with Spirit, Presence, and Authenticity* (Jossey-Bass/Wiley, 2014) and *Creative Social Change: Leadership for a Healthy World* (Emerald, 2016). She earned her PhD at Columbia University (NY) as a sociologist. She has trained professionally in somatically grounded systems learning with Dr Moshe Feldenkrais and engaged Buddhist chaplaincy with Roshi Joan Halifax. Currently, she facilitates groups, bringing mindfulness and joy into everyday life.

Charlotte Hardie is an art, equine, and yoga educator in Charlotte, Vermont. She is passionate about animals, education, creativity, and the wild landscape. She makes art to understand her relationship to the world and to others. She celebrates expression, and encourages her students and herself to find voice and boldness in art. She holds a Master's degree in Engaged Humanities and the Creative Life with an emphasis in Depth Psychology from Pacifica Graduate Institute.

Aaron Monts is a scholar, writer, and executive director of a therapeutic, alternative high school. He believes that we are strengthened by and through constructive dialogue around the issues of faith and theology, justice and politics, and transparent yet gracious conversations about our shortcomings. Serving as a consultant, he serves internationally with leadership development, organizational change, and strategy formulation services. He holds an Executive Leadership Certificate from Harvard Kennedy School, a PhD in Leadership Studies from Johnson University, and an MA in Contemporary Theology and Philosophy. An emerging scholar, relevant scholarship includes his dissertation: Racial Narratives: A Sociohistorical Analysis of Michael Brown and Ferguson, Missouri and "Critical Race Theory: A Prophetic Voice for the Church and the Stone-Campbell Movement."

Julian Norris is an educator and guide who lives in the Treaty Seven territories of the Canadian Rockies. He is a Professor at the Haskayne School of Business, where he teaches courses in leadership, complexity, and sustainability, and is the founding director of the Wolf Willow Institute, a charitable foundation focused on cultivating the leadership capabilities required to address complex socio-ecological challenges. He has previously served as the Director of Systems Learning at the Banff Centre and the Associate Director of Outward Bound Canada and currently chairs the board for the Animas Valley Institute. He is known for his ability to combine a big-picture systems perspective with the "inner" work of human development and considers himself, above all, to be a grateful student of – and occasional teaching assistant to – the beauty and intricate complexity of the natural world and the wild mysteries of the human psyche.

Eve Ridgeway is an ordained Anglican minister in the UK and the Associate Rector of St. George's Church, Leeds. She completed her MA in Theology and Ministry with Sheffield University and is currently a PhD student in systematic theology at the University of Aberdeen. She has also been improvising since 2017, in long and short forms, performs with *Right Here Right Now and Fool(ish)* across Yorkshire and has trained with Chicago improviser Craig Uhlir. She studied music initially and is a singer, cellist, and guitar player. Eve loves introducing people to the gift and joys of improvisation.

Danny Smith is a modern-day Romantic poet, a tarot reader, and a digital artist. She holds a Master's degree in Engaged Humanities and the Creative Life with an emphasis in Depth Psychology from Pacifica Graduate Institute. She authored (2023) *Catharsis: A Collection of 21 Poems*.

Brendan Ellis Williams, is a poet, priest, religious scholar, spiritual director, herbalist, and teacher. His work is often concerned with rewilding the human soul, the role of landscape in human life and meaning, animism, worldview formation, esoteric religious expressions, comparative historical theology, and the reclamation of indigenous European traditions—particularly those of his own Gaelic ancestral inheritance. He holds an MFA in poetry from St. Mary's College of California, an MDiv from the Graduate Theological Union at Berkeley, and is presently a candidate for the PhD in religion at the University of St. Andrews, Scotland. He thinks, breathes, dreams, and creates with the wild landscapes of the American Mountain West, the Northern California Coast, and the West of Ireland.

Michael R. Young is a Lecturer in the Humanities PhD program and Professor in the Great Books program at Faulkner University. He is certified in Spiritual Direction and holds a PhD and MA in Philosophy from the University of Dallas and an MDiv and MS in Biblical Studies and Ministry from Abilene Christian University. Relevant publications include: *Where Has All the Beauty Gone?* (*Consortium Journal*/Spring 2023); *Spiritual Formation, the Intellectual Virtues, and the Acquisition of Knowledge* (*Journal of Faith and the Academy*, VIII(2)/Fall 2015).

Foreword

The landscape of leadership development has many modalities that are often experienced as polarities or tensions. For example, is the purpose of development to gain improved performance, or deeper meaning? Do we develop leaders through instruction or by experience? Such tensions have become particularly acute in our current era, described variously as a polycrisis, crisis of meaning, or crisis of consciousness. Traditional leadership models seem inadequate in the face of these challenges. We are constantly called to grow and expand our knowledge and practice of leadership. To do that, we need to look for influences beyond the usual theories and research to reinvigorate how we lead. Alicia Crumpton's *Artful Leadership: Retreat, Recenter, and Rewild* invites us into a modality that extends the range of our leadership thinking, feeling, and acting.

Having spent decades exploring the intersection of leadership development, adult development, and integral theory, I have witnessed many approaches that attempt to bridge the gap between effectiveness and authenticity. What makes this present volume distinctive is its recognition that genuine leadership transformation requires more than cognitive understanding or behavioral modification – it demands a fundamental shift in how we relate to ourselves, others, and the world around us.

Navigating such a shift is demanding. The three-stage journey that Crumpton articulates – Retreat, Recenter, and Rewild – helps us meet this demand. It does this by mirroring the process described by developmental psychology about how humans navigate major transitions of identity. The retreat phase acknowledges that transformation often begins with a dissolution of our previous sense of identity – who we were no longer fits current reality and we step back from it. We are then disoriented as we enter the liminal space of transformation.

Eventually we emerge from the liminal space. The expanded consciousness that emerges comes through a process of making sense of or integrating the new distinctions our transformed identity enables. This allows us to recenter. The new self becomes the source of leading. Our inner compass guides us to align action with deeper purpose.

However, this is not enough. The rewilding phase offers perhaps the most radical proposition: that we need to take one more step, to connect our inner compass with more than ourselves. We need to integrate our fundamental interconnectedness with all life. This ecological, even cosmological perspective challenges the anthropocentric assumptions that underlie much of our current leadership thinking and invites us into what systems theorists call "participatory consciousness" – a way of being that recognizes our embeddedness in and creation of larger wholes.

This is easier said than done. What strikes me most about how the approach this volume presents can help with this is its integration of multiple ways of knowing. The inclusion of artistic practices, somatic awareness, contemplative disciplines, and ecological wisdom creates what we might call a "transmodal methodology" for leadership development. This is not merely intellectual eclecticism but a sophisticated understanding that transformation occurs through and across multiple dimensions of human experience simultaneously.

The collaborative nature of this work, bringing together voices from diverse fields, embodies the very principles it espouses. Rather than presenting a single authoritative voice, it creates what we might call "polyphonic wisdom," or multiple perspectives harmonizing around shared themes while maintaining their distinctive contributions.

For practitioners in the field of leadership development, this volume offers both theoretical depth and practical applicability. The integration of somatic practices, creative exercises, and reflective inquiries provides concrete tools for facilitating the kind of transformative experiences that lead to the deeper transformations described. For leaders, it offers a pathway through what can feel like an impossible maze of competing demands and expectations.

Perhaps most importantly, *Artful Leadership* arrives at a time when we take yet another turn in the evolution of collective consciousness. The ever-accelerating fragmentation the world presents for leaders to deal with requires thinking and acting from an ever-expanding wholeness. The crises we face are not just in the world, be they ecological, social, political, or spiritual. The crises are in us, requiring self-leadership that can hold paradox, navigate complexity, and inspire collective action while remaining grounded in authentic presence.

This volume is not merely about improving leadership effectiveness; it is about reimagining what leadership could become when rooted in creativity, connection, and care. It invites us to consider that our current leadership challenges may be evolutionary pressures calling forth new capacities for conscious, integral, and life-affirming ways of being.

I invite you to receive this work not just as information to be consumed but as a living invitation to your own transformation. May it serve as both mirror and map for your journey toward the kind of leadership our world needs.

Jonathan Reams
Co-founder and Chief Creative Officer, Center for Transformative Leadership
Editor, *Maturing Leadership: How Adult Development Impacts Leadership*
Associate Professor, Norwegian University of Science and Technology (2007–2024)

Preface

Leadership is a journey, one that weaves through uncharted terrains of challenges, creativity, and transformation. This book, *Artful Leadership: Retreat, Recenter, and Rewild*, is both a reflection of my own path and an invitation for others to embark on their unique journey toward authentic and holistic leadership. It emerges from a time when I, too, felt adrift – creatively numb, untethered from vision, and uncertain if the spark that had once fueled my life and work would return.

Rather than surrender to that sense of loss, I turned inward, seeking the roots of imagination, creativity, and wholeness. My journey led me to Pacifica Graduate Institute, where I explored the confluence of engaged humanities, depth psychology, and the creative life. There, in moments of vulnerability and discovery, I began to reimagine what leadership could look like when grounded in the wisdom of art, the power of images and storytelling, and the interconnectedness of all life.

This book is not just my story. It is enriched by the voices of contributors I personally invited to participate – an interdisciplinary group of scholars and creatives, many of whom are emergent scholars. It was important to create an opportunity for these emergent scholars' voices to be heard. To my delight, each person, when asked, said "yes," generously offering their perspectives, insights, and experiences. Their contributions exemplify the kind of collaborative spirit and creative energy that this book seeks to inspire in leadership.

Artful Leadership is the culmination of this collective journey. Divided into three transformative stages – *Retreat*, *Recenter*, and *Rewild* – the book offers tools, insights, and exercises to help leaders explore the shadows of their knowing, reconnect with their creative essence, and embrace their role as stewards of a flourishing and sustainable future.

The arts, as this book reveals, are not merely esthetic embellishments but profound pathways to healing, growth, and transformation. By engaging with creative practices, fostering dialogue, and honoring the wisdom of natural systems, leaders can cultivate the presence, imagination, and interconnectedness necessary to inspire change – not just within themselves but within their organizations and communities.

I invite you to step into this journey with curiosity and courage. May you find, as I have, that artful leadership powerfully illuminates not only the path ahead, but also the beauty of our shared human experience.

– Alicia D. Crumpton

Acknowledgments

The impetus for this book emerged reflectively following my experience of being part of a cohort exploring humanities, the creative life, and depth psychology at Pacifica Graduate Institute. I want to thank my instructors and fellow cohort members who held space for my retreat, recentering, and rewilding.

Thank you to Debra DeRuyver from the International Leadership Association, who guided the process, asked great questions, and encouraged throughout. Also, thank you to Fiona Allison from Emerald, who provided publication technical guidance and support.

Thank you to Jonny, my husband, who rolled his eyes and smiled when I said I thought I would propose an edited book. Rolled his eyes because at this stage of life, I could be eating bon bons and having fun, but instead I am driven to talk about something that I'm passionate about. He's my number one supporter in all things.

Thank you to Mom, who is the most creative person I know. She can look at a rock and a string and imagine possibility. Her esthetic eye is keen, particularly for wild color combinations. I love our conversations, which often begin with a question such as wondering how many colors of green there are. She inspires me toward esthetic sight, imagination, and creativity.

Finally, thank you to the contributors, who when I asked them to participate, said yes.

Introduction

Alicia D. Crumpton

Abstract

This book explores artful leadership as a holistic integration of artistic sensibility, mindful presence, and ecological consciousness. A three-part journey leads a leader toward authentic, creative, and holistic leadership in an increasingly complex world. In Part 1, "Retreat," readers step back from conventional leadership paradigms to explore the shadows of our knowing and being. Chapters examine art as a form of esthetic leadership, the transformative power of human–animal relationships, the unintended consequences of technology, virtue-based approaches to knowledge acquisition, and the sacred dimension of silence as pathways to deeper self-understanding and leadership presence. Part 2, "Recenter," focuses on realigning leadership identity through creative practice, narrative power, and collaborative processes. Chapters explore how leaders can cultivate esthetic sensibility, harness the power of storytelling, reconcile internal values with external image, engage with inspiration through dialogue, employ improvisational techniques to navigate complexity, and explore art as a vehicle for social change. Part 3, "Rewild," guides leaders toward reconnecting with their innate wholeness and the web of life. Through explorations of the ecological self as a foundation for leadership, lessons from natural systems, and the reclamation of metaphysical relationality, readers discover how leadership can foster resilience, creativity, and systemic transformation. Throughout, somatic, creative, and reflective exercises are provided to cultivate presence, spark imagination, and develop the capacity to lead from a place of authenticity, interconnectedness, and vision. Artful leadership is offered that honors human creativity and the wisdom of natural systems, ultimately guiding leaders toward creating more sustainable, just, and flourishing organizations and communities.

Keywords: Artful leadership; mindfulness; ecological consciousness; esthetics; inspiration; imagination; narratives; resilience; creativity

We live in an age where the unraveling of our social fabric, pandemic-related apocalyptic associations and memories, loss of trust in leadership, and erosion of democratic norms contribute to profound feelings of alienation and disorientation. Grief and a sense of loss emerge as a person senses a loss of their capacity to imagine, create, and take necessary steps to affect one's surroundings. As Margaret Wheatley (2023) described it, we inhabit "the age of threat when everything we encounter intensifies fear and anger" (p. 8).

Leaders are not immune to these forces. They speak of wanting to quit, feeling disconnected, and experiencing a pervasive sense of disease. Many describe a state of exhaustion so complete they wonder if recovery is possible. We all desire connection, rootedness, and spaces filled with imagination and wonder – yet the weight of our collective challenges can leave us in what Wheatley (2023) called "survival mode ... [where] we can no longer stop the forces of harm and destruction that have been set in motion" (p. 8).

For such a time as this, many of us find ourselves at pivotal life moments, recognizing a deep desire to live, work, and play authentically – emerging from a renewed awareness of who we are and the life we are called to lead. Yet we struggle with the enchantment of habitual ways of being accompanied by the false comfort of success, power, and productivity. We experience tension between the safety of familiar identity and the persistent call toward new experiences of vitality and wholeness.

Within this darkness lies an invitation.

What if our current challenges aren't merely obstacles to overcome but portals to transformation? What if this moment of collective disorientation actually presents an unprecedented opportunity to rediscover what it means to lead with wholeness, creativity, and purpose?

As we collectively face uncertainty and flux, we can (re)discover our true selves. We can learn to unite soul, role, and calling – to experience an undivided life. The purpose of this book is to explore the healing power of artful leadership through the journey of retreat, recentering, and rewilding.

Transformative Journey: Retreat, Recenter, and Rewild

This book offers a pathway forward through three interconnected journeys: Part 1: Retreat, Part 2: Recenter, and Part 3: Rewild. There are 15 chapters and three poetic responses, one for each part.

Part 1: Retreat reimagines withdrawal as an intentional act that allows leaders to confront inner shadows emerging with transformative insights. Drawing on Parker J. Palmer's (2000) wisdom, retreat becomes a practice of spiritual engagement and self-exploration essential for illuminating interiority and leadership. Through explorations of esthetic leadership, equine relationships, technology boundaries, virtue ethics, sacred silence, and contemplative practice, Part 1 illuminates retreat as an integrative process of stepping away to confront, understand, and transform.

By engaging with art, Carol Burbank, in Chapter 1, reminds us that individuals step away from conventional hierarchies, entering a realm of imagination and possibility, sparking personal and societal evolution. This esthetic form of leadership models the essence of retreat – a movement away from the known to discover the transformative power of questioning, "What if?"

In Chapter 2, Retreat becomes an act of reconnection with embodied presence and instinctual wisdom, explored by Charlotte Hardie using the lens of human–horse relationships. Interspecies connections potentially heal the Cartesian mind–body split, offering a path toward psychological integration and authentic leadership.

Chapter 3 uses my study of Mary Shelley's *Frankenstein* to explore the unintended consequences of technology design, where retreat is framed as an opportunity to reflect on technological impacts, recover balance, and create a healthier relationship with social media.

Michael R. Young encourages creating space in Chapter 4 for cultivating intellectual and moral virtues essential for knowledge acquisition and leadership. Retreat refers to our intentional reflection on our knowing and how we might reconnect with virtuous knowledge.

Silence is put forth as a sacred dimension of retreat, where a person transcends the "noise" of modern existence to rediscover connection to Being. In Chapter 5, I explore poet Octavio Paz and philosopher Max Picard's writings, where silence emerges as a catalyst for metamorphosis.

In Chapter 6, Bradley D. Davidson explored mindfulness as a retreat, where contemplative practice recenters one's identity and purpose.

In Part 1's poetic conclusion, Danny Smith's poem invites readers into the sacred slowness that true retreat demands – a counterpoint to our frantic world. Through lyrical imagery of winter's necessary stillness, the poem reveals the wisdom associated with withdrawal, echoing the season's invitation to come home to ourselves in ways that analytical prose alone cannot capture.

Together, the chapters in Part 1 illuminate retreat as an integrative process of stepping away to confront, understand, and transform. By engaging with shadows, silence, creativity, and mindfulness, leaders cultivate deeper awareness and authentic presence, enabling personal and collective transformation.

Part 2: Recenter explores the transformative power of aligning leadership with core values, creativity, and collaboration. Rooted in the metaphor of the potter's wheel, recentering emphasizes shedding dualistic paradigms and stepping into wholeness. Drawing inspiration from Joseph Campbell's wisdom on embracing life's possibilities, Part 2 highlights how leaders can refine their identity and purpose through inspiration, creative practice, narrative power, inclusive collaboration, and improvisation. This part positions recentering as an integrative practice where creativity and collaboration become essential tools.

The role of creativity and esthetic sensibility in leadership is explored in conversation by Catherine Etmanski and me, emphasizing the importance of inclusive practices that celebrate diverse voices and perspectives. In Chapter 7, we explore leadership as an art form where collective creativity flourishes, fostering environments of inspiration and collaboration.

Aaron Monts underscores the role of narratives in shaping individual and collective realities. Recentering, described in Chapter 8 as "re-storying" and sense-making, harnesses narrative power to inspire positive change, unite communities, and foster deeper cultural and personal connections.

Images we hold of ourselves shape our identity. In Chapter 9, Sarah Andreas posited that leaders can recenter their identity through creative engagement and critical reflection, building resilience and fostering authentic presence.

Kevin D. Collins explored creativity in Chapter 10 as an intra-active process rooted in dialogue and collaboration. The idea of inspiration and the muse was revisited through Barad's agential realism, where recentering embraces relational creativity that transcends individual inspiration, emphasizing process over product and collective innovation.

Drawing on the principles of improvisation, Chapter 11 highlights the power of playfulness, adaptability, and presence in leadership. Eve Ridgway articulates how improvisation provides a model for recentering leadership in communal discovery, where creativity and intuition are cultivated in a shared environment.

Courage in Motion, presented as Chapter 12, refers to the personal journey of nonprofit *Life On Art* founder and artist Tracy Ferron. Rewilding as transformative effect achieved through art creation represents an outcome for the healing power of creativity. Creative expression becomes a vehicle for empowerment and collective liberation, and imagination inspires radical inclusion and resilience in addressing societal challenges.

Danny Smith's Part 2 poetic response, with its vibrant exploration of recentering as both artistic practice and leadership necessity, offers readers a glimpse into the transformative moment when scattered energies align and purpose crystallizes, mirroring the potter's wheel metaphor that shapes this part, revealing through verse finding one's center in a fragmented world.

Part 2 centers on the journey of realigning leadership identity, values, and practices to create balance and foster imagination. Using the metaphor of the potter's wheel, recentering emerges as shedding limiting dualities and embracing integration. Each chapter offers unique insights into how leaders can deepen their connection to self, others, and the creative forces shaping leadership.

Part 3: Rewild embraces a return to our original wholeness, activating a sense of interconnectedness with all life. Grounded in ecological, psychological, and metaphysical perspectives, rewilding challenges leaders to see themselves as part of an intricate web of relationships cultivating practices that honor creativity, responsibility, and inclusivity. Chapters explore transformation through art, the ecological self, lessons from natural systems, and metaphysical relationality – offering a vision of leadership rooted in the rewilding of self and society.

Drawing from ecology and Indigenous wisdom, Kathryn Goldman Schuyler introduces the concept of the ecological self in Chapter 13, which transcends anthropocentric worldviews to embrace interconnectedness with all living systems. Rewilding provides a way to address the current polycrisis and nurture collective flourishing.

Julian Norris used the reintroduction of Yellowstone wolves as a metaphor to explore how leadership can mirror natural ecosystems. In Chapter 14, leaders are invited to *rewild* their psyches, adopting relational and holistic practices that allow them to thrive amid complexity and promote systemic transformation.

Brendan Ellis Williams examines the philosophical divide between dualistic worldviews and relational, animistic ontologies, advocating for a metaphysical shift honoring all beings as conscious agents within an interconnected web. Through contemplative practices and animistic perspectives presented in Chapter 15, leaders are guided to rewild their souls, fostering relationships that honor the consciousness and agency of all life forms, thereby contributing to a global *communitas*.

Danny Smith's poem *Woodspell* concludes Part 3 with a mesmerizing journey into the untamed terrain of the rewilded soul, where a poet ventures beyond civilization's constraints. The poem's vivid imagery of stormy woods and primordial wisdom beckons readers to experience the transformative power of rewilding, not just intellectually, but through the embodied, emotional language of poetry that mirrors the wildness it celebrates.

In its entirety, Part 3 offers a vision of leadership rooted in the rewilding of self and society – a call to return to the essence of our humanity while embracing ecological and metaphysical interconnectedness. Leaders are inspired to cultivate creativity, reimagine systems, and embrace relational practices that align with the natural world's wisdom. Together, these chapters build a roadmap for cultivating a leadership grounded in wholeness and collective responsibility.

Your Invitation to Artful Leadership

Interweaving insights from artists, activists, ecologists, contemplative practitioners, philosophers, religious leaders, scholars, teachers, and business and nonprofit leaders, you are invited on a leadership journey that honors your inner wisdom, imagination, and creativity.

Whether you're seeking renewal amid exhaustion, integration of your creative capacities, ecological perspectives on systemic change, or simply a more authentic expression of your leadership calling, the pathways of retreat, recentering, and rewilding offer practical wisdom for navigating these uncertain times.

This book invites you into a community of practice where artful leadership emerges through intentional withdrawal, creative recentering, and courageous reconnection with our fundamental wholeness.

Using Artful Leadership: A Guide to Personal Transformation and Purposeful Practice

This book is designed for leaders interested in personal change and transformation. Each chapter is written using an accessible tone, with each retaining the unique voice of its contributor to deliberately highlight the varying ways people from diverse disciplines approach these topics. Additionally, this book serves as both a source of inspiration and a practical toolkit; each chapter includes one or more somatic breathing, creative, and reflective practices designed to facilitate a deepening of each chapter's meaning and application to your life.

Overview: The book is divided into three parts: Retreat, Recenter, and Rewild. Each part represents a phase in your journey toward deeper self-awareness and purposeful leadership. A poetic response at the end of each part invites you to connect, engage, and explore the part's deeper meanings. Follow the steps below to support your reading and reflection.

Step 1: Create a personal space conducive to deep reading, introspection, and reflection. Attend to the esthetics and comfort within the space so that you are comfortable eliminating distractions (e.g., cell phones). Consider setting specific reading times and using mindfulness techniques to stay focused.

Step 2: Gather supplies such as a journaling notebook, pens, colored markers, sticky notes, highlighters, or digital tools for notetaking.

Step 3: Actively read a part's introduction and then a chapter. Each chapter is designed to stand alone. However, you are encouraged to consider the part (i.e., retreat, recenter, or rewild) within which the chapter is included to orient your movement through the journey.

Step 4: As you read, use your notebook to capture questions, aha's, or anything that comes to mind. Revisit and reflect on these notes periodically.

Step 5: Answer the following questions in your notebook after reading an article:

- What key insights or strategies are presented?
- What memories, emotions, or feelings are evoked?
- How does what you read align with or challenge who you are, your experiences, or how you lead?
- What new questions or thoughts does this spark about who you are or your leadership?
- How do you want to respond to what you learned from this?
- What actionable goals will you set based on your reflections?

Step 6: Practice one or more of the somatic breathing, creative, or reflective practices included near the end of each chapter. These activities are designed to help you embody a chapter's lessons and apply the content. Consider how to integrate these practices into your daily leadership activities.

Think of the book as a companion that leads you to uncover deeper self-awareness, reconnect with your values, and foster transformation. In an era of disconnection and disorientation, *Artful Leadership* invites you on a journey to retreat from the noise, recenter your purpose, and rewild your leadership – discovering the creative power that lies at the heart of meaningful change.

Your journey begins now.

References

Palmer, P. J. (2000). *Let your life speak: Listening for the voice of vocation*. Jossey-Bass.
Wheatley, M. J. (2023). *Who do we choose to be? Facing reality, claiming leadership, restoring sanity* (2nd ed.). Berrett-Koehler.

Part 1

Retreat

> If we, as leaders are to cast less shadow and more light, we need to ride certain monsters all the way down, explore the shadows they create, and experience the transformation that can come as we "get into" our own spiritual lives. (Palmer, 2000)

To retreat is an overt act of trying to escape from a particular situation. Retreat also holds a connotation of retreating for a time to "get away." We speak in terms of respite, vacating, being in nature, those opportunities where we cease what we are doing to spend time in nature, quiet, or solitude. We associate retreating, in this sense, with a reset, taking a break to recoup from the dailiness of life. Retreat, in this book, is considered in the sense of human understanding where a person suspends their usual ways of thinking, creating an opening to explore new possibilities and to gain new perspectives.

Part 1 reframes the concept of retreat as more than an escape; it becomes an intentional act of stepping away to examine the shadows that obscure clarity in leadership and life. Palmer's quote from "Let Your Life Speak" underscores the necessity of engaging deeply with their inner "monsters," shadows, and spiritual dimensions to illuminate pathways for personal and communal growth. Retreat, in this sense, transcends its superficial interpretation as leisure or respite and is instead elevated to a transformative practice rooted in philosophical inquiry; intentional withdrawal, and somatic, creative, and reflective practices.

Retreat is an exercise in suspending conventional ways of thinking, allowing individuals to explore alternative paradigms and access wisdom concealed by daily distractions. This involves confronting and understanding the impacts of technology on the psyche, acknowledging how modern life shapes perceptions of reality, and navigating the interplay between personal and collective consciousness. Shadows – representing unseen or neglected aspects of the self and society – are explored as a necessary counterpart to light, offering insight into the complexity of human understanding.

The retreat framework emphasizes the importance of silence, solitude, and nature as catalysts for renewal, inviting leaders to reconnect with their authentic selves and the deeper truths that guide their vocation. By retreating from noise and engaging with reflective practices, individuals uncover new possibilities for leadership and knowledge, paving the way for transformative experiences that resonate beyond the individual level.

Reference

Palmer, P. J. (2000). *Let your life speak: Listening for the voice of vocation.* Jossey-Bass.

Chapter 1

Art as Esthetic Leadership: The Creative Power of the "What If?"

Carol Burbank

Scholar/Practitioner, USA

Abstract

This chapter explores the concept of art as a form of creative leadership that operates through the radical question "What if?" Artists serve as leaders by creating works that mirror, challenge, and celebrate the human experience, inviting audiences into transformative relationships with their creations. Through this engagement, art establishes a liminal space where both individual and collective consciousness can evolve, fostering social change and cultural development. Artistic expression represents a form of leadership that transcends conventional hierarchies, offering a unique power to inspire transformation through authenticity, beauty, and witness. In societies facing crisis or autocratic control, esthetic leadership becomes particularly vital as both a refuge and catalyst for healthy change, providing spaces where empathy, curiosity, and creative possibility can flourish.

Keywords: Esthetic leadership; creative transformation; social imaginary; artistic authenticity; cultural evolution

Introduction

There is a reason that a healthy, active presence of diverse artists and writers reflects a healthy, evolving society. Artists mirror, challenge, and celebrate the human experience, with all its universal emotional power reflected through specific cultures. Artists lead from a place that is defined by possibility, supported by the willingness to start from the unknown to make something new. Those

Artful Leadership: Retreat, Recenter, and Rewild, 3–12
Copyright © 2026 by Carol Burbank
Published under exclusive licence by Emerald Publishing Limited
doi:10.1108/S2058-880120250000010002

possibilities live in the art itself, illuminating imaginary worlds that impact personal and social realities by awakening the liberating force of the "what if?"

"What if?" is the radical question at the heart of every creative vision. Whether the question leads us to explore abstract or personal storytelling, it tests our courage, resilience, and vision because the question asks us to live consciously. By helping us move into new ways of thinking and knowing, art invites us to explore creative ways of being present. This invitation is a vital form of leadership, often difficult to measure, but always transformative and engaging.

Thinking of art itself as creative leadership requires a shift in mindset. Normally, we elevate individuals as leaders and track their impact as personal or organizational. But leadership is always experienced in relationship – profoundly human, and at its best, innately improvisational. At the same time, the terms we use to define leadership are more about the process of living those relationships, with results connected to experiencing positive values like service, transformation, vision, creativity, and spirituality. If we consider art the dynamic expression of the artist leader, it doesn't take a big leap to understand that art itself stands in as creative leadership. More specifically, because we generally interact with art as the representative of the artist, then we can say that the relationship between art and audience activates and embodies leadership. Through engaged reception and responsive interpretation, the relationship opens the potential for inspiration for shifts in mindset, beliefs, or actions.

With this turn, we redefine the usual roles of leader and follower, beyond conventional thinking about leadership hierarchies. By creating new narrative and visual containers for ideologies, identities, and insights, artists open a liminal space that is both public and private. Reception is an internal experience, unique to each person who chooses to connect with art, in whatever form it may take. This space cannot be regulated, although public access to the art itself can be pushed underground or closed off through censorship.

Over time, some artists become symbolic leaders, claiming a public leadership role because of their work. The more innovative or politicized an artist's work, the more likely their personal identity will become a leadership brand, speaking to a circle of supporters and critics eager to confront or affirm their message and esthetic. In parallel, the work itself is highlighted as a leadership interface, increasing in controversy and influence, taking on a transformative leadership role, and establishing different relationships with different audiences. Artists and art gain power and visibility. By occupying what Chiara Bottici (2019) calls the social imaginary, a sociopolitical bridge between individual and collective spaces, art activates cultural mythologies that are negotiated, contested, and lived as part of social evolution.

The social imaginary is a space of invention and possibility where both art and artists claim a central leadership role in social change. The root cause of their influence is their ability to harness the "what if." Creative innovation creates community consciousness in an evolutionary step toward complexity and away from inauthentic dogma. Audiences building a relationship with the "what if" in any genre take on a co-creative role, activating their own psyche as they connect with another's vision dialogically, emotionally, and authentically.

Even art and writing that might be pigeonholed as propaganda, sharing a simple message meant to sway opinion, creates a potential dialogue of discovery, if it engages daily with expansive questions. Here, consider the British street artist, Banksy (n.d.), whose anti-authoritarian social commentary combines whimsy, pathos, and clear political messages that transform public spaces with provocative images. These offerings impact public and private symbologies, becoming memes, part of a cultural lexicon of self-expression, resistance, and community. In literature, George Orwell's (1949/1983) *1984* identifies a clear theme – totalitarianism depends on absolute conformity, at the cost of our humanity – with a complexity that has kept both the book and its ideas culturally relevant. The specter of Big Brother, for example, has become a meme adapted by artists, writers, reality-TV creators, and pundits, offering a shorthand for experiences of surveillance, pressures to conform, and the dangers of a single story to shape identity and behavior. We situate ourselves thanks to these experiences, adapting and learning.

The resulting depth of expression brings energy to communication and reception, making it possible for art itself to take a leadership role. This effect cannot be underestimated. It explains the power of certain works, which stand alone and are sustained both by form and message, sometimes long after the artists' death. Consider Picasso's (1937) *Guernica*, painted in response to the 1937 bombing of a Basque town, with long-term impact as both political and esthetic exploration of fascism and violence. In literature, Toni Morrison's (2007) *Beloved*, a sociohistorical, vividly surreal story of a former slave haunted by an impossible choice, also leads by representing the complexity of surviving brutality and bondage. This is creative leadership to inspire justice, grounded in witness.

But esthetic leadership is not limited to representing negative aspects of human experience. Beauty can lead just as powerfully. Art that holds a space for beauty brings us to a liminal space of grace, reframing the way we see the world, our experiences, and stories. Moving into a relationship with esthetic beauty can give us a different relationship with nature, people, and ourselves. Consider Robin Wall Kimmerer's (2015) book, *Braiding Sweetgrass*, an intimate scientific & cultural history that deepens our connection with traditional plants and their relationship with native culture. In visual art, Georgia O'Keefe (n.d.) created remarkable images of flowers, landscapes, and cityscapes, moving beyond literal representation into heightened portraits and stylized and sensual portraits of human and non-human worlds.

Here, we also need to acknowledge the emotional force of music. For example, in the movie *The Shawshank Redemption* (Darabont, 1994), Andy Dufresne (Tim Robbins) locks himself in the prison office in an act of defiance against prison authorities and plays Mozart's *Duettino-Sull'aria* over the loudspeakers, creating a sense of the sublime throughout the grimly imagined prison yard. The 2024 film, *A Complete Unknown* (Mangold, 2024), tracks the power of music as countercultural community building through the story of Bob Dylan's rise to fame, becoming a voice for a generational moment, and a space for connecting emotionally with transformative leadership. Music inspires a fluid, often wordless connection with the imaginal, a generative and fundamental human creative force where collective and individual consciousness blend and energize our psyches and accompany our daily lives.

Of course, art can serve both beauty and witness, because craft and mastery bring esthetic power to an artist's purpose, and each masterwork has its own layers of meaning and style. In this process, familiar genres become powerful tools for persuasion, and experimental work articulates new architectures for understanding. Whether art is elevated as controversial, innovative, or beautiful, as long as it speaks with an authentic voice or vision, it carries the energy of transformation and pleasure. It leads us forward or inward, challenges our perceptions, and engages us in a world beyond pragmatic daily experience. As a result, the influence of art is non-linear, existing fluidly within and outside ideological or capitalist exchange, uniquely navigating the space of psyche and society. It often affirms or offends audiences in a specific niche, so measuring impact feels subjective, anecdotal, and very personal.

This challenging fluidity makes it easy to dismiss art and artists as fringe-dwellers. In a capitalist society, where money and fame equate with success and influence, art's non-transactional impact is often minimized as irrelevant and criticized as corrupt. Even artists whose work earns mainstream acclaim are objectified as special or different, and sometimes both. Within capitalism, art is othered primarily because it must be, in most cases, an avocation. Vocations make money and create economic security; avocations are hobbies, and therefore personal, not professional.

As a result, perhaps the only kind of leadership *not* represented in the creative space is transactional: trading money, goods, or services that codify leaders and followers in hierarchies of exchange. Art leads from a transformational impulse, fueled by questions that adapt, reframe, and challenge so-called certainties. Within that space, artists create works that offer leadership through service, vision, and other leadership values. When we experience the vulnerability and power of possibility, we recognize the personal, subjective experience of art as vital to our well-being. This experience offers leadership that can arguably only come from specific locations in specific communities, generated by cultural outliers who ask and answer big questions that inspire social change and long-term cultural evolution.

Trying to contain or control the "what ifs" generated in our liminal relationships with art is a symptom of autocracy. Even when creativity is simply celebratory self-expression, authoritarians are threatened by the pleasure and self-expression of authentic individual exploration. In *The Power of the Powerless*, Vaclav Havel (1978/1990) described Czechoslovakia's Velvet Revolution as evidence of the power of authentic art to challenge state-controlled ideology, which he called post-totalitarianism. Autocrats depend on citizens willing to live within the lie that justifies state control, imposing ritualized state doctrine that institutes "a profane trivialization of ... inherent humanity [in service of ideological] utilitarianism" and conformity (p. 145). Repression of the arts and exiling artists is "a desperate attempt to plug up the dreadful wellspring of truth, a truth which might cause incalculable transformations in social consciousness, which in turn might one day produce political debacles unpredictable in their consequences" (p. 150).

Art as Esthetic Leadership   7

Masterful artistic expression is characterized by exploratory authenticity, a process of discovery and questioning, defining and renewing unpredictable internal truths. The "what if" is a space of freedom. Havel (1978/1990) wrote:

> If the suppression of the aims of life is a complex process, and if it is based on the multifaceted manipulation of all expressions of life, then, by the same token, every free expression of life indirectly threatens the post-totalitarian system politically, including forms of expression to which, in other social systems, no one would attribute any potential political significance, not to mention explosive power. (p. 151)

In such a society where spontaneous public or private self-expression is distrusted and monitored, any authentic art, writing, music, or creative production, overtly political or not, becomes a potential site for dissidence. Even in democratic societies, art that highlights non-normative identities, viewpoints, or experiences can be controversial and is seen as disruptive. The "what if" expressed in art awakens a hunger for diversity, freedom, and self-expression. Artists lead by creating work that lives in that relational space of dialogic authenticity, creating a community experience of co-leadership.

This collaborative leadership reception and self-invention generates both collective connection and personal individuation. Psychologist Carl Jung defined individuation as developing self-awareness through active engagement with collective consciousness and an evolving, authentic Self. Like an artist's work, which rises out of a process of evolving awareness, "the self is relatedness... The self only exists inasmuch as you appear. Not that you are, but that you *do* the self" (Jung, 1988, p. 73). Art and the Self are therefore enacted through simultaneous states of being and doing, making and receiving, experiencing and becoming. Through their relationship with art, audiences move into conscious relationship with the Self of the artist, through the leadership space where doing and being coincide in the imagination. What is perhaps most remarkable is that the artist need not be present, if their work is authentic; furthermore, the work need not be a masterpiece for the authentic experience to translate the "what if" into possibility.

Art's fluid leadership power is even easier to see when we acknowledge that genres and venues change over time, forms subverted or reinvented to serve new purposes and tell different stories. Formerly innovative genres are adopted as mainstream expression. Impressionist paintings that now claim a place of pride in museums and collections were once damned as unfinished, careless vulgarities. The very name *Impressionism* was created as an insult to the paintings themselves, in a satirical article that mocked the suggestive brushstrokes and sketched details (Leroy, 1874/2019). That is why it's so important to recognize that, whether a work is considered avant-garde or conventional, there is nonetheless a relationship established with the audience/viewer/reader, a moment of esthetic leadership engagement that is fluid through time and place.

With a long-term lens, we are less likely to dismiss art, writing, and music that is celebrated in mainstream culture as less powerful than art from the fringes of contemporary culture. We can see the power of esthetic leadership in the evolution of popular entertainment. Even the impact of art for pure entertainment's sake changes over time, mirroring and generating cultural change. Consider the sitcom, a genre Saul Austerlitz (2014) called a form obsessed with "the preservation of equilibrium … the repetition compulsion of eternal sameness conjoined to a desire to overturn the established order; a profound esthetic conservatism bundled with an ingrained desire to shock" (p. 7). In short, this purposely banal genre of TV entertainment is a wolf in sheep's clothing, the Wonder Bread of early television that filled living rooms with episode after episode of mainstream *Father Knows Best* (James & Tewksbury, 1954–1960) stereotypes amounting to middle-class domestic comfort food. It has become an art form in its own right, with more and more social commentary embedded in the storytelling and increasing levels of meta-commentary signaling our discomfort with the conventions of child-man husband, harried mother-wife, and children in various comically redeemed states of disarray.

The most vivid recent example is the 2021 dark comedy, *Kevin Can F* Himself* (Armstrong, 2021–2023), launched as a direct attack on the most standardized versions of the sitcom, directly satirizing the particularly shallow flop, *Kevin Can Wait* (2016), widely dismissed by critics as "a terrible and unimaginative show" (Chaney, 2016, p. 1) that killed off characters, basic TV credibility, and good taste for cringe-worthy laugh-track humor. Any sitcom equilibrium is demolished in the recent grimly satirical version, in which Allison, the harried wife, plots Kevin's murder and her own escape from the laugh-track world of her husband's abuse. Scenes with Kevin are played in a brightly lit, standard sitcom set, with the husband's put-downs rewarded with a jarring laugh-track. Scenes outside his sphere of influence are naturalistic, but seem dark in comparison, documenting the bleak reality of Kevin's increasingly desperate wife. The blended storytelling is often masterful, combining suspense and entertaining contradictions that became more and more surreal and disturbing as the series continued to the end, when Kevin dies as a result of his own hapless sitcom unconsciousness.

This last example brings us into the messy territory leadership theorists also struggle to define: how to talk about leadership that offers positive processes and results (classically, Winston Churchill), as opposed to negative processes and results (classically, Adolf Hitler). In the world of esthetic leadership, ideas about good and bad artistic work are passionately debated, without the clear cultural markers that give Churchill's stabilizing leadership a moral high ground when compared to Hitler's devastating violence. For our purposes, it is enough to note that some artworks embody deeper values and purposes than others, depending on the artist's intention, vision, and abilities.

The most immersive esthetic leadership relationships activate specific audiences, invigorating community values and empathy by sharing stories that acknowledge differences as well as universalities. Here, consider the groundbreaking poetry by Diné writer, Jake Skeets (2019), shattering form into a landscape of beauty and devastation that is both highly literary and indigenous. Skeets' poetry leads us into a new relationship with both language and history, redefining the politics of beauty and loss in gorgeous, sometimes shocking poems. We have to work hard and dig deep in our own consciousness to connect with this kind of challenging esthetic leadership.

On the other hand, some esthetic works (reality TV, for example) initiate relationships with audiences that seem more like highly controlled escapist trances than conscious co-creative relationships. Here, consider the popular pablum of *Love After Lockup* (Sharp Entertainment, 2018–2025), a redundantly edited and highly scripted series of vignettes tracking relationships between recent parolees and the people who try to marry them. It's a familiar structuring of the genre: multiple stories weave together in short scenes of conflict or passion, with confessional moments revealing secrets and concerns, and recaps and future events peppering the new materials. Yet even this prescriptive esthetic creates a relationship with the viewer, generating emotional loyalties and opinions, leading with stimulating engagement that offers esthetic popcorn. This, too, creates a space where – however unconsciously – the viewers' psyche connects with collective storytelling.

Inevitably, the "what if" of esthetic leadership always takes us somewhere new, even as the experience affirms aspects of our own evolving Self. Deep or shallow, the journey is characterized by an imaginary relationship defined by strategically developed creative expression, played out in both public and private contexts. The most masterful works connect us with expansive spaces for storytelling, self-awareness, and cultural understanding. They are a direct link to an evolving social imaginary, at its best co-creative and consciously engaging. Each artist designs their work with intent and craft, choosing genres, forms, and creative solutions to answer whatever form of "what if" they have the courage to explore. Depending on the mastery of the artist, esthetic leadership becomes a space for transformative leadership and social change.

In a time of global crisis and fracturing nationalism, esthetic leadership becomes even more important as a tool for justice, self-awareness, and problem-solving. In struggling democracies, esthetic leadership is quickly othered and criticized, labeled a danger to an autocratic state or community control, and limited wherever possible. Shallow and programmable experiences are more easily manipulated and generally proliferate as a way for the social imaginary to conform to narrow definitions of self and culture. Although these experiences can never be entirely transactional, they can be formalized into rigid reinforcements leading toward conformity rather than creativity.

But reinforced by beauty and complexity, art can create a haven for healthy change. In the face of crisis, transformative esthetic leadership is a refuge and a launching pad. It provides a place to privately and publicly engage with community, practice empathy, and explore the unfamiliar with curiosity. Leadership values of service, transformation, innovation, stability, and vision are holistically expressed through creative action, experiential and interpretive. Leading from possibility, artists make works that embody leadership potential, artists make works that embody leadership potential, co-creating healthy personal and social realities by awakening the full, liberating force of the "what if?"

Cultivating Creative Possibility: Engaging with the "What If?"

Leadership, like art, flourishes at the intersection of vision and possibility. Drawing from the transformative power of artistic expression, this collection of exercises invites leaders to explore the radical question of "What if?" by engaging in a deeper relationship with esthetic leadership. By engaging with these practices, you'll discover how esthetic principles can enhance your leadership approach, fostering authentic connections and creating spaces where transformation becomes possible.

Somatic Breathing Exercise: Embodying Creative Possibility in Relationship with Art

- Choose a favorite musical, visual, or short literary work.
- Find a comfortable seated position and connect with that work of art. Listen, read, observe. Breathe naturally and deeply.
- When you feel connected with the work, close your eyes. Continue breathing deeply and naturally or use a meditation breathing technique you prefer.
- As you continue breathing deeply, focus on the ideas, images, and energy of that creative experience you value.
- As you breathe, clear your mind and open to the "what if" this artist is asking and answering. What question rises that resonates with you most?
- Once a question rises clearly, open your eyes and reconnect with the work. In connection with the art, what answers rise in you and in the work that is leading you forward?
- Notice any sensations, images, or ideas that arise without judgment.
- Gradually bring your awareness back to the room, carrying this expanded sense of possibility with you.

Creative Leadership Group Reflection Exercise: The Art of Your Leadership

- Gather a small group of people that share leadership and community connections. The goal is to learn about each person's creativity and open possibilities and connections, whether or not you enjoy the artwork you share in your circle.
- Have each person bring three art objects (music, poetry, painting, etc.) that resonate with them deeply (e.g., poetry, music, painting). They can choose which one, or all, to share in the circle.
- Take turns sharing the work, using these prompts as a starting place to explore the creative ways each of you explores esthetic leadership:

  o What emotions does this work evoke in you?
  o What does the art form stir up in you, bring forth in you?
  o What questions and ideas inspire you in this work?
  o What invitation or inspiration emerges for you?
  o How does this reflect your values and leadership qualities?

Esthetic Leadership Practice: Creating Your Inspiration Gallery

- For 1 week, document moments when you encounter something that inspires awe, beauty, or inspiration.
- Create a physical or digital "gallery" of these moments through photographs, quotes, or brief descriptions.
- Actively engage with the materials to consider:
  - What specifically caught your attention (be precise about details)?
  - Your immediate emotional and physical response
  - Any questions or insights that arose from the experience
  - What patterns (stories, images, words, energies) do these moments have in common?
  - How this moment might inform your leadership approach

Make Esthetic Leadership a Conscious Choice

- For 1 week, keep a log of the TV shows, artworks, movies, music, plays, or other esthetic experiences you choose.
- As you look at that log, circle the experiences that elevated you. Underline the experiences that moved you into a negative or unconscious space.
- By becoming aware of the esthetic relationships you're inviting, you can become conscious about the ways you are creatively connecting with the social imaginary, and make choices that are expansive and authentic, supporting your own unique creative leadership skills and mindset.

References

Armstrong, V. (Creator). (2021–2023). *Kevin can f*ck himself* [TV series]. Mr. D Productions.

Austerlitz, S. (2014). *Sitcom: A history in 24 episodes from I Love Lucy to Community*. Chicago Review Press.

Banksy. (n.d.). *Website*. https://www.banksy.co.uk/

Bottici, C. (2019). Imagination, imaginary, imaginal: Towards a new social ontology? *Social Epistemology*, *33*(5), 433–441. https://doi.org/10.1080/02691728.2019.1652861

Chaney, J. (2016). Kevin Can Wait is exactly as awful as you imagined. *Variety*, 9/19. https://www.vulture.com/2016/09/kevin-can-wait-is-just-as-bad-as-you-imagined.html

Darabont, F. (1994). *The Shawshank Redemption* [Film]. Castlerock Entertainment.

Havel, V. (1990). The power of the powerless. In P. Wilson (Ed.), *Open Letters* (pp. 125–214). Vintage. (Original work published 1978)

James, E. (Creator), & Tewksbury, P. (Director). (1954–1960). *Father knows best* [TV series]. Rodney Young Productions.

Jung, C. (1988). *Nietzsche's Zarathustra: Notes on the seminar given in 1934–1939* (J. L. Jarrett, Ed.). Princeton University Press.

Kimmerer, R. W. (2015). *Braiding sweetgrass*. Milkweed Editions.

Leroy, L. (2019). Louis Leroy's scathing review of the First Exhibition of the Impressionists. *Artsmarts*, *3*(2). (Original work published 1874). https://arthive.com/publications/1812~Pictorial_Louis_Leroys_scathing_review_of_the_First_Exhibition_of_the_Impressionists

Mangold, J. (2024). *A complete unknown*. Searchlight Pictures.

Morrison, T. (2007). *Beloved*. Vintage.

O'Keefe, G. (n.d.). *Georgia O'Keefe museum*. https://www.okeeffemuseum.org/

Orwell, G. (1983). *1984*. New American Library. (Original work published 1949)

Picasso, P. (1937). *Guernica*. Museo Nacional Centro de Arta Reina Sofia. https://www.museoreinasofia.es/en/collection/artwork/guernica

Sharp Entertainment. (2018–2025). *Love after lockup* [TV series]. Sharp Entertainment.

Skeets, J. (2019). *Eyes bottle dark with a mouthful of flowers*. Milkweed Editions.

Chapter 2

The Alchemical Horse: Equine Relationships and the Path to Individuation

Charlotte Hardie

Independent Researcher, USA

Abstract

This chapter explores the transformative potential of human–horse relationships in fostering psychological integration and individuation. Drawing on Jungian psychology, biosemiotics, and complexity theory, the author describes how horses serve as unique mirrors and guides in the journey toward wholeness. As prey animals with heightened sensitivity, horses demand authentic presence and embodied intelligence, challenging humans to reconcile internal experiences with external expressions. The paper examines how equine partnerships help heal the Cartesian mind–body split prevalent in Western society by inviting humans into relational awareness and somatic intelligence. Through these interspecies connections, individuals develop leadership qualities that prioritize cooperation over dominance while reconnecting with their instinctual wisdom. While horses offer a powerful pathway to individuation, the principles of embodiment and presence can be cultivated through various mindful practices that ground humans in their physical experience and intuitive knowing.

Keywords: Equine; alchemy; transformation; biosemiotic; complexity

Introduction

Alchemy is transformation, a collaboration between symbols, meanings, images, and substance. Traditionally, alchemy is known as transforming lead into gold.

Artful Leadership: Retreat, Recenter, and Rewild, 13–20
Published under exclusive licence by Emerald Publishing Limited
doi:10.1108/S2058-880120250000010003

Jungian analyst Nathan Schwartz-Salant (1995) wrote that alchemy attempts "to deal with the complexities of change, the transformation from one state or form to another" (p. 2). In psychological terms, alchemy can describe the process of moving toward wholeness, which C.G. Jung (1928/1953) called individuation – the path of deepening connection with the Self. Jung wrote, "Individuation means becoming an 'in-dividual,' and, in so far as 'individuality' embraces our innermost, last, and incomparable uniqueness, it also implies becoming one's own self. We could therefore translate individuation as 'coming to selfhood' or 'self-realization'" (p. 173). Rather than acting from external influences, individuation involves an ongoing process of inner connection, integrating lived experience, values, and personal insight.

Equine collaborations offer a unique pathway toward individuation. Horses, as sentient and highly perceptive beings, mirror the emotional and energetic states of those who interact with them. Their nonverbal communication and ability to respond to human authenticity make them profound partners in the individuation process. When we engage with horses, we are invited to embody presence, emotional honesty, and self-awareness. Horses demand congruence between our inner experience and outer expression, teaching us to trust our instincts and refine our ability to navigate the complexities of human relationships. In this way, equine collaboration serves as an alchemical process, fostering transformation, integration, and a return to our innate wholeness.

A connection with horses facilitates this path. Humans often resist discomfort, avoiding difficult conversations or stillness. Instead of embracing vulnerability, we allow impulses and reactivity to manifest through substance use, busyness, or drama. Transformation requires a willingness to be with discomfort and engage in the alchemical process. Horses, an animal integral to human evolution, demand presence and compel us to confront the uncomfortable aspects of our psyche. Psychologist James Hillman (2010) stated, "The psyche animates the world it inhabits" (p. 17). Horses provide access to emotional, energetic, and physical realms far beyond what we experience independently. To develop a meaningful relationship with a horse, a human's psyche must expand to match the equine's high sensitivity and instincts.

Horses are prey animals, and their survival in the wild depends on acute awareness of their surroundings. Their nervous systems are attuned to the energy of the land and creatures around them. Being in the presence of horses requires sensory engagement. Horses pick up on excitement, fear, and dishonesty, responding with either disinterest or reactivity. Horses are massive, elegant, and expressive beings that embody distinct individuality while forming deep partnerships with humans. Engaging with them is an invitation into relationship and mystery, expanding our psyche in the process.

Modern culture teaches humans to control emotions and bodies and to suppress instincts. Especially for women, societal conditioning discourages loudness, dominance, or eccentricity. This suppression constricts consciousness, leading to psychological disease and emotional disassociation. To interact with a horse effectively, one must be assertive yet relaxed, strategic yet responsive, and firm yet soft. Horses demand an embodied intelligence that balances these qualities. They become mirrors, reflecting back our state of being and encouraging an alchemical transformation. Dr Susan Rowland (2012) wrote in *The Ecocritical Psyche*, "True alchemy is a heritage of balancing the two creation myths/forms of consciousness" (p. 44). Horses provide a distinct consciousness that challenges the dominant masculine paradigm, inviting us into greater harmony within ourselves and with our environment.

Biosemiosis

Communication with horses is nonverbal. They respond to energetic cues such as body language, breath, and presence. If horses detect flightiness or dishonesty, they disengage. Connecting with a horse happens on a cellular level, dissolving traditional concepts of communication and fostering a somatic relationship. Biosemiosis emerges when we listen beyond words, attuning to another's presence at an embodied level. Biosemiotics is "the study of meaning internal to cells" (Favareau, 2012, p. 26). This principle extends beyond human language, encompassing interspecies communication influenced by thought but driven by presence.

Humans often assume communication is reliant on speech, but the reality is a lot of our communication derives from what is unspoken. Psychologist Albert Mehrabian's (1972) research on nonverbal communication found that 93% of communication is nonverbal (p. 182). As well as language, communication is determined by behavior, facial expressions, and subtle body exchanges. People attuned to subtle body cues are often perceived as charismatic or gifted, yet this ability stems from an awareness of nonverbal communication. Horses sharpen this awareness. They give immediate feedback to every tight muscle, constricted breath, or clenched jaw. When a human softens and breathes into their body, moving from a place of embodiment rather than solely from the mind, a horse becomes more willing, reinforcing confidence in instinctive communication.

Horses operate with a technology that evolves from authenticity and wholeness. Equine expert and dancer Paula Josa-Jones (2017) attributes their congruent behaviors to their prey nature: their inside feelings and intentions match their outer behaviors and expressions (p. 7). In contrast, humans – conditioned by power-driven societies – often exhibit contradictions between internal intentions and outward behaviors. Horses, as highly attuned beings, reflect these incongruences back to us, and if we wish to strengthen our relationship with these equines, we are invited to find alignment between our internal and external realities. If a person approaches a horse with internal fear masked by forced confidence, the horse will sense the underlying emotion and respond accordingly, often with agitation or withdrawal. This mirroring teaches humans to embody authenticity and presence, developing a refined awareness of biosemiotic intelligence.

This capacity to connect with subtle and unseen forces holds profound implications for meaning-making. Jungian analyst Jerome Bernstein (2005) wrote, "Everything animate and inanimate has within it a spirit dimension and communicates *in that dimension* to those who can listen" (p. 8). Nature reflects human consciousness, and horses provide a bridge to this wisdom. The earth supports galloping hooves, the mountains provide a backdrop for our dreams, and the wind carries messages of presence. On a windy day, horses become restless, their acute hearing disrupted, making them more alert. Similarly, humans in overstimulating environments experience heightened reactivity and irritability. By stepping out of high-arousal states and attuning to the body's wisdom, we reclaim biosemiotic intelligence and reconnect with the rhythms of the natural world.

Healing the Mind–Body Split

Western culture has evolved through Cartesian dualism, which suggests a fundamental separation between the mind and the outside world. Philosopher René Descartes' famous phrase, "I think, therefore I am," prioritizes the mind over felt experience. Scholar Lee Bailey (2005) critiqued this rationalistic tradition, stating it symbolized "the rationalistic goal of a disembodied consciousness, an intellectual tradition devoted to the enchantment of pure logic and theory" (p. 64). This split contributes to an experience called the subject–object divide, in which humans view themselves as separate from the world, rather than as interconnected participants within the world.

Horses help heal this divide by drawing us into embodied experience. They operate in a world of interconnection, responding to subtle energetic shifts in their environment. To communicate with a horse effectively, one must abandon the notion of separateness and engage through presence, breath, and physical awareness. Horses teach us to shift from the detached, objectified self to the "bottomless subject" – a world of endless potential and wholeness (Bailey, 2005, p. 59). This process fosters an intuitive intelligence that reconnects us to the rhythms of nature and our own instincts.

The history of human civilization is deeply intertwined with horses. For thousands of years, horses have shaped human development, enabling transportation, agriculture, warfare, and trade. In turn, humans have selectively bred horses for strength, speed, and endurance, influencing equine evolution. This mutual evolution represents a co-adaptive relationship where both species have influenced each other's survival and behavioral patterns.

Beyond their historical utility, horses have played a profound role in shaping human leadership and emotional intelligence. The qualities necessary for successful horsemanship – patience, presence, adaptability, and mutual trust – mirror those required for effective leadership. Unlike hierarchical, dominance-based leadership models often seen in human society, horses function within a herd dynamic that prioritizes clear communication, cooperation, and emotional attunement. Observing and working with horses provides insight into nonverbal leadership, reinforcing the importance of authentic presence over authoritative control.

Horses require humans to lead with clarity and intention rather than force or coercion. They do not respond well to dominance but thrive under confident, steady guidance. This lesson translates directly to human leadership, where true influence arises not from exerting control but from fostering trust, alignment, and relational awareness. By studying equine behavior and relationships, humans can learn to navigate complex social and professional landscapes with greater emotional intelligence and adaptability. Horses have evolved alongside humans, witnessing our shifting relationship with connection and disconnection through-out history. As we stand at the threshold of our next evolution, they offer a bridge back to ourselves – guiding us toward reintegration, embodiment, and a deeper sense of wholeness.

Complexity Theory

Through relationships with horses, humans, and nature, new forms of conscious-ness emerge. Complexity theory suggests that "order emerges spontaneously from complex, dynamical systems inherent in the organism" (Bernstein, 2005, p. 48). The interconnectedness of these relationships fosters transformation. Horses embody qualities that challenge and rework human functionality. As prey animals, their psychology is rooted in non-predatory behaviors. Equine expert Linda Kohanov (2003) describes their relational approach as valuing "coopera-tion over competition, relationship over territory, responsiveness over strategy, emotion and intuition over logic, process over goal, and a creative approach to life" (p. xxx). In contrast, human culture prioritizes predatory traits such as pro-ductivity, profit, and domination over nature. By observing and learning from horses, we can rediscover balance and embrace alternative models of leadership and relationship.

Horses possess immense power but use it judiciously, reserving their energy for attunement and awareness. When humans enter their space, we gain access to highly efficient forms of perceiving, healing, and connection. Likewise, horses expand their own potential through human relationships. As herd-oriented ani-mals, they must learn to act independently when with humans. Instead of relying on their equine companions for guidance, they connect with their instincts and form a unique bond with their human partner that can encourage them to evolve in ways that expand upon their strength and capacity.

Horses live in a constant state of awareness and responsiveness to their sur-roundings. As prey animals, their survival depends on their ability to sense subtle environmental cues and make split-second decisions. They do not operate from rigid patterns but rather from an ability to adapt to what is happening in the pre-sent moment. This is a crucial skill for humans, particularly in modern leadership, where uncertainty is an unavoidable aspect of life. Working with horses teaches individuals how to become comfortable with the unknown, to move beyond fear-based reactions, and to engage with the world in a state of fluid awareness.

Equine relationships also highlight the value of nonlinear problem-solving. Unlike traditional hierarchical thinking that seeks control and predictability, complexity theory suggests that growth emerges through interaction, feedback, and adaptability. Horses challenge humans to be present, to listen beyond spo-ken words, and to trust the process of unfolding relationships. By embracing this approach, individuals can develop resilience, intuition, and the capacity to engage with life's inherent uncertainty.

Horses offer a gateway into the *borderland*, a term Bernstein (2005) described as "the psychic space where the hyper-developed and overly rational Western ego is in the process of reconnecting with its split-off roots in nature" (p. 9). In relationship with horses, humans soften their egos, moving beyond intellectual dominance and into embodied, instinctual awareness. This reconnection provides an antidote to modern fragmentation, offering pathways to healing through interspecies relationships. Horses provide a pathway for psychological integration, bridging the gap between intellect and instinct. As Jungian scholar Keiron Le Grice (2013) stated, individuation begins when we recognize that "the unconscious roots of our personality misalign with the conscious plan of our life" (p. 82). Horses help us realign with our authentic selves by demanding presence, responsiveness, and embodied intelligence, reinforcing the idea that transformation emerges through relationship.

Bridging Connection Beyond Horses

While this paper focuses on the transformative potential of human–horse relationships, the principles explored extend beyond equine interactions. Any relationship that invites us out of our intellect and into embodied presence – whether through movement, nature, art, or deep human connection – can serve as a catalyst for individuation. Horses are one path, but the essence of this work is about reconnecting with the wisdom of the body and the intelligence of intuition.

By engaging in experiences that ground us in our physicality and instincts, we cultivate wholeness, resilience, and a greater sense of belonging to ourselves and the world. These small acts of awareness bring us into the present moment, reconnecting us with the wisdom and potential held within the body. By embracing these practices regularly, you'll discover that true leadership power emerges not from intellectual force but from embodied presence – the ability to remain centered, responsive, and attuned to the subtle energies that shape our interactions and organizations.

Somatic Breathing Practice

This somatic breathing practice introduces an intentional breathing technique that connects mind and body to reduce stress, increase awareness, and promote overall well-being.

Grounding Breath

Stand with feet shoulder-width apart. Visualize roots extending from your feet into the earth. Breathe deeply, allowing tension to release with each exhale, flowing down through your imagined roots. Start by noticing which parts of the body are touching the ground – if standing, spread through the toes; if sitting, press your seat into the chair. Next, soften and lengthen the breath, paying attention to where it travels in the body. Another practice is to gently run the fingers along the hands, noticing the sensitive nerve endings. Additionally, observe the textures around you – the fabric of your clothing, the fur of a pet, or the grain of wood beneath your fingers. Engage the senses further by tuning into smells, tastes, and ambient sounds. This practice mirrors how horses maintain constant ground connection through their hooves.

Creative Practice

Journaling, as a creative practice, is an expressive activity that fosters mind–body connections.

Biosemiotic Journaling

After meetings or important interactions, write freely about the nonverbal elements you observed, body language, energy shifts, and what remained unspoken. Consider: What was communicated beyond words? This develops your capacity for reading subtle cues.

Reflective Practice

Reflective practice encourages introspection and conscious examination of thoughts, emotions, and experiences to deepen self-knowledge and personal growth.

Complexity Meditation

Sit quietly for 15 minutes. Observe the natural rise and fall of your breathing. Contemplate a current leadership challenge not as a problem to solve but as a system to witness with curiosity. Ask: *What is trying to emerge here?* Allow insights to arise without forcing conclusions.

Effective leadership emerges not from intellectual dominance but from embodied presence, authentic communication, and attunement to subtle energies within complex systems. Regular practice will help cultivate the balance of assertiveness and receptivity that horses naturally model.

Conclusion

Western culture prioritizes intellect and productivity over feeling and rest, leading to individual and collective imbalance. Reconnecting mind and body, rational thought and emotional awareness, fosters healing. Horses demand this integration, requiring humans to engage with presence and embodied wisdom. In our culture, we are taught to act with confidence while suppressing instincts and uniqueness. Horses demonstrate how to embody both expression and instinct in balance. Standing beside a horse heightens bodily awareness. Sitting on a horse's back synchronizes human and equine intelligence. Engaging in partnership with horses expands human consciousness, opening new pathways for healing, connection, and transformation in the modern world.

References

Bailey, L. W. (2005). *The enchantments of technology*. University of Illinois Press.

Bernstein, J. (2005). *Living in the borderland: The evolution of consciousness and the challenge of healing trauma*. Routledge.

Favareau, D. (2012). *A more developed sign: Interpreting the work of Jesper Hoffmeyer*. Tartu University Press.

Hillman, J. (2010). The therapeutic value of alchemical language: A heated introduction. In J. Hillman (Ed.), *Alchemical psychology* (Uniform ed., Vol. 5, pp. 9–19). Spring Publications.

Josa-Jones, P. (2017). *Our horses, ourselves: Discovering the common body*. Trafalgar Square Books.

Jung, C. G. (1953). *Two essays on analytical psychology* (R. F. C. Hull, Trans.). Princeton University Press. (Original work published 1928)

Kohanov, L. (2003). *Riding between the worlds*. New World Library.

Le Grice, K. (2013). *The rebirth of the hero: Mythology as a guide to spiritual transformation*. Aeon Books.

Mehrabian, A. (1972). *Nonverbal communication*. Aldine-Atherton.

Rowland, S. (2012). *The ecocritical psyche: Literature, complexity evolution and Jung*. Routledge.

Schwartz-Salant, N. (1995). *Encountering Jung on alchemy*. Princeton University Press.

Chapter 3

Exploring the Frankenstein-ian Progression of Social Media's Architecture

Alicia D. Crumpton

Kaleidoventure LLC, USA

Abstract

This chapter examines parallels between Victor Frankenstein's creation and modern technological innovations, particularly social media platforms. In the summer of 1816, Mary Shelley's Frankenstein emerged from a ghost story challenge, creating an enduring narrative about creation, responsibility, and unintended consequences. Through this literary lens, we explore how both creators pursued ambition without fully considering ethical implications, resulting in unforeseen consequences for human well-being and social cohesion. For leaders navigating technological innovation, Frankenstein offers a powerful framework for understanding the responsibilities of creation, the importance of ethical foresight, and the necessity of digital boundaries. The analysis explores philosophical shifts in human–technology relationships, draws connections to present-day technology development, and introduces somatic practices and reflective exercises for leaders seeking to foster healthy technology engagement for themselves and their organizations.

Keywords: Technology ethics; social media; digital well-being; leadership; innovation ethics; Frankenstein; technological responsibility; digital design ethics

Introduction

In the summer of 1816, a group of writers, including Mary Shelley, gathered in Switzerland and challenged each other to write ghost stories. From this creative exercise emerged *Frankenstein*, a tale of creation, abandonment, and destruction

Artful Leadership: Retreat, Recenter, and Rewild, 21–32

Copyright © 2026 by Alicia D. Crumpton

Published under exclusive licence by Emerald Publishing Limited

doi:10.1108/S2058-880120250000010004

that continues to resonate today. Writer J. Paul Hunter (2012) reflected, "Frankenstein (the name) became a kind of all-purpose watchword for creativity gone wrong and monstrosity gone wild." Furthermore, our captivation, suggested clinical psychologist Robert Romanyshyn (2019), presents a rationale for further interrogation, specifically related to technological innovations.

Our continued fascination with this narrative suggests it holds valuable insights for our technological age. Through a close reading of *Frankenstein*, this chapter examines parallels between Victor Frankenstein's creation and today's technological innovations, particularly social media platforms. The Center for Humane Technology (n.d.) asserted that our society is being hijacked by technology: "What began as a race to monetize our attention is now eroding the pillars of our society: mental health, democracy, social relationships, and our children." Thus, a sense of urgency for this chapter, where a comparison reveals how creators in both contexts pursued ambition without fully considering ethical implications, lost control of their creations, and witnessed unintended consequences unfold.

For leaders navigating technological innovation along with their own usage, *Frankenstein* offers a powerful framework for understanding the responsibilities of creation, the importance of foresight, and the necessity for digital boundary setting. This analysis explores philosophical shifts in human–technology relationships, summarizes key elements of Shelley's story, draws connections to present-day technology creation and adoption, and introduces somatic practices and reflective exercises for leaders seeking to foster healthy technology engagement for themselves and their organizations.

Historical Context: Shifting Worldviews

To understand the relevance of *Frankenstein* to modern technology debates, we must first consider the philosophical context in which Shelley wrote. The early 1800s marked a profound transition from worldviews that emphasized human interconnection with creation to a scientific paradigm prioritizing objectivity, rationality, and progress.

From Interconnection to Mechanism

Within the Judeo-Christian tradition, creation stories portrayed a harmonious, unified relationship between humans, nature, and the divine. Humanity's interconnection with creation was "acknowledged and thought of as binding together self, society, and the cosmos" (Goodman, 2003, p. 31). This worldview was giving way to a scientific perspective that validated knowledge through empirical observation and experimentation.

Philosopher Hannah Arendt (1958/1998) documented how this shift profoundly altered humans' self-perception, purpose, and sense of responsibility. The world transformed from a sacred space to a mechanistic system that could be manipulated, controlled, and consumed. Earth itself, once humanity's nurturing home, became "a prison for men's bodies" (p. 2), fostering alienation from both nature and other humans.

From Community to Commodity

As society embraced scientific rationalism, the private sphere of home, family, and subjective experience became subordinate to the public domain of objectivity, production, and consumption. Progress came to mean "the accelerated consumption of nature and the quantitative increase in produced goods" (Arendt, 1958/1998, p. 105). Humans themselves became viewed as "the same and interchangeable" (p. 123) within systems of labor and exchange.

This mechanization produced what Arendt (1958/1998) called "universal unhappiness" and "survival consumption" (p. 134), with society "dazzled by the abundance of its growing fertility and caught in the smooth functioning of a never-ending process, [but] no longer able to recognize its own futility" (p. 135). Human value became tied to production capacity and wealth, creating conditions for the dehumanization of those with fewer economic resources.

From Contemplation to Automation

The technological worldview encouraged "automatism in man, actions without thinking" (Arendt, 1958/1998, p. 155). Humans became less capable of discerning meaning or attributing intrinsic value to nature and art. Evidence of alienation included rising superstition, decreasing common sense, and declining trust in one's capacity to reason.

Arendt (1958/1998) observed that "the world of experiment seems always capable of becoming a manmade reality ... this puts man once more into the prison of his own mind" (p. 288), diminishing transcendence, mystery, and contemplation. This historical context sets the stage for understanding how *Frankenstein* critiques unbounded scientific ambition and creation without ethical consideration.

Frankenstein: A Summary of Key Elements

Mary Shelley's narrative begins with explorer Robert Walton writing to his sister from the Arctic. Describing his scientific expedition, Walton laments his isolation: "I have one want which I have never yet been able to satisfy ... I have no friend" (Shelley, 1831/2012, p. 10). In this remote setting, Walton encounters Victor Frankenstein pursuing his creation across the ice who proceeds to tell his story.

Victor Frankenstein was shaped by his reading works about alchemy, the occult, and the supernatural, including works by Cornelius Agrippa, Paracelsus, and Albertus Magnus. His father said, "do not waste your time upon this; it is trash" (Shelley, 1831/2012, p. 23). Instead, Frankenstein procured all the works and continued to read remarking, "My dreams were therefore undisturbed by reality; and I entered with the greatest diligence into the search of the philosopher's stone and the elixir of life" (p. 23). Alchemists believed that the philosopher's stone held the ability to transmute base metals into gold or silver, and most importantly was capable of healing the body, securing immortality. Frankenstein dreamed, "what glory would attend the discovery, if I could banish disease from the human frame and render man invulnerable to any but a violent death" (p. 23).

After years of study, he experienced a breakthrough moment: "I succeeded in discovering the cause of generation and life; I became myself capable of bestowing animation upon lifeless matter" (p. 32). Rather than questioning whether he should proceed, Frankenstein envisioned how "a new species would bless me as its creator" (p. 33).

In a moment of moral reasoning, Frankenstein recalled how "I doubted at first whether I should … [but], my imagination was too much exalted by my first success to permit me to doubt of my ability" (Shelley, 1831/2012, p. 32). Frankenstein, so filled with possibility, did not consider potential consequences or even question whether he should proceed with the creative act. Instead, he envisioned how, "A new species would bless me as its creator" and "I might in process of time renew life where death had apparently devoted the body to corruption" (p. 33). He envisioned introducing the possibility of overcoming death, and his motivation was amplified through his ego.

Working feverishly and neglecting relationships, nature, and his own well-being, Frankenstein assembled a creature from human remains and brought it to life using electricity. When his creation opened its eyes, Frankenstein's triumphant vision collapsed: "now that I had finished, the beauty of the dream vanished, and breathless horror and disgust filled my heart" (Shelley, 1831/2012, p. 36). He abandoned his creation without guidance or support.

The abandoned creature, learning language by observing a family from afar, developed sophisticated moral reasoning and self-awareness. Reading Milton's *Paradise Lost*, the creature identified with both Adam (the first of his kind) and Satan (the rejected outcast). What he desired most was acceptance and relationship: "My heart yearned to be known and loved by these amiable creatures" (Shelley, 1831/2012, p. 92). When humans rejected him based on his appearance, the creature turned to vengeance, declaring "everlasting war against the species" (p. 95).

Confronting Frankenstein, the creature demanded a female companion, promising they would retreat from human society. Frankenstein initially agreed but later destroyed the female creation, fearing they might reproduce a "race of devils" that would threaten humanity. In retribution, the creature murdered Frankenstein's friend Henry, his bride Elizabeth, and indirectly caused the death of his father.

At the story's conclusion, Frankenstein dies pursuing his creation. The creature, standing over his creator's body, acknowledges his crimes but asks poignantly: "Am I to be thought the only criminal when all humankind sinned against me?" (Shelley, 1831/2012). The story ends with the creature planning his self-destruction on a funeral pyre.

From Frankenstein to Facebook: Parallels in Creation

Mary Shelley's tale of creator and creation gone awry provides a powerful metaphor for modern technological innovation, particularly in social media development. Many have critiqued unquestioned notions of progress and ethical considerations associated with technological adoption and advancement (cf. Bailey, 2005; Baym, 2010; Carr, 2010; Song, 2021; Turkle, 2011). Just as Frankenstein pursued God-like power without fully considering its implications, today's tech innovators have created digital platforms that have evolved beyond their original intentions. While Frankenstein's creation was physical, social media architects have created psychological architectures that reshape human behavior, attention, and social relationships at a massive scale.

The Evolution of Digital Technology

Computing transformed from a human profession to a technological revolution that reshaped society. In the early 20th century, "computers" were skilled humans who performed calculations manually. Highlighted in the film *Hidden Figures* (Melfi, 2016), women, instead of computers, manually performed calculations that supported, for example, space flight. The film illustrates how the introduction of the mainframe computer shifted humans' role, requiring specialized expertise. The development of mainframe computers in the mid-20th century led to innovative programming languages, networking capabilities, and graphical interfaces. By the mid-1960s, "computers for business had become well established" (Campbell-Kelly & Aspray, 1996, p. 207).

The creation of transistors and microprocessors miniaturized computers from room-sized machines to personal devices, accelerating access for everyone. Microsoft, founded in 1975 by Bill Gates and Paul Allen, and Apple, founded in 1976 by Steve Jobs and Steve Wozniak, revolutionized personal computing. This innovation was so significant that in 1983, *Time Magazine* named the personal computer "Machine of the Year," with Roger Rosenblatt (1983) characterizing society's anticipation: "Deep in your all-American heart ... you crave this little honey, which will count for you and store for you and talk for you."

The internet, created by Tim Berners-Lee, connected these computers globally, while the Mosaic browser (later Netscape) increased accessibility.

The cell phone, in various forms, emerged in the 1960s. Watchers of the TV show *Get Smart* (Brooks & Henry, 1965–1970) watched Agent 86 talk into his hidden shoe phone. In Stone (1987), the stockbroker Gordon Gecko in *Wall Street* used a Motorola DynaTAC mobile phone, characterized affectionately as a brick phone due to its shape and size. The character *Jerry Maguire* in the Crowe's (1996) film of the same name conducted his sports business on a cell phone. In the first *Sex and the City* film released in King (2008), the character Samantha Jones handed Carrie Bradshaw an iPhone. Film and television chronicled the adaptation and adoption of cellular technology. Meanwhile, mobile phones evolved from bulky novelties in the 1980s to essential devices by the 2000s. Apple's iPhone, introduced in 2007, fundamentally changed our relationship with technology by putting internet-connected computers in our pockets, complete with cameras that turned everyone into documenters of daily life.

Technologies like electronic mail (email) and instant messaging transformed personal communication and collaboration. Social media applications such as Amazon, Google, Facebook, Twitter, and Instagram were designed to leverage technology to influence our buying, communication, querying, sources of information, and interaction. Cultural commentator, Craig Detweiler (2014), coined the terms *iGods* when referring to these applications, critiquing how often people adopt and adapt to their usage "without pausing to consider whether they are good or bad, helpful or hurtful." What can be a naïve assumption related to creation and notions of progress is the assumption of do no harm.

The Intentional Design of Social Media

Unlike Frankenstein's creation, which was abandoned without guidance, social media platforms were deliberately designed to capture and maintain user attention. Economist Herbert A. Simon's (1997, *The Economist*, 2009) assessment of administrative behavior posited that attention is a scarce resource in decision-making, so you need to structure processes to manage and direct attention effectively. Drawing on Simon's theory of attention as a scarce resource, creators built systems to direct and exploit human attention. For example, Nir Eyal (2012b), who teaches companies how to capture attention, openly advocated for "variable rewards" that "drive [users] crazy." This approach leverages the same psychological mechanisms as gambling machines. Social media incorporates several key design elements including: algorithms, the pull-to-refresh mechanism, the like button, notifications, and the hooked model of variable rewards, all collectively shaping human behavior and experience in profound ways.

1. *Algorithms* determine what content users see, personalizing experiences to increase engagement. In so doing, "filter bubbles" (Pariser, 2011) curates our feed only showing us "what it thinks we should see."
2. *The pull-to-refresh mechanism* mimics slot machines, creating anticipation and dopamine release with each new content load. This potentially increases screen time due to persistent desire for updates and new content.
3. *The like button* provides instant social validation but fosters unhealthy comparison and addiction to approval.
4. *Notifications* keep users engaged with real-time updates but create distractions and anxiety.
5. *The Hooked Model* uses triggers, actions, intermittent rewards, and investment to build habits, intentionally fostering addictive behaviors. Developed by Nir Eyal (2012a), the hooked model introduces users to a trigger, action, reward, and investment strategy that serves to build habits.

Together, these elements create a dynamic and engaging social media environment, while also presenting significant challenges related to well-being and ethical use.

Creators' Remorse

Just as Frankenstein came to regret his creation, many social media architects now express grave concerns about their innovations, alleging that social media creators took on a puppet master role driven by a vision for manipulative, persuasive omniscience.

Loren Brichter, who created the pull-to-refresh mechanism, compared his invention to a slot machine that "could easily retire" but continues to serve "a psychological function" (as cited in Lewis, 2017).

Tristan Harris, former Google employee, considers technology's impact on attention "the most urgent problem," affecting "our democracy and our ability to have the conversations and relationships that we want" (as cited in Lewis, 2017). Chris Marcellino, who helped invent notification systems, acknowledges that these technologies "affect the same neurological pathways as gambling and drug use" (as cited in Lewis, 2017).

Sean Parker, Facebook's first president, admitted: "I don't know if I really understood the consequences … it literally changes your relationship with society, with each other" (as cited in Ong, 2017). Justin Rosenstein, creator of Facebook like button, acknowledged there is a "growing concern" about user addiction, partial attention, "severely limiting people's ability to focus, and possibly lowering IQ" (as cited in Lewis, 2017).

James Williams, former Google strategist, described the attention economy as "the largest, most standardized and most centralized form of attentional control in human history" (as cited in Lewis, 2017). Furthermore, the Internet, according to Williams, "[is becoming] an all-encompassing, persuasive environment, one that ultimately contributed (contributes) to humans giving up goals, subsuming to fake news and persistent outrage … contributing to a kind of 'supercharged narcissism'" (as cited in Lewis, 2017).

Written in 2001, prior to the advent of smartphone technology, specifically the iPhone, Naisbitt et al. (2001) presciently argued that we need to intentionally question "what place technology should have in our lives and in society" (p. XX). They described life with technology as being in the *technologically intoxicated zone* characterized as "spiritually empty, dissatisfying and dangerous, and impossible to climb out of unless we recognize that we're in it" (p. 11).

Human Consequences: The Monster Returns

While digital technology has empowered humanity in countless ways, it has also created significant social and psychological challenges. Like Frankenstein's creature, whose suffering led to destructive behavior, social media's unintended consequences include (Haidt, 2024):

1. *Social Isolation:* Despite greater connectivity, heavy social media use correlates with reduced in-person interaction and increased loneliness.
2. *Digital Addiction:* Constant access to social media creates problematic patterns of overuse, reduced productivity, and attention difficulties.
3. *Destruction of Shared Reality:* Jonathan Haidt (2024) compared our current social fragmentation to the Tower of Babel, noting "something went terribly wrong … we are disoriented, unable to speak the same language or recognize the same truth."

4. *Mental Health Impacts:* Social media use correlates with increased anxiety, depression, and other mental health issues, particularly among adolescents.
5. *Sleep Disruption:* Blue light from screens and nighttime use disrupt sleep patterns, creating downstream effects on physical and mental well-being.

As we navigate our shared digital landscape, we see that it is a blessing and a curse. The parallels to Frankenstein's cautionary tale remind us that innovation without foresight and responsibility can lead to unintended suffering.

Key Parallels Between Frankenstein and Social Media

Mary Shelley's Frankenstein and today's social media landscape share striking parallels in their creation stories, impacts, and unintended consequences – both representing powerful innovations that eventually escaped their creators' control and vision. What follows is an examination of the similarities in worldviews, identity formation, intentional design choices, and ethical considerations illuminating technology's double-edged nature and our responsibility as both creators and consumers of digital experiences.

Differing Worldviews

Victor Frankenstein represented a hybrid worldview combining alchemy's mysticism with modern science's empiricism. This combination fueled his hubris and belief he could transcend natural limits. Similarly, social media creators embrace a technological worldview emphasizing connectivity, optimization, and progress, while sometimes neglecting human and social consequences.

Identity, Isolation, and Obsession

Both narratives center on identity fragmentation, isolation, and obsession. Frankenstein's identity became consumed by his scientific ambition, while his creature struggled with rejection and alienation. Similarly, social media creators often shape their identities around their work, while users curate idealized online personas that can lead to fragmented self-perception.

In terms of isolation, Frankenstein withdrew from relationships to pursue his work, while his creature experienced profound loneliness due to social rejection. Likewise, social media creators can become distanced from the ethical implications of their work, and users often experience isolation despite apparent connectivity. Despite being more connected than ever, many social media users experience feelings of alienation and isolation. The curated nature combined with affirmative nature of social media can amplify a sense of inadequacy and loneliness as compared to the lives of others.

The theme of obsession manifests in Frankenstein's single-minded pursuit of creation and his creature's quest for revenge. Similarly, social media creators became fixated on user engagement, metrics, and revenue potential, while users develop dependency behaviors that impact mental health. Many social media users develop obsessions with social media, constantly looking at their phone and struggling to unplug, an obsession that can lead to addictive behaviors.

Intentional Design Versus Abandonment

Frankenstein abandoned his creation without vision or guidance for its future. In contrast, social media creators implemented highly intentional design strategies focused on attention capture and retention. These include algorithmic curation, data collection, engagement maximization, and emotional amplification – all aimed at building profitable platforms rather than prioritizing human well-being.

Ethical Abdication and Unforeseen Consequences

Victor Frankenstein pursued creation without considering moral implications, then abandoned his responsibility when confronted with the reality of his work. This neglect led to tragedy for everyone involved. Similarly, social media creators often prioritized engagement and profit over ethical considerations, creating systems that facilitate addiction, polarization, misinformation, and mental health challenges.

The unintended consequences in both cases stem from creators' failure to anticipate potential negative outcomes and establish ethical guidelines. As social media platforms have grown to unprecedented scale, their effects have rippled through society in ways their architects did not predict or prepare for.

Contemplating these parallels between Frankenstein's monster and our technology use, a question arises about how to engage with technology more mindfully. By reflecting on our individual relationship with social media and technology, we can reclaim agency, transforming ourselves from passive consumers into conscious participants shaping technology's role in our lives.

Somatic Breathing, Creative and Reflective Practices

Leaders navigating today's digital landscape face unique challenges that parallel Frankenstein's dilemma. Frankenstein neglected his physical health and emotional needs during his obsessive creation process; likewise, today's leaders need practices to reconnect themselves with their bodies, breath, and present–moment awareness. Consider integrating somatic breathing practices, creative exploration, and intentional digital detox into your leadership routine.

Somatic Breathing

By reconnecting with your body's wisdom through conscious breath work, you create space for clarity and presence that technology often disrupts.

Box Breathing for Stress Regulation

Inhale slowly through the nose for a count of four. Hold the breath for a count of four. Exhale completely through the mouth for a count of four. Hold the empty lungs for a count of four. Repeat for 1–3 minutes.

Diaphragmatic Breathing for Focus

Place one hand on your chest and one on your abdomen. Breathe deeply through your nose, ensuring your abdomen expands. Exhale slowly through slightly pursed lips. Practice for 1–3 minutes before important decisions or meetings.

Creative Practices

Creative practices – whether writing, movement, or artistic expression – activate different neural pathways, generating fresh perspectives on persistent challenges.

Morning Pages (Cameron, 2002)

Find a quiet and comfortable space where you can write without distractions. Just let the words flow onto a page, stream of consciousness, do not overthink. Continue writing until you have written, drawn, or doodled on three pages. Once finished, take a moment to reflect on the experience. Notice any shifts in your mood, mindset, or clarity.

Technology-Free Walk

Set a timer for 20–30 minutes. You can walk more or less, key is establishing a set time every day to foster a habit of walking. Before you begin, stand still for a moment. Let your body relax, take a few deep breaths. Note how you're feeling and thoughts you're having. Start walking at a slow, deliberate pace. As you walk, pay attention to your breathing, noticing the rhythm and how it synchronizes with your steps.

Reflective Practices

Voluntarily refraining from using technology, specifically smartphones and computers, creates a space wherein you can regain control over time and attention, opening up spaces for things you want to pursue within intention.

Technology Detox

Establish regular periods when you disconnect completely from technology. Before the detox, reflect and journal about the following: Why am I doing this? What is my motivation to do this? What is important to me? What does a healthy relationship with technology look like? How do I want to spend my time? What would success look like? Set a goal such as staying off technology from dinner until the next day or on Saturdays.

During the detox, plan outdoor activities that allow you to connect with nature, incorporate daily breathwork, participate in a hobby such as painting, cooking, welding; and write in your journal a reflection of what you are thinking, feeling, and experiencing.

Following the detox, reflect upon the following: What did you learn? What will you change permanently? What do you want others to know?

Establish Technology Boundaries

Establish clear expectations about work-related after-hours communication. Turn off the sound and notifications on your computer and cell phone during certain periods of the day. Set daily specific time limits and ensure a healthy balance with other activities. Maintain a reflection journal, writing or drawing about the experiences, specifically questioning the effects that changing technology habits has and how changing the amount of time spent on technology has affected what you pay attention to.

References

Arendt, H. (1998). *The human condition* (2nd ed.). University of Chicago Press. (Original work published 1958)

Bailey, L. W. (2005). *The enchantments of technology*. University of Illinois Press.

Baym, N. K. (2010). *Personal connections in the digital age*. Polity Press.

Brooks, M., & Henry, B. (Creators). (1965–1970). *Get smart* [TV series]. CBS Productions.

Cameron, J. (2002). *The Artist's way: A spiritual path to higher creativity* (10th Anniversary ed.). Putnam Books.

Campbell-Kelly, M., & Aspray, W. (1996). *Computer: A history of the information machine*. Basic Books.

Carr, N. G. (2010). *The shallows: What the Internet is doing to our brains*. W.W. Norton.

Center for Humane Technology. (n.d.). http://humanetech.com/

Crowe, C. (Director). (1996). *Jerry Maguire* [Film]. Tristar Pictures.

Detweiler, C. (2014). *IGods: How technology shapes our spiritual and social lives*. Brazos Press.

Eyal, N. (2012a). *The hooked model: How to manufacture desire in 4 steps*. https://www.nirandfar.com/how-to-manufacture-desire/

Eyal, N. (2012b). *Want to hook your users drive them crazy*. TechCrunch. https://techcrunch.com/2012/03/25/want-to-hook-your-users-drive-them-crazy/

Goodman, A. (2003). *Now what? Developing our future: Understanding our place in the unfolding universe*. Peter Lang.

Haidt, J. (2024). *The anxious generation: How the great rewiring of childhood is causing an epidemic of mental illness*. Penguin Press.

Hunter, J. P. (2012). Introduction. In M. Shelley (Ed.), *Frankenstein* (2nd Norton critical ed., pp. ix–xviii). W.W. Norton.

King, M. P. (Director). (2008). *Sex and the city* [Film]. New Line Cinema.

Lewis, P. (2017, October 6). "Our minds can be hijacked": The tech insiders who fear a smartphone dystopia. *The Guardian*. https://www.theguardian.com/technology/2017/oct/05/smartphone-addiction-silicon-valley-dystopia

Melfi, T. (Director). (2016). *Hidden figures* [Film]. Fox 2000 Pictures.

Naisbitt, J., Naisbitt, N., & Philips, D. (2001). *High tech high touch: Technology and our accelerated search for meaning*. Nicholas Brealey.

Ong, T. (2017, November 9). Sean Parker on Facebook: 'God only knows what it's doing to our children's brains'. *The Verge*. https://www.theverge.com/2017/11/9/16627724/sean-parker-facebook-childrens-brains-feedback-loop

Pariser, E. (2011). *Beware online "filter bubbles"*. Ted Talk [Video, 9:05] https://youtu.be/B8ofWFx525s

Romanyshyn, R. D. (2019). *Victor Frankenstein, the monster and the shadows of technology: The Frankenstein prophecies*. Routledge.

Rosenblatt, R. (1983). A new world dawns. *Time*. https://time.com/archive/6598096/a-new-world-dawns/

Shelley, M. (2012). *Frankenstein* (2nd Norton Critical ed.). W.W. Norton. (Original work published 1831)

Simon, H. A. (1997). *Administrative behavior: A study of decision-making processes in administrative organizations* (4th ed.). Free Press.

Song, F. W. (2021). *Restless devices: Recovering personhood, presence, and place in the digital age*. IVP Academic.

Stone, O. (Director). (1987). *Wall Street* [Film]. American Entertainment Partners.

The Economist. (2009). Herman Simon. *The Economist*. https://www.economist.com/news/2009/03/20/herbert-simon

Time Magazine. (1983). *Cover page*. https://content.time.com/time/covers/0,16641,19830103,00.html

Turkle, S. (2011). *Alone together: Why we expect more from technology and less from each other*. Basic Books.

Chapter 4

Being and Knowing: A Virtue-based Approach to Leadership and Knowledge Acquisition

Michael R. Young

Faulkner University, USA

Abstract

This chapter explores the fundamental relationship between epistemology, virtue ethics, and leadership through a philosophical examination of how we acquire and apply knowledge. Beginning with an exploration of our intrinsic human curiosity and desire to understand the world, classical and contemporary perspectives on knowledge acquisition, including rationalism, empiricism, testimony, intuition, and faith-based understanding, are explored. Drawing from Aristotle, Plato, and contemporary philosophers, a virtue-based framework for becoming "good knowers" is presented that integrates intellectual and moral development. The Golden Mean framework is applied to intellectual virtues such as curiosity, autonomy, and thoroughness, demonstrating how leaders can cultivate these qualities both personally and organizationally. By connecting epistemological foundations with practical leadership applications, it is argued that virtuous knowledge-seeking is foundational to effective leadership and provides specific practices for developing intellectual virtues in leadership contexts. The "beauty of virtuous leadership" lies in its transformative power to effect positive change through small but significant virtuous acts.

Keywords: Virtue ethics; epistemology; intellectual virtues; Aristotle's Golden Mean; knowledge acquisition; moral formation; practical wisdom; philosophical leadership

Artful Leadership: Retreat, Recenter, and Rewild, 33–49
Copyright © 2026 by Michael R. Young
Published under exclusive licence by Emerald Publishing Limited
doi:10.1108/S2058-880120250000010005

Introduction

Well, here we are. We exist. We exist in a world. It is a world of objective things and living others. The famous 20th-century philosopher, Martin Heidegger (1927/1962), in his work, *Being and Time*, provides a phenomenological analysis (that is, a study of the phenomena that appear to us in our consciousness) of our experience of being or existing. He refers to this experience of being as our *thrownness* into the reality of existing as a *being-in-the-world* (pp. 78–86). With finely nuanced terminology, Heidegger attempted to describe our way of finding ourselves thrust into the world with no choice on our part to exist, or choice of "worlds" in which to exist in, we simply exist, here, now. We encounter our life-world (Husserl, 1970, p. 154), like waking up in the morning to a new day. We greet this world with a certain past, with a particular attunement or mood to understand it, and with the possibilities we project into the future. Pope Francis (2024) referred to Heidegger's insight stating, "philosophy does not begin with a pure concept or certainty but with a shock," and "without deep emotion, thought cannot begin. The first mental image would thus be goosebumps." So again, we find ourselves here, alive, in the world, and our first response should be one of wonder and even excitement. It is such wonder and excitement of existence that moves us to seek knowledge and understanding of the world and others about us – and to want to share such knowledge with others.

We are curious creatures. It is intrinsic to our nature. We want to know and understand things. As Aristotle (350 B.C.E./2003) noted long ago,

> All men by nature desire to know. An indication of this is the delight we take in our senses; for even apart from their usefulness they are loved for themselves; and above all others the sense of sight. For not only with a view to action, but even when we are not going to do anything, we prefer seeing (one might say) to everything else. The reason is that this, most of all the senses, makes us know and brings to light many differences between things. (*Metaphysics*, Bk. 1, Ch. 1, 980a)

As knowers, we can find ourselves in three different possible states in relation to knowledge (Gordon, 2018):

1. knowing (spurred on by a question and arrived at a particular answer),
2. not knowing, but aware that you do not know (a lingering question with a set of possible answers or no answer), or
3. not knowing and not aware of not knowing (absence of a question).

Amid the distinct states of knowing, not knowing, or not knowing one does not know, "the human mind privileges certain uncertainties over others" (Gordon, 2018, pp. 37–42). We are curious about different questions that arise. The range of the quality of our curiosity can range from the frivolous to the profound. The motivations for satisfying our curiosity can range from the simple pleasure in the satisfaction of knowing to the intense anxiety of needing to know for life's sake and life's meaning. Thus, our desire to know is largely utilitarian for our own purposes, but this utility of seeking knowledge can be immature and self-centered or mature by seeking knowledge for the common good of all. Our motivating utility to know requires maturation through education (learning how to know and what to know), modeling (from examples and stories of mature knowers), habituation (practice of coming to knowledge and understanding), and desiring to know for the common good (seeking to know and understand what is excellent for oneself and others).

What is Knowledge?

Here is an attempt to define knowledge from Plato via Socrates' dialogue with Theaetetus from long ago:

> Now when a man gets a true judgment about something without an account, his soul is in a state of truth as regards that thing, but he does not know it; for someone who cannot give and take an account of a thing is ignorant about it. But when he has also got an account of it, he is capable of all this and is made perfect in knowledge. (Plato, 4th century B.C./1997, *Theaetetus*, 202c)

Yet, by the end of the dialogue, both Socrates and Theaetetus reject this definition because of the lack of clarity of how one gives an *account* of some knowledge claim. The frustration of ending with no conclusion for a definition is common within Platonic dialogues.

Nevertheless, in another dialogue, *Meno* (Plato, 385 B.C./1997), the subject is addressed once again. The young slave, Meno, and Socrates tackle the subject of the nature of virtue. Both agree that knowledge of virtue is of excellent value for living virtuously. However, during the course of the dialogue, they acknowledge that one can live virtuously without having knowledge of virtue. The qualifier is that they can do so only by having a true opinion of what virtue is, and it so happens to align with actual knowledge of the nature of virtue. So, we have opinion (a right opinion) versus knowledge, with both achieving the same results. Which is better? Both Socrates and Meno agree that it is better to have knowledge over opinion, which can be wrong, that is, the opinion does not happen to align with true knowledge. But how does one distinguish between knowledge, true opinion, and false opinion? Plato returns to the need to give an account for a knowledge claim, that is, to be able to provide justification that supports a knowledge claim:

> For true opinions, as long as they remain, are a fine thing and all they do is good, but they are not willing to remain long, and they escape from man's mind, so that they are not worth much until one ties them down by giving an account of the reason why... After they are tied down, in the first place they become knowledge, and then remain in place. (Plato, 385 B.C./1997, *Meno*, 98a)

Thus, the difference between knowledge and opinion, and even true opinion, is that knowledge can provide a reason, a justification for its truth claims, whereas an opinion, even a true opinion, cannot. With this distinction achieved, we can further assert that the definition of knowledge is a belief that can be justified by reason or experience, which establishes a claim of truth. The three key terms in this definition are belief, justification, and truth. Belief is an initial requirement for establishing knowledge. While belief cannot be equated with knowledge, since a belief can be wrong, it is, nevertheless, the first step in seeking to establish a claim of knowledge as true. Justification is the means of verifying a belief as true. Different truth claims involve different modes of justification depending on the nature of the content or type of knowledge. For example, a scientist employs measurements, physical tests, etc., to justify the truth of a knowledge claim, whereas an historian relies on documents, records, testimonies, etc., for claims of historical truth. Justifications for knowledge can be of various strengths or quality of validity. Justification is not equivalent to truth automatically but requires examination or testing of its strength or validity. Hence, many scientific claims of knowledge of the past have been overturned due to further examination, experimentation, and newly acquired information. With these nuances acknowledged, our proposed definition of knowledge above as "a belief that can be justified by reason or experience which establishes a claim of truth" stands as a functional working definition of the nature of knowledge (Dew & Foreman, 2020, pp. 16–20).

A Brief History of How We Know

We can now have a look at the history of the various schools of thought about how we acquire knowledge. The survey is limited to Western thought. This limitation is due to acknowledging that it is philosophy that has most significantly influenced western civilization. However, it is also acknowledged that western philosophy was significantly influenced by medieval Islamic philosophers and earlier, by eastern mathematicians. With this attempt to provide even a brief overview of the history of thought concerning epistemology, even just Western thought, it must first be acknowledged that it is a bit artificial, if not potentially a distortion to excise the various epistemologies from the more comprehensive philosophy of any given philosopher. And second, there is the reality of briefly covering 2,500 years of philosophical development of understanding how we know is, well, ludicrous. One should turn to the masterful work by Frederick Copleston (1993) and his nine-volume work, *A History of Philosophy*, for such a feat. Shy of tackling this expansive and intensive work, and more specifically for our purposes, we will look elsewhere to grasp the general historical contours of epistemological thought. And indeed, we have something to look at for a display of the history of some of the epistemological (epistemology: the study of how we acquire knowledge) schools of thought.

The famous painting by Raphael, *The School of Athens* (1511), depicted in Fig. 4.1, portrays numerous ancient philosophers, including Raphael himself, who is barely visible wearing a black beret peaking around the corner of the column in the lower right-hand corner of the painting. The painting is one of four wall frescoes in the *Stanza della Segnatura*. Each wall represents one of the

Fig. 4.1. The School of Athens by Raphael.

four branches of knowledge during the Renaissance – theology, literature, justice, and philosophy. I highlight this painting of the philosophers because it provides a beautiful and vivid introduction to the early history of some of the foundational schools of thought as to how we know things in the world. I will highlight just a few figures that represent some of the primary options to think about our means of arriving at knowledge.

First and foremost, we have the two central figures framed by the archway in the center-back, Plato to the left with his hand pointing upwards to the realm of the forms or ideals (the realm of metaphysics, non-material reality) and Aristotle on the right with his hand outstretched pointing to this world of knowable physical objects. These two key figures represent a dividing line within epistemology, namely, rationalism (we know what we know by reason) and empiricism or objectivism (we know what we know by our sensory perceptions).

One of the figures to the left of Plato is his master teacher, Socrates, in the green toga. He is portrayed here in discussion with some up-and-coming young men of Athens. Socrates was noted for his annoying discussions of critical matters such as justice, beauty, truth, etc. His approach to discover definitions of such significant topics was by way of dialectic, that is, by asking questions and seeking answers which aroused further questions. This back-and-forth dialogical approach has frustrated many a student of Socrates since his discussions never end with a clear conclusion. However, this is not relativism nor throwing up one's hands claiming that we do not know anything. Rather, by means of the question-and-answer method (partial though they might be), we do gain ground on knowing what something is through a process of elimination and partial insights. The abrupt endings of the Socratic dialogues are intentional. It indicates that such subjects require ongoing thought, reflection, and discussion. Gains in knowledge and understanding are made, but the open-endedness process allows for further insights to be gained.

The gentleman slouching on the steps is Diogenes the Cynic. He is known for his strange behavior and anti-society antics, calling for a kind of simplistic, naturalistic (almost animal-like) utopia. But for our purposes, I direct you further down to the figure writing, leaning on the block of marble, looking rather despondent. This is Heraclitus (actually, a portrait of Michelangelo). He is famous for his comment, "Upon those who step into the same stream ever different waters flow" (as cited in Wheelwright, 1966, p. 71). Heraclitus uses the image of the ever-moving waters of a stream to indicate that it is never the same stream and so points to the world as ever-changing. The result of this insight is that one cannot claim knowledge at all because change is ever pervasive. Any claim of knowledge has already slipped into the past, for the present is now different from that which occurred before. Hence, Heraclitus represents for us the epistemological school of skepticism; all claims of knowledge are questionable due to the flux of reality. The most radical conclusion within skepticism is that one cannot know anything. This epistemological stance creates a difficult and despondent way to live.

Our last group of figures representing another epistemological school of thought are the scientists, science understood in the broader and original conception, which simply includes a subject to study and a proposed method by which to study it. In the lower left side is Pythagoras, a mathematician and observer of the movement of the stars. On the lower right side, we have Ptolemy and Zoroaster holding spheres. We might refer to them as early cosmologists, students of the cosmos, but in general they too were mathematicians attempting to figure out the movement of the stars by mathematical calculations. They can represent science in general, or more specifically the scientific method: measurement, experimentation, and repeatable and demonstrable (repeatable) proofs. The sciences are another school of thought as to how we know things. It seeks to establish justifiable truth beliefs by way of demonstrable, verifiable, objective proofs.

Leaping over the medieval, early modern, and modern developments of epistemological debate (and it is a mighty leap!), our current philosophical context is often referred to as postmodern. It manifests an emphasis on the fluid nature of language and our historical and cultural conditionedness, which renders one's knowledge claims as merely personal subjective assertions lacking in any justification. The epistemological developments within the modern philosophical era are complex and extensive. Nevertheless, returning to our pictorial reference of Raphael's painting, we can detect that it does provide a peek at the major influential schools of epistemological thought that were certainly developed further and differently in the modern period, but nevertheless, continue to demonstrate their influence upon us today. Thus, to gather up and set before us the possible schools of epistemology, the study of how we come to knowledge, we can choose from rationalism (we know by way of reason, our rational powers), empiricism (we know by way of what we experience via our sensory perceptions), or we know by way of some combination of these two. And then there is the choice of throwing our hands up and drowning in what Edmund Husserl (1970) called the "skeptical deluge" (p. 14), claiming we cannot know anything – which, of course, is a logical contradiction in that it is a claim to know that one cannot know!

Sources of Knowledge

Beyond the pictorial representative figures of the different schools of how we know within Raphael's painting, we now catalogue the various sources for acquiring knowledge. As demonstrated in Table 4.1, leaders have multiple sources for knowledge, each with distinct strengths, pitfalls, and strategies for optimization:

Table 4.1.   Knowledge Pathways, Application, Pitfalls, and Mitigation Strategies.

Description	Leadership Application	Potential Pitfall	How to Optimize
Testimony			
Information received from people (experts, team members, reports, advisors)	• Making decisions based on specialized input • Gathering market intelligence • Learning from mentors and experts • Seeking specialized knowledge	• Unreliable sources • Echo chambers and groupthink • Political filtering of information • Over-reliance on single sources • Information silos	• Triangulate important information • Develop diverse networks of trusted sources • Systematically verify critical information
Intuition			
Immediate understanding without conscious reasoning; gut feelings based on experience	• Quick decision-making in time-sensitive situations • Identifying unspoken dynamics • Sensing when a strategy isn't working • Detecting deception or hidden agendas	• Confusing bias with intuition • Overconfidence in gut reactions • Ignoring contradictory data	• Balance intuition with objective analysis • Develop intuition through deliberate practice • Recognize when intuition is most reliable • Use intuition as a starting point for deeper inquiry

(*Continued*)

Table 4.1.   (*Continued*)

Description	Leadership Application	Potential Pitfall	How to Optimize
Natural Understanding			
Universal principles that humans grasp across cultures (ethics, fairness, dignity)	• Building a values-based organizational culture • Establishing ethical frameworks • Cross-cultural leadership • Conflict resolution • Creating fair systems and policies	• Cultural bias in application • Assuming universality where none exists • Over-generalizing principles • Imposing personal values as "natural" • Neglecting cultural nuance	• Balance universal principles with cultural context • Co-create values with diverse stakeholders • Regularly examine ethical foundations • Test assumptions about what is "naturally" understood
Faith-Based Understanding			
Knowledge derived from core beliefs and foundational assumptions	• Providing vision and purpose • Making decisions aligned with core values • Persisting through uncertainty • Leading with authenticity	• Dogmatic thinking • Confirmation bias • Imposing beliefs on others • Rejecting evidence that challenges beliefs • Lack of critical examination	• Integrate faith and reason in decision-making • Remain open to evidence that challenges assumptions • Respect diverse belief systems • Create space for multiple perspectives

Already addressed is the use of our reason and our senses. Another major source of knowledge that we depend upon daily is the realm of human testimony. We rely on trusted others to provide us with information about the world around us. Our knowledge of history is almost entirely from the voices of others from the past. We can read textbooks about different historical events, visit actual sites of historical significance, and view documents written by key figures. All this knowledge is dependent upon the testimony of others. As well, we daily rely on the testimony of the weatherman to decide what to wear, and we listen to family and friends to know about things they have seen and heard from the day. A moment's reflection on our part belies the reality that we depend upon the testimony of others for much, if not most, of our knowledge claims. Of course, there can be inaccurate or outright false testimony from other people, so we seek confirmation from more trusted people or go to *see for ourselves*. Testimony is thus potentially less reliable and requires verification or confirmation via other means or sources of knowledge. J. D. Trout (1998) refers to this as the *method of triangulation*, where one piece of a larger web of resources is engaged to acquire knowledge. One might seek further testimony from other sources or rationally reflect on the testimony, reasoning, and any physical evidence to draw a conclusion as to what is true. While testimony from others might be considered a more problematic source of knowledge, it is certainly a common, if not predominant means of acquiring knowledge.

Another source of knowledge, though controversial, is intuition, roughly defined as an immediate grasp of something or proposition as true apart from any inference (reason) or observation (experience). It is controversial since some argue that claims of knowledge by way of intuition are merely opinions, or that intuitions are pre-disposed tendencies to believe something. Yet humanity demonstrates a remarkable natural acquisition of the knowledge of basic rational principles and general ethical principles. For instance, a child instinctively recognizes the truth that the whole is greater than the sum of the parts when it is explained to them. This intuitive capacity can also manifest itself morally. It is intuitively and universally acknowledged that killing an innocent person is wrong morally. "It is called *natural* because humans are made in their nature to be able to grasp ethical principles" (Budziszewski, 1997, p. 93). This natural capacity of human beings is historically referred to as natural law. John Finnis points to seven basic goods manifested within the concept of natural law: "life (living, health, procreation), knowledge, play, aesthetic experience, friendship or sociability, a plan of life for the moral good, and religion or holiness" (Hill, 2016, pp. 81–82).

Natural law is criticized, however, for assuming all cultures have agreed on all of these principles and manifest them in the same form, while the truth is there are many variations of ethical practices from culture to culture and throughout history. This argument is countered by pointing out that the principles of natural law's ethical framework operate as

> general principles to be supplemented by sound practical thinking, conscience, and civil law, tailored to the particularities of a given society ... each society has different social and cultural circumstances and so will interpret each general principles of natural law in different particular ways. (McDermott, 2012, p. 94)

Despite all the variations of ethical practices manifested among various cultures across time, the reality is that there is a remarkable consistency of these ethical principles manifested among all peoples. There appears to be something built in humanity to naturally grasp the knowledge of these ethical principles as well as some conceptual realities such as mentioned; the whole is greater than the sum of the parts.

One final source of knowledge, and perhaps the most controversial, is faith. Can faith be a legitimate source of knowledge? Recall earlier it was stated that our movement toward acquiring knowledge begins with a belief that something is true that in turn moves us to seek to establish that such a belief is true. Yet, this belief dynamic involved in knowledge does not indicate that belief or faith is knowledge. In contrast, faith is a response to initial knowledge claims. Faith in the existence of God, for example, is based on two possible sources of knowledge, namely, nature (order, intricacy, beauty, etc.) and revelation (religious documents and testimony). Nevertheless, faith here is not itself a source of knowledge, but rather a response to knowledge claims, in this case the knowledge claims discerned from the order of nature and the testimonies of divine revelation.

What is significant for us to consider, however, is the relationship of faith to reason (cf. Pope John Paul II, 1998, *Fides et Ratio*). The options of how one can understand the relationship of faith to reason can be summarized as follows. One, the relationship can be visualized as two separate circles. This first circle represents the realm of reason, and the second, totally separate and apart from reason, is the realm of faith. They simply do not have any connection or relationship. The second way of understanding faith and reason is to envision them as one larger circle representing reason with a smaller circle within the larger circle representing faith. Faith is understood as some minor constituent part of the operation of reason. Third is the opposite of the second relationship. In this case, reason is swallowed up as a subset of faith. This is often referred to as *fideism*, all knowing relies upon faith in some manner. And finally, one can conceive the relationship of faith and reason as two partially overlapping circles. Both have their own separate domain and means of acquiring knowledge but also have a domain in which both reason and faith are integrated and operate together to acquire knowledge. Again, the initial statement that a belief or faith in something as true, moves one to seek knowledge to begin the process of knowledge acquisition might fall into this latter category of the relationship of faith and reason.

To apply this discourse on the nature of knowledge to leadership, we can assert that a leader not only is aware of how one knows and the various sources of knowledge as well as how to assess them, but also seeks to understand how others learn, know, and act upon their knowledge. This leads us to the task of being good knowers.

Being Good Knowers

We are indeed knowers, as cited in the introduction, and we now know the means of how we know as well as the sources for knowing. It is appropriate to marvel at the achievements of humanity in literature, the arts, and sciences across the millennia and in all cultures. Yet a haunting dark shadow hovers over the great achievements of humanity. The history of the peoples of the earth also manifests a great deal of, well, stupidity. A stupidity entailing not so much a lack of knowledge but knowing and doing just the opposite of what is known or even a disregarding of what is known. Certainly, there are times when humanity has acted mistakenly out of ignorance, and we can be sympathetic toward others and ourselves on such occasions. But often it is the case that mankind takes actions that counter or dismiss knowledge embedded within our minds, which is publicly known and affirmed within the culture. We exclaim, *Why did I do that, I know better!* To address this universal human frustration, we should listen to this insight from the Russian dissident, Aleksandr Solzhenitsyn (1976):

> I was convinced that I was doing good, and I was well supplied with systematic arguments. And it was only when I lay there on rotting prison straw [in a Russian prison] that I sensed within myself the first stirrings of good. Gradually it was disclosed to me that the line separating good and evil passes not through states, nor between classes, nor between political parties either – but right through every human heart. (p. 597)

This insight by Solzhenitsyn won only through suffering, vividly depicts our human condition. It is the front line of our battle between good and evil – and it starts, as always, in our own hearts, in the depths of our very being. As Solzhenitsyn spoke elsewhere, "The meaning of life lies not, as we have grown to thinking, in prospering, but in the development of the soul" (as cited in Morson, 2024, pp. 41–48). Might this development of the soul also influence how we come to knowledge?

Again, all have experienced the internal conflict within themselves and witnessed it among others of knowing something, but for whatever reason choose to disregard the knowledge and act apart from what we know. And we also witness the failure to know due to the difficulty or challenging demands of knowing something. Then there is the refusal to know something, either out of laziness or disregard for the value of specific knowledge content. Aside from human limitations in acquiring knowledge, such failures in obtaining knowledge just cited display an inherent weakness in ourselves as knowers. How are we to wage this frontline (internal) war and develop right thinking by properly following the knowledge we already have and discipline ourselves in properly seeking new knowledge? Thus far, our considerations of how we know, displayed in the history of the development of epistemology, have focused on the mechanics of the intellectual operation of coming to knowledge. But what of the quality or character of the knower themselves? Might the character dispositions and intentions of the knower influence what and how well one knows? The answer, of course, is yes. The dilemma is how do we overcome such a pervasive problem? The answer, at least partly (at least!), is grounded in education, an education of a particular kind.

The intent of education through the centuries of Western Civilization placed the emphasis upon the cultivation of virtue. In the mid-20th century, however, the emphasis turned toward career preparation, perhaps due to the overwhelming sense of needing to rebuild society after World War II. Be that as it may, antiquity displayed an intense interest in virtue formation as exemplified by the Stoics (cf. Roman Emperor Marcus Aurelius, *Meditations*, 170s B.C./2003).

In the New Testament, the apostle Paul admonishes followers of the Way to put off the old corrupted evil self and put on the new: the good self is in the likeness of God (*New American Standard Bible*, 1995, Eph. 4:22–24). The New Testament contains several virtue lists to be manifested among Christians (Gal. 5:22–23; Col. 3:12–14; James 3:17–18; II Pet. 1:5–7) and even calls upon us to have the very mind (*phronema* – a mindset) of Christ (Phil. 2:5). But again, how do we put these virtues on? How does this grand transformation occur?

To answer this question, we will work through the definition and application of Aristotle's (325–323 B.C.E./1984) virtue formation description in his *Nicomachean Ethics*. And then close with some practical practices highlighted from the work of Jason Baehr (2011) for developing specifically the intellectual virtues but are applicable to the development of the moral virtues as well. The final claim is that becoming virtuous people is foundational for good leadership and the source for changing the world by one small virtuous act at a time, manifesting the beauty of a well-formed virtuous knower. In Dostoyevsky's (1998) novel, *The Idiot*, the character, Prince Myshkin, declares, "Beauty will save the world." The beauty of virtuous leadership can in some measure support such a declaration.

Traditionally, drawing from Plato, Aristotle, and later from Thomas Aquinas, the virtues are categorized into three types: intellectual, moral (also known as the Cardinal Virtues), and theological. The intellectual virtues are listed as understanding, knowledge, and wisdom by Aquinas. Aristotle cites the key moral virtues of prudence, justice, temperance, and courage. Drawing upon Biblical scripture, Aquinas lists the theological virtues as faith, hope, and love. Shy of doing the excellent work of defining each of the virtues, I highlight two of the moral virtues, prudence and temperance, since these terms are less familiar in common parlance. Prudence has to do with wise, practical action. Aristotle states that prudence "has to do with a good attainable by action; ... a man who deliberates well ... by judgment, can aim well at the things which are attainable by action and are best for man" (Apostle, 1984, p. 107). Temperance "is a mean with regard to pleasures" (Apostle, 1984, pp. 52, 53) and specifies that the pleasures in question are of the body, not of the soul, and more particularly, they are the pleasures of touch. The term *mean* in the description of temperance will come to light as we turn to Aristotle's definition of virtue and will enhance our understanding of all the virtues.

Next, we find pragmatic support in developing the virtues from Aristotle's *Nicomachean Ethics*. Embedded within Aristotle's definition of virtue, we find pragmatic support for a program to develop both intellectual and moral virtues through the habituation of practice to form one's disposition of character. Aristotle provides us with this succinct definition: "Virtue, then, is a habit disposed toward action by deliberate choice being at the mean relative to us, and defined by reason and as a prudent man would define it" (Apostle, 1984, pp. 28, 29). To unpack this definition, which leads us to the practice of forming such virtues, we need to pay special attention to the key terms of habit, action, choice, mean, reason, and prudence. Virtues can be described as follows:

- Habit – a reasoned, chosen act practiced repeatedly until it becomes part of one's disposition.
- Action – an embodied act, via word and/or deed, substantiating a virtuous behavior.

- Choice – a reasoned selection of an act to conduct.
- Mean – (the Golden Mean; see Fig. 4.2), the virtuous act falls between the extremes of lack or excess of the virtuous act.
- Reason – the virtuous act is intellectually selected considering the goodness of the act in contrast to the extremes of action (or inaction) and the desire (attraction) for enacting the action.
- Prudence – Aristotle (325–323 B.C.E./1984) defined prudence (*phronesis* – application of knowledge) as "a true and reasoned state of capacity to act with regard to the things that are good or bad for man" (1140b5–7). Basically, a prudent person knows the right thing to do in each situation and acts rightly upon that knowledge.

In general, Aristotle's definition and program for virtue formation can be pictured as a bell curve depicted in Fig. 4.2.

The horizontal axis measures the lack of appropriate virtuous action to the left and the excess of appropriate proportion of virtuous action to the right. The center section and apex of the bell curve represents the mean (often called the Golden Mean) between the two extremes. The apex is curved and somewhat wide in range to represent the variable particulars of an action that takes into consideration the specific circumstances in which the action is taken as well as the capacities of the individual enacting the virtue. As an example, the virtue of courage falls between the lack thereof, cowardice, and the excess, foolhardiness. Running away from any strange little sound in the woods is cowardice, but taking on a charging grizzly bear is foolhardiness.

Now let's play out Aristotle's habituation program for virtue formation among one of the intellectual virtues.

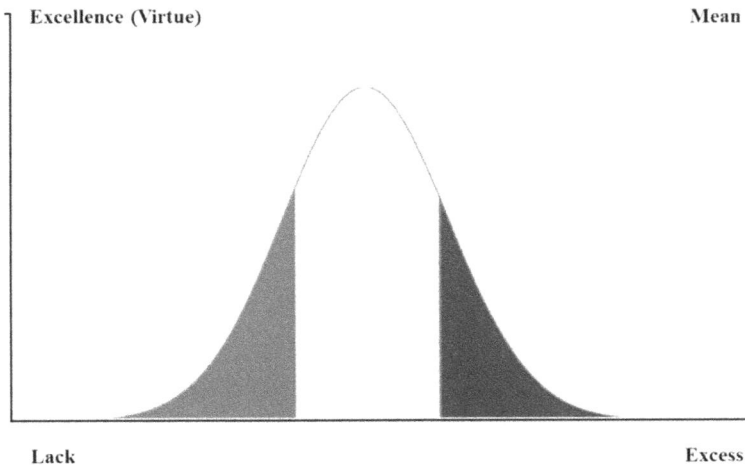

Fig. 4.2.   Bell Curve.

The Practice of Knowing

Following Aristotle's lead, Jason Baehr (2011) wrestled with understanding the distinctions and possible connections between intellectual and moral virtues. Wading through the different theories to distinguish the intellectual moral virtues, Baehr proposed his own criteria for distinguishing the intellectual virtues from the moral. I would simply add that the theological virtues of faith, hope, and love provide a wholeness to virtue or character formation that enables one to understand that both the intellectual and moral virtues are united, or at least overlap, in service to and in practice of the theological virtues.

In his most recent work, Baehr (2021) listed nine key intellectual virtues, their definitions, and each with a memorable slogan to help embed them within one's mind and heart. As demonstrated in Table 4.2, each of Baehr's virtues suggests a leadership application and action.

Some of these virtues and slogans can be enriched with examples and models drawn from figures acting virtuously, both past and present. Modeling and instilling these intellectual virtues in those whom we lead would certainly be of great service to all.

Along with models and stories of the various virtues being enacted, there is the helpful use of metaphorical thinking, comparing one thing to another for understanding. In fact, this type of thinking is the predominant means of gaining understanding (Lakoff & Johnson, 2003). For instance, the book of Proverbs can serve as a resource to discover what the sages of old understood to be the tools necessary for informing and forming the souls of the young (and old!), often in the form of metaphors or poetic parallel assertions. David Bland's (2015) study of the Proverbs explicates the practical advice and wise practices used to shape a person's life in relationship to others and to God. These formation tools include:

- Verbal instruction and reinforcement, both positive and negative. (Prov. 25:11–15; 26:1–9; 27:14–19)
- Observation of life experiences, as well as role-playing, and discernment. (Prov. 15:13–17, 33; 16:9)
- Communal practice in the context of specifically defined communities such as a family, neighborhood, town, or cultural group. (Prov. 22:6; 31:10–31)

The effective use of the proverbs for moral virtue development manifests these elements (Bland, 2015, 71–88):

- Memorable
- Flexible
- Situational
- Familiar
- Brief and Witty
- Universal

The literary nature and practical function of the proverb are attractive due to these characteristics and are well suited for leading others in developing virtuous attributes and practices.

Table 4.2.   Intellectual Virtues Adapted to Leadership.

Virtue	Definition	Leadership Application	Action
Curiosity	A disposition to wonder, ponder, and ask why	Continuously questioning assumptions	Ask questions!
Autonomy	Capacity for self-directed thinking	Making decisions without unnecessary deference to authority	Think for yourself!
Humility	Owning intellectual limitations and mistakes	Acknowledging when you don't have answers	Admit what you don't know!
Attentiveness	Being "personally present" in learning	Giving full focus to important issues	Look and listen!
Carefulness	Noticing and avoiding intellectual pitfalls	Checking assumptions before decisions	Get it right!
Thoroughness	Seeking deeper explanations	Not settling for easy answers	Go deep!
Open-mindedness	Thinking outside conventional boundaries	Considering diverse perspectives	Think outside the box!
Courage	Persisting despite fear of failure	Taking necessary risks	Take risks!
Tenacity	Embracing intellectual challenge	Working through difficult problems	Embrace struggle!

Note: Adapted from Baehr (2021).

Practices and Reflections

We are indeed curious creatures. We desire to know. For leaders of people, one needs to know how to know, to know well, and to know what is good and beneficial for all. To accomplish such a feat, one must be virtuous intellectually and morally. Again, Aristotle provides us with a program to obtain the virtues. Know what they are, practice them, and practice them more until the virtue becomes embedded within your character.

Self-Assessment

Begin with a self-assessment of what virtues you already routinely exercise in acquiring knowledge and enabling others to know and understand. As an example, the intellectual virtue of curiosity. Become mindful of how you engage your surroundings with curiosity in various situations and in relationships with other people. Such awareness of when and how you employ curiosity can sharpen your understanding of how to develop other virtues.

Including in this self-assessment is the difficult task of being honest with yourself about which virtues you lack or are weak in practicing. To overcome such deficiencies, select a virtue, say, persistence or tenacity, and intentionally embrace the challenge of tackling a problem or issue that appears insurmountable and try again, try a different angle, and keep at it. Practice this discipline of embracing challenge in numerous circumstances and ways until it becomes a habit, a normal behavior for you.

Developing Virtues

Then, as leader, how might you aid those you lead in developing virtues? As you are wrestling with developing virtues within yourself, invite those around you to join in the habituation of a particular virtue. Jointly select a virtue for all to work on. Together, create a clear, pithy definition, making sure everyone has a clear understanding of what the virtue is and what it looks like in practice. Perhaps place visuals in the workspace as reminders of the virtue to be practiced. Meet weekly for a short debriefing session to share success, failures, and new strategies for developing the stated virtue. Mutual encouragement can be a strong incentive to persist in habituating a virtue. Be consistent in recognizing those who display the chosen virtue during the workday. This joint effort in virtue development can instill an enjoyable workplace environment because it can, with creativity, involve a bit of levity. But, more importantly, it will be recognized as doing good for oneself and others.

References

Apostle, H. G. (1984). *Nicomachean ethics* (H. G. Apostle, Trans.). The Peripatetic Press.
Aristotle. (1984). *Nicomachean ethics* (H. G. Apostle, Trans.). The Peripatetic Press. (Original work published 325–323 B.C.E.)
Aristotle. (2003). *Metaphysics. Modern library* (G. Hayes, Trans.). (Original work published 350 B.C.E.)
Aurelius, M. (2003). *Meditations. Modern library* (G. Hays, Trans.). (Original work published 170s B.C.)
Baehr, J. (2011). *The inquiring mind: On intellectual virtues & virtue epistemology.* Oxford University Press.
Baehr, J. (2021). *Deep in thought: A practical guide to teaching for intellectual virtues.* Harvard Education Press.
Bland, D. (2015). *Proverbs and the formation of character.* Cascade Books.
Budziszewski, J. (1997). *Written on the heart: The case for natural law.* IVP Academic.
Copleston, F. (1993). *A history of philosophy, Vols. I–IX.* Image Books.
Dew, J. K., & Foreman, M. W. (2020). *How do we know* (2nd ed.). InterVarsity Press.
Dostoyevsky, F. (1998). *The Idiot. Wordsworth classics.* (Original work published 1868–1869)
Francis, P. (2024, October 24). *Dilexit Nos (He loved us)* [Encyclical Letter]. https://www.catholicnewsagency.com/news/260051/pope-francis-releases-first-sacred-heart-encyclical-in-nearly-70-years-connects-devotion-to-ai-digital-age
Gordon, G. (2018). *The new science of curiosity* (G. Gordon, Ed.). Nova Science.
Heidegger, M. (1962). *Being and time* (J. Macquarrie & E. Robinson, Trans., 7th ed.). Harper & Row. (Original work published 1927)

Hill, J. L. (2016). *After the natural law: How the classical worldview supports our modern moral and political values*. Ignatius Press.

Husserl, E. (1970). *The crisis of European sciences and transcendental phenomenology: An introduction to phenomenological philosophy*. Northwestern University Press.

Lakoff, G., & Johnson, M. (2003). *Metaphors we live by*. University Press.

McDermott, J. L. (2012). *How American law lost God*. New Hope Publications.

Morson, G. (2024). Faith and Russian literature. *First Things*. https://firstthings.com/faith-and-russian-literature/

New American Standard Bible. (1995). Zondervan Publishing House.

Paul, J. (1998). *Fides et Ratio* [Encyclical Letter]. https://www.vatican.va/content/john-paul-ii/en/encyclicals/documents/hf_jp-ii_enc_14091998_fides-et-ratio.pdf

Plato. (1997). Meno. In J. M. Cooper (Ed.), *Plato: Complete works* (pp. 870–897). Hackett. (Original work published 385 B.C.)

Plato. (1997). Theaetetus. In J. M. Cooper (Ed.), *Plato: Complete works* (pp. 157–234). Hackett. (Original work published 4th century B.C.)

Raphael. (1511). *The school of Athens* [Artwork]. Wikimedia Commons. https://commons.wikimedia.org/wiki/File:Raphael_School_of_Athens.jpg

Solzhenitsyn, A. (1976). *The Gulag archipelago part 1* (T. P. Whitney, Trans.). Whitney Fontana.

Trout, J. D. (1998). *Measuring the intentional world: Realism, naturalism, and quantitative methods in the behavioral sciences*. Oxford University Press.

Wheelwright, P. (Ed.). (1996). *The Presocratics*. Macmillan.

Chapter 5

Retreat from Noise: Silence as Sacred Space

Alicia D. Crumpton

Kaleidoventure LLC, USA

Abstract

This chapter explores the ontological and existential significance of silence as a sacred dimension of human experience through a dialogical examination of the works of Max Picard and Octavio Paz. In an era characterized by increasing environmental, informational, and cognitive noise, people have become alienated from the transcendent qualities of silence that once fostered authentic connection to Being. Drawing on Picard's concept of silence as "an independent being" and Paz's notion of "the other shore," modern consciousness and how it has separated humans from their original state of wholeness is explored. Through analysis of cosmological narratives, the human condition in modernity, and the nature of poetic inspiration, creative expression, particularly poetry emerges from and returns us to sacred silence. Practical somatic, creative, and reflective practices designed to help leaders reconnect with silence as a source of wisdom, inspiration, and authentic presence are included. These embodied approaches offer pathways to transcend the noise of modern existence and access the transformative power of silence as a sacred space where the self becomes properly situated within the cosmos, enabling what Paz describes as a "metamorphosis" that returns one to their original being.

Keywords: Silence; sacred space; transcendence; poetry; inspiration; cosmology; being; noise; modernity; alienation; wu wei

Introduction

I can't hear myself think. Scientists have noted how "As the global population soars, cities and towns sprawl out, and roads stretch into even the most remote

Artful Leadership: Retreat, Recenter, and Rewild, 51–59
Copyright © 2026 by Alicia D. Crumpton
Published under exclusive licence by Emerald Publishing Limited
doi:10.1108/S2058-880120250000010006

parts of the world, quiet is becoming increasingly scarce" (Morber, 2020). Physical and environmental noise, when combined with informational, cognitive, and social noise, affect our ability to hear ourselves think. Philosopher Max Picard (2002) described how humans are so part of the noise around them that they do not notice what the noise is doing: "the noise is the main thing: man is only the place occupied by the noise." A question Vaclav Havel (1991), former Czech Republic president, pondered was how people "accommodate something within them which paralyzes every effort of their better selves to revolt ... [each] can be alienated from themselves only because there is something in them to alienate" (p. 148). Considering Havel's question through the lens of Picard suggests that the noise of machination becomes emptiness, an emptiness that "follows [you] home" (Picard, 2002, p. 190). Furthermore, Picard postulated that in the world of the machine, "the word of the poet can never be born, for the word of the poet comes from silence" (p. 191). Mexican poet and essayist Octavio Paz (1973) explored the "poetic phenomenon" in his book *The Bow and the Lyre*.

Both Picard and Paz explored the sacred inspiration as travel to a transcendent space beyond our dailiness, a place of Being and revelatory experience. The purpose of this chapter is to merge their voices dialogically, thereby creating a harmonious existential and ontological discussion about the nature of Being, transcendence, and inspiration. Important elements brought forth by each include the fall in relation to cosmology, language, and the human condition; inspiration, including the importance of transcendence and poetry; and poetic experience and revelation.

Cosmology

"In the beginning" starts Genesis 1 (*New International Version*, 1973/2011), a story about the beginning of the cosmos describing God (Being) as creator of place (cosmos) and duality (light/darkness, evening/morning, wet/dry, masculine/feminine, and nature/human). In Genesis 2:25, Adam and Eve's lack of shame at being naked suggested there was a time when humankind was solely aware of Being versus self-awareness, including a duality perspective. Adam and Eve were told to eat of any tree but the tree of the knowledge of good and evil (Genesis 2:17). But they ate of the tree, with the aftermath described in Genesis 3:10–12 as *the fall* of humankind: "Adam answered, I heard you [God] in the garden, and *I was afraid* because I was naked; *so I hid*. And [God] said, *Who told you that you were naked* [emphasis added]?" The fall began a period of individual consciousness combined with separation between man and woman, humankind and nature, and humankind and Being.

Both Paz and Picard referred to a cosmological time "pre-fall." Paz (1973) noted man's preference for himself and subsequent alienation from Being because we "live in a fallen [emphasis added] world" (p. 130). Humankind is reminded "of that state in which the fall [emphasis added] ... had not yet taken place" (Picard, 2002, p. 46). We are presented with a before and after.

Heavens are commonly referred to as cosmological, transcendent space of Being, God, or gods. The *other shore* and *silence* represent Paz and Picard's constructions descriptive of heavens or the transcendent. The other shore, according to Paz (1973), is a place where humankind is detached from objectivity, where there is no life or death, and a place of dying and being born (p. 106). Silence is a phenomenon described by Picard (2002) using phrases such as: "an independent being," the space of Being, the "Holy Wilderness," "primary objective reality," or "quality of infinity." Whether the other shore or silence, each are experiences of the transcendent.

The wholeness of creation was once experienced as a wholly interconnected existence. With the fall, humankind developed a consciousness and separation, especially into objective and subjective spheres. This separation results in man being "uprooted like a tree and thrown ... to the other shore, to the encounter of himself" (Paz, 1973, p. 107). Language is central to the way humans make sense of their experiences.

Language and the Human Condition

Language aids humans with engagement, description, and sense-making. Paz (1973) assumed that "as soon as man acquired consciousness of himself, he broke away from the natural world and made another world inside himself." This consciousness of self and other, a subject–object distinction, fosters a perceived separation from the whole. Words, then, become "bridge[s] by which man tries to traverse the distance that separates him from external reality" (Paz, 1973, p. 25). Disconnection from silence contributes to a language "surrounded by the dark rim of melancholy" (Picard, 2002, p. 37).

Visions of deus ex machina and other enchantments (cf. Bailey, 2005) further alienate humankind such that our aim becomes "finding the old path, the forgotten way of communication between both worlds [ancient beliefs versus modernity]" (Paz, 1973, p. 89). Whereas Paz suggested that humankind's connection to Being fosters a sense of trying to return or find the path, Picard painted a bleaker picture. Picard (2002) suggested that the West has almost destroyed silence, but acknowledged some hope in recognizing, "a man who still [emphasis added] has the substance of silence within himself."

If language emerging from silence has a spiritual quality, then if disconnected from silence, words become "noise" (Picard, 2002), wherein noise contributes to humankind's alienation. Picard explained, "Noise is the enemy of silence; it is opposed to silence. The noise of words is not merely opposed to silence: it makes us even forget that there was ever any such thing as silence at all" (p. 172). Ultimately, noise tends to alienate by destroying our sense of unity and connection to the whole. Inspiration, then, represents the interplay of silence, the poet, and a poem in critically activating humankind's remembrance of and connection to silence.

Inspiration and Poetry

Poetry, then, as creative language, moves beyond superficialities to capture the essence of the transcendent. Brueggemann (1989), in his essay, *Finally Comes the Poet*, asserted that "the poet/prophet is a voice that shatters settled reality and evokes new possibility." Echoing the prophetic role that Brueggemann suggested,

Paz (1973) described poets as those who travel to the other shore and bring forth a poem. In this sense, poetry is a way to "transcend the limits of language" (Paz, 1973, pp. 13, 25), perhaps providing a clarion reminder for those who have forgotten the silence suggested by Picard (2002), who stated that "poetry comes out of silence and yearns for silence."

Through poetry, a poet speaks with a "strange voice, his voice and his word are the strange ones" (Paz, 1973) because the poem comes from a different world. This is an important aspect of Paz's ideas – that a poem is not bound by this world or language; it is beyond this world, coming from a different world known as the other shore. Paz reminded, "We are in a world that is, another world" where the poet experiences the supernatural (Paz, 1973, pp. 109, 112). This seems to reflect Jung's (1971) distinction of visionary art that "transcends our human feeling and understanding," visionary art is that which taps into primordial archetypes "speaking to the heart of mankind" (p. 101). Specifically, poetry's connection to silence "not only brings the things out of the silence; it also produces the silence" (Picard, 2002, p. 147).

With visionary art, the poet is but an instrument within the creative process, which raises questions about free will. Paz (1973) asserted:

> The will intervenes little or participates in a paradoxical way. If he has been chosen by the great wind, it is useless for man to try to resist it ... the will is inextricably mingled with other forces, exactly as at the moment of poetic creation. (p. 107)

When pulled to the other shore, the poet is transported beyond his will. This seems to confirm neuroscientist's Sam Harris' (2012) viewpoint that "free will doesn't even correspond to any subjective fact" but instead, "the emergence of choices, efforts, and intentions is a fundamentally mysterious process." Paz (1973) explained the poet's experiences of the other shore as *tremendum mysterium*.

The variable sources of inspiration are topics for speculation (Forster, 2007; Sacks, 2012; Smith, 2007). Paz (1973) described the poet as allowing himself to be "seduced by the forces of attraction and repulsion of language" (p. 58). In his attempts at describing the poet's influences, Paz drew upon a variety of experiences:

1. A sudden appearance of phrases fallen from heaven. No one has summoned them (p. 41).
2. "Suddenly the rhyme appears" (p. 141).
3. A collaboration ... the form of an intrusion ... some call it demon, muse, spirit, genius (p. 141).
4. A mysterious alien collaboration, with the uninvolved apparition of another voice ... irruption of an alien will (p. 142).
5. The other voice, the strange will, other, that is, God or nature with its gods and demons (p. 144).

Inspiration is, as journalist Daniel Smith (2007) observed, "artists continue to experience inspiration intuitively as a natural conduit of their art" (p. 114).

Poetic Experience and Revelation

Paz and Picard critique modernity and the alienation of humankind, encouraging a movement back to the beginning to the other shore or silence. Poetry facilitates a revelatory opportunity for what Paz (1973) described as a "metamorphosis, change, an alchemical operation" in which humankind is "outside himself and, simultaneously ... return[s] to his original being: returns him to himself" (Paz, 1973, p. 98). The poetic experience provides the poet and the experiencer an opportunity for transcendence, where the original being was before the fall.

This view of poetic creation and poetic experience represents a spiritual dimension of wu wei, defined by philosopher Edward Slingerland (2014) as "no trying" or "no doing." Slingerland (2014) noted people experience wu wei as a "gap between an 'I' and various forces that take over when they enter wu wei" (p. 26). Integral to the spiritual dimension of wu wei is that a person is "properly situated in the cosmos" or an "absorption of the self into something greater," a giving yourself up to something bigger than yourself (Slingerland, 2014, pp. 40, 47, 52), in other words, the other shore or silence.

Poetic experience becomes a "spiritual exercise ... a means of interior liberation" (Paz, 1973, p. 3). For spiritual people, Picard (2002) noted that "When the substance of silence is present in a man, all his qualities are centered in it; they are all connected primarily with the silence and only secondarily with each other" (p. 70). This sort of connection to the other shore or silence is an ontological connection to something beyond oneself. Bohm and Nichol's (2004) discussion of the implicate order suggests the importance of inspiration in creating what he described as a "common culture," asserting that we "must start to establish a coherent meaning for the whole" (p. 139). Thus art, a poem, becomes the vessel through which humankind remembers connection and experiences connection to something greater.

Somatic, Creative, and Reflective Practices

Having explored the profound philosophical landscape of silence through the lenses of Paz and Picard, we now turn our attention to the critical question of how a leader might engage with these insights. The theoretical discussions of transcendence, inspiration, and the sacred space of silence are not merely abstract concepts but living principles that can be embodied through deliberate practice. The following exercises are structured approaches to experiencing silence, practices inviting leaders to move beyond intellectual understanding and into a direct, somatic engagement with the "substance of silence" that Picard described. Each exercise offers a pathway to reconnect with the deeper dimensions of leadership – not as a set of strategies but as a way of being that emerges from silent receptivity.

Somatic Practices

The Sacred Pause – Reconnecting with Silence

The purpose of this exercise is to experience the "substance of silence" within yourself, creating space between noise of your environment and your inner wisdom.

- Find a comfortable seated position, preferably away from technology or distractions.
- Close your eyes and take three deep breaths, extending your exhale longer than your inhale.
- Place one hand on your heart and one on your belly.
- As you breathe, silently ask: *Where in my body do I feel the noise of life?*
- Notice any sensations of tension, constriction, or agitation.
- Now ask: *Where in my body do I feel silence?*
- Breathe into any space that feels open, calm, or quiet.
- For 5–7 minutes, simply breathe and observe the interplay between noise and silence in your body.
- Before ending, silently ask: *What quality of leadership emerges from my silence?*

Consider: What did you notice about the difference between "noise" and "silence" in your body? How might Picard's notion that "a man who still has the substance of silence within himself" relate to your own experience? As a leader, how might pausing for silence change your decision-making process?

Crossing to the Other Shore – Embodied Visualization

The purpose of this exercise is to experience Paz's concept of "the other shore" as a place of inspiration and reconnection with the wholeness of Being.

1. Stand with your feet shoulder-width apart, feeling grounded to the earth.
2. Close your eyes and breathe deeply, imagining yourself standing at the edge of a body of water.
3. With each inhale, feel yourself gathering courage and intention.
4. With each exhale, imagine yourself releasing what separates you from *the other shore*.
5. Begin to sway gently, feeling the rhythm of the water.
6. When ready, take seven steps forward, each step representing movement toward the transcendent.
7. After your seventh step, stand still and imagine yourself arriving at "the other shore."
8. Breathe deeply for 1–2 minutes, noticing what you sense, feel, or intuit in this place.
9. When ready, open your eyes and write down or draw what you experienced.

Consider: What qualities of "the other shore" did you experience? How does movement from one shore to another relate to your leadership transitions? What might it mean for you to return from "the other shore" with inspiration to share with others?

Silence as Sacred Space – Moving Meditation

The purpose of this exercise is to create an embodied understanding of silence as "an independent being" with "quality of infinity" (Picard, 2002).

1. Clear a space in your room where you can move freely.
2. Stand in the center of this space, eyes closed, breathing deeply.
3. Extend your arms outward, slowly turning in a circle.
4. As you turn, imagine you are creating a sacred circle of silence around yourself.
5. When you've completed the circle, begin to move within it in any way your body wishes to move.
6. Allow movement to arise from stillness rather than planning.
7. Notice the quality of movement that emerges when you remain connected to silence.
8. After 5–7 minutes of free movement, gradually return to stillness at the center.
9. Before opening your eyes, sense the quality of the space you've created.

Consider: How did creating a "sacred space" change your experience of movement? What qualities of leadership might emerge from a foundation of sacred silence? How might you create "circles of silence" in your organizational spaces?

Creative Practice

The Poet's Journey – Creative Expression

The purpose of this exercise is to experience being "an instrument within the creative process," as Paz (1973) described, where inspiration comes through you rather than from you.

1. Gather paper and drawing/writing materials.
2. Sit in silence for 3–5 minutes, allowing yourself to become receptive.
3. Place your non-dominant hand on your heart center.
4. With your dominant hand, begin to draw or write without planning or judging.
5. If thoughts arise about what you "should" create, acknowledge them and return to being receptive.
6. Continue for 10–15 minutes, allowing whatever emerges to take form.
7. When complete, place your creation before you and observe it as if someone else made it.
8. Notice what messages or wisdom it might hold.

Consider: What was your experience of creating without the "will" interfering? How does this relate to Paz's (1973) description of the poet as "allowing himself to be seduced by the forces of attraction and repulsion of language"? In what ways might your leadership benefit from this receptive stance rather than always driving action?

Reflective Practice

Daily Silence Practice

The purpose of this practice is to bring the wisdom of silence into everyday leadership through consistent practice.

1. Commit to 5–10 minutes of silence at the beginning of each workday.
2. Find a quiet space (even if it's your car before entering the building).
3. Begin with three deep breaths, extending your exhale.
4. Place one hand on your heart, one on your belly.
5. Ask silently: "What quality of presence does my leadership need today?"
6. Listen for the answer that emerges from silence, not analytical thinking.
7. Before ending, set an intention to return to this silence briefly before important meetings or decisions.
8. Consider keeping a "silence journal" to track insights that emerge.

Consider: How does regular silence practice affect your leadership presence? What changes do you notice in your decision-making when you pause for silence? How might creating "silence rituals" transform your organizational culture?

These embodied approaches offer pathways to transcend the noise of modern existence and access the transformative power of silence as a sacred space where the self becomes properly situated within the cosmos, enabling what Paz (1973) described as a "metamorphosis" that returns one to their original being. Through these practices, you are cultivating not just moments of quiet but a fundamental reorientation to leadership that springs from the sacred space of silence.

Summary

New York Times book reviewer Helen Vendler (1974), after reading Paz, reflected:

> The work of creation is as mysterious to [poets] at it is to us; it is only the poets who can speak with authority of what takes place as the invisible becomes visible, the blank page is filled, and the ear hears that "unheard music," as Keats called it, which addresses the spirit.

Both Paz and Picard articulated an existential reality and source of inspiration as revelatory of teachings from this other realm. Artists, poets, and creatives are but instruments of this other dimension where connection and a sense of the whole reigns! Sadly, some, according to Picard (2002), are silenced by noise to the point where they no longer experience silence. There is hope in knowing the possibility of traveling to the other shore where knowing is made visible, that we then use language or other forms to communicate, and in so doing help people remember.

References

Bailey, L. W. (2005). *The enchantments of technology*. University of Illinois Press.
Bohm, D., & Nichol, L. (2004). *On creativity*. Routledge.
Brueggemann, W. (1989). *Finally comes the poet: Daring speech for proclamation*. Fortress Press.
Forster, J. (2007). *Muses*. Pocket Essentials.
Harris, S. (2012). *Free will*. Free Press.

Havel, V. (1991). Open letters: Selected writings, 1965–1990. Alfred A. Knopf.

Morber, J. (2020). The world is noisy. These groups want to restore the quiet. *Wired.* https://www.wired.com/story/the-world-is-noisy-these-groups-want-to-restore-the-quiet/

Jung, C. G. (1971). *The spirit in man, art, and literature*. Princeton University Press.

New International Version. (2011). Biblica Inc. https://www.biblegateway.com/passage/?search=genesis%201&version=NIV. (Original work published 1973)

Paz, O. (1973). *The bow and the lyre: The poem, the poetic revelation, poetry and history* (R. L. C. Simms, Trans.). University of Texas Press.

Picard, M. (2002). *The world of silence* (Reprint ed.). Eighth Day Press.

Sacks, O. (2012). *Hallucinations*. Alfred A. Knopf.

Slingerland, E. G. (2014). *Trying not to try*. Spring Publishing.

Smith, D. B. (2007). *Muses, madmen, and prophets: Rethinking the history, science, and meaning of auditory hallucination*. Penguin Press.

Vendler, H. (1974). The bow and the lyre. *New York Times*. https://www.nytimes.com/1974/06/30/archives/the-bow-and-the-lyre-diary-of-the-poetic-process.html

Chapter 6

Mindful Leadership: Rediscovering Identity and Purpose Through Contemplative Practice

Bradley D. Davidson

The Bradley Davidson Company LLC, USA

Abstract

This chapter explores how mindfulness practices can address the growing crisis of leadership identity and purpose in today's fast-paced professional environment. Drawing from both ancient wisdom traditions and contemporary research, how the frenetic pace of modern leadership has fostered mindless automaticity, disconnecting leaders from their authentic selves and contributing to widespread burnout, is explored. The chapter presents a framework for understanding how mindful awareness practices facilitate the rediscovery of leadership identity, meaning-making, and purpose – three interconnected elements essential for effective and sustainable leadership. Mindfulness serves as the foundation for leadership transformation. The chapter concludes with a comprehensive set of practical mindfulness exercises categorized into somatic breathing, creative, and reflective practices that leaders can implement to reconnect with their core identity and purpose. By prioritizing these contemplative practices, leaders can not only enhance their own well-being but also foster greater alignment, engagement, and effectiveness within their organizations.

Keywords: Meaning; purpose; self-awareness; mindfulness; remembering

Artful Leadership: Retreat, Recenter, and Rewild, 61–73

Copyright © 2026 by Bradley D. Davidson

Published under exclusive licence by Emerald Publishing Limited

doi:10.1108/S2058-880120250000010007

Introduction

In Disney's film, *The Lion King* (Allers & Minkoff, 1994), Simba heard an unexpected message from his deceased father, King Mufasa. Simba was the son of King Mufasa and Queen Sarabi. He was being groomed to be the next king when his father was killed while attempting to rescue Simba from a danger caused by Simba's carelessness. After Mufasa rescued Simba and was killed in the process, Simba tried to escape his guilt and grief by running away to live a life of *hakuna matata*, a life of *no worries*. In running from his feelings of grief and deep remorse, he abandoned the destiny of leadership for which Mufasa had been preparing him. During this period of regret-driven escapism, Mufasa appeared to Simba in a vision. Having seen Simba's attempts to run from his feelings of guilt and grief, Mufasa said to him, "You have forgotten who you are ... look inside yourself, Simba. You are more than what you have become. You must take your place in the circle of life ... Remember who you are" (Allers & Minkoff, 1994). Mufasa's words were a call for Simba to pause, remember who he was, and reimagine his future. This profound moment of mindful awareness was a significant turning point for Simba who, in avoiding reality, was heading toward a future of meaninglessness and wasted potential.

Like Simba, many leaders have lost connection with their authentic selves through mindless living. Their life and leadership have drifted from alignment with their true identity and purpose. Research suggests that the volatility, stress, and unsustainable pace of modern leadership are driving this disconnection as well as fueling an epidemic of burnout (Bocheliuk et al., 2020; Future Forum, 2022; Leka et al., 2010). The frenetic speed of professional life causes leaders to prioritize merely keeping up rather than engaging in mindful acts of noticing, reflecting, and savoring – practices that research suggests are essential to living and leading authentically (DeGreeff et al., 2010). This crisis of pace, identity, and purpose has generated a sense of malaise. Instead of continuing to mourn for their potential, leaders must regain their sense of identity and purpose to lead their lives and their organizations into the future.

The purpose of this chapter is to explore how mindfulness practices can address this crisis of leadership identity and purpose. Contemplative practices can provide a pathway for leaders to reconnect with their authentic selves and rediscover purpose in their work. Throughout, emerging trends in mindfulness research, identity formation, purpose, and leadership psychology are discussed. The chapter reveals how mindful awareness practices offer powerful tools for gaining a clearer sense of leadership identity and purpose, closing with practical mindfulness practices for leaders.

Mindlessness and Identity Erosion

There is a growing crisis of mindlessness in leadership. When leaders operate on autopilot, they lose touch with their authentic identity – their answer to the question, "Who am I as a leader?" This mindful self-awareness serves as a powerful rudder, determining direction and purpose (Tan et al., 2023). A leader's self-identity also strongly influences the self-identity of their followers (van Dick & Schuh, 2010).

Leaders who operate without mindful awareness often develop faulty views of their identity. Some adopt an overly idealized definition of leadership, causing distress as they attempt to fit into rigid expectations while ignoring contextual elements crucial for authentic identity formation (Nyberg & Sveningsson, 2014). Others experience internal conflicts when perceiving a gap between their true self and what is expected of them, leading to projections of false constructs (Sinclair, 2011).

Those who fail to cultivate mindful awareness of their authentic leadership identity are more likely to face burnout affecting their leadership and resulting in higher turnover and decreased performance among followers (Brooks et al., 2023; van Dick & Schuh, 2010). This mindless disconnection from authentic identity and purpose, combined with increasing demands on time and energy, results in diminished well-being (Future Forum, 2022; Thoits, 2012).

The Burnout Epidemic: A Crisis of Mindlessness

Leaders are experiencing increased burnout, which contributes to negative outcomes for the leader, workforce, organization, and community (Campbell & Gavett, 2021; Future Forum, 2022; Microsoft, 2022; Parent-Lamarche & Biron, 2022). Recent studies reveal that more than 50% of leaders and 40% of employees are experiencing burnout (Future Forum, 2022; Microsoft, 2022). Between August 2021 and August 2022, one study reported a 20% decline in work–life balance and a 40% deterioration in stress and anxiety levels among executives (Future Forum, 2022). The lack of mindful awareness is contributing to the burnout epidemic. Without the mindful ability to notice and tend to stress, volatility, and uncertainty, we have little hope of avoiding burnout within ourselves and our organizations (Levy & Levy, 2019).

The consequences of this mindless approach to leadership affect both personal and organizational well-being. Leader burnout leads to declining mental health, depersonalization, disconnection from others, and diminished self-esteem (Omrane et al., 2018). Physical health suffers too, with burnout increasing risk of pre-hypertension by 85% and cardiovascular disease hospitalization by 10% (John et al., 2024).

Perpetuating these crises, many leaders have fallen into what mindfulness researchers call *automatic thinking* (Zhang et al., 2020), drifting through professional life guided by shifting circumstances and routines rather than intentional awareness. Without mindful engagement with these challenges, leaders risk accelerating the downward spiral of purpose in both their leadership and the organizations they lead.

Mindfulness at the Intersection of Identity, Meaning, and Purpose

As an executive coach, I regularly engage with leaders questioning their identity and purpose. While they may not use these exact terms, questions of *who am I* and *why am I here* remain perennial inquiries. These questions fundamentally require mindful awareness to answer authentically.

Mindful Awareness of Role Identity

Our identities are definitions of ourselves within social roles that require mindful attention to discern accurately (Sinclair, 2011; Thoits, 2012). Leader identity specifically refers to the mindful understanding and integration of the facets that define oneself as a leader (Munusamy et al., 2010). Effective leaders are those who mindfully adapt and present their identity in ways that positively impact their leadership context (Sinclair, 2011).

In *The Lion King* (Allers & Minkoff, 1994), Mufasa told Simba, "You must take your place in the circle of life," encouraging mindful awareness of his true identity. Consider Dr Martin Luther King's leadership, likely rooted in mindful awareness of values including equality, justice, change, and hope. Similarly, Mother Teresa's leadership emerged from mindful attention to values of compassion, empathy, and service.

Mindful Creation of Meaning

Meaning emerges from our mindful ability to notice and attribute significance to our experiences (Ivtzan et al., 2016; Mead, 1910). Viktor Frankl (1992, 2014), Holocaust survivor and psychologist, observed that prisoners who mindfully looked beyond immediate suffering to find meaning were most likely to survive. Frankl created the equation $D = S-M$, where despair equals suffering minus meaning. Mindful identification of meaning in difficulty rescues us from despair and redirects us toward purpose.

Henri Nouwen (1972) described another benefit of mindful meaning-making during challenges:

> Whether we try to enter into a dislocated world, relate to a convulsive generation, or speak to a dying person, our service will not be perceived as authentic unless it comes from a heart wounded by the suffering about which we speak.

This concept of the *wounded healer* emerges from mindful attention to our experiences, preparing us for deeper service to others.

We often fail to discover meaning because of mindless, automatic thinking (Zhang et al., 2020). When mindfully engaged with challenges, we pause, reflect, and discern meaning in life-giving ways. This mindful awareness provides insights about aligned leadership contexts where our unique experiences contribute to authentic leadership influence.

Purpose Through Mindful Awareness

Purpose is the strategic vision that mindfully directs our thoughts and actions. While meaning-making often occurs during or after experiences, purpose represents the mindful vision motivating future action. Identity, meaning, and purpose demonstrate interplay; identity creates meaning, meaning drives awareness of purpose, and purpose reciprocally enhances meaning and identity (Thoits, 2012).

Kavita Shukla's (TED^{x}Manhattan, 2012) story illustrates this mindful integration. After drinking unsafe water while visiting her grandmother in India, she was given spices that prevented illness. This experience, coupled with mindful awareness of her identity and interest in food security, led to developing *Freshpaper*, spice-infused paper extending produce freshness. Her mindful meaning-making transformed into purpose, resulting in innovation improving lives globally.

Identity, meaning, and purpose are distinctive yet complementary processes requiring mindful attention. Each contributes to bringing our authentic leadership to life, enhancing personal well-being and organizational success (Thoits, 2012).

Why Mindful Leadership Matters

Why did Mufasa care about Simba remembering who he was through mindful reflection? Because mindful awareness of meaning and purpose is foundational to making sense of life and finding motivation to live it authentically. This mindful discernment strengthens a leader's ability to align organizations with meaningful purpose. According to Northouse (2021), "Leadership is the act of influencing a group of people to achieve a common goal bigger than themselves." Mindful leadership naturally connects personal identity with organizational purpose.

As an executive coach, I've observed that successful leaders demonstrate mindful awareness of purpose for themselves and their organizations. They mindfully see beyond current circumstances to discern compelling visions. As James Burns (1978) stated, "Leadership is nothing if not linked to collective purpose … social change measured by intent and by the satisfaction of human needs and expectations" (p. 3). Purpose itself is *silent leadership* (Hickman & Sorenson, 2013); like space between musical notes, the mindful presence of purpose creates an irresistible shared vision.

The Centrality of Mindfulness and Contemplative Practices

Mindfulness and contemplative practices form the foundation for discerning leadership identity and purpose. When Mufasa appeared to Simba, his message was essentially an invitation to mindfulness: stop, look around, look inside, and return to purpose. The current leadership crisis stems largely from decreased mindful awareness amid increasing pace (Bocheliuk et al., 2020).

Unless we embrace mindful practices to retreat, recenter, and reconnect, we have little hope of understanding our life-giving identity and purpose. Research suggests that mindful remembering of who we are drives meaningful work, professional effectiveness, and satisfaction (Cardona et al., 2019; Southwick et al., 2021; Thoits, 2012).

This emphasis on mindful awareness is rooted in ancient wisdom. Taoist and Buddhist traditions espouse the benefits of inward attention and present–moment awareness (Brown & Ryan, 2003; Zu, 2019). The Judeo-Christian tradition encourages contemplative time for rest and renewal (*New International Version*, 1973/2011, Mark 6).

Contemporary research reinforces these ancient insights. Nader and Mahesh-wari (2023) noted that the greatest leadership triumphs result from mindful self-knowledge and purpose. Emotional intelligence, crucial for leadership effectiveness, depends fundamentally on self-awareness (Goleman, 2011). Parker Palmer (2000) emphasized listening mindfully to our interior life for purpose guidance. Reflective practice is essential for authentic identity formation (Sinclair, 2011).

Despite compelling evidence, practices of mindful quieting, inward attention, and discernment remain underutilized (Davidson, 2019; Mols et al., 2016). Mindfulness and introspection are effective for uncovering important characteristics and insights (Mols et al., 2016), leading to greater meaning and purpose (Chu & Mak, 2020). The value of these practices remains widely underestimated and deprioritized (Mols et al., 2016).

Framework for Mindful Leadership

From my coaching experience, three factors most impact our sense of identity and purpose:

1. mindful understanding of our positive core (strengths, values, interests, and needs),
2. mindful alignment of this core with meaningful focus, and
3. engagement in mindfulness practices creating this awareness and alignment.

To invite these factors into the process of remembering who we are, we create a space and curate a set of practices enabling us to step out of the rapid pace that drives our automatic thinking and responding, find our true self in this place of quietness, and to reorient ourselves to our true identity and purpose.

To engage in new and unfamiliar ways of thinking, we need support. When we purchased our home, one of the characteristics of the home that attracted us the most was the beautiful garden created by the previous owner. In a corner of the garden is a lovely wooden trellis arch. Each spring, a spindly blooming vine finds its way out of the warming earth to the bottom of that trellis. Gradually it grows, hugging the trellis as it grows upward and over. Eventually, the vine has taken the shape of the trellis in a lovely arch of leaves and blooms. Our lives are like the delicate and vulnerable vine. We need a trellis to guide our growth. Just as a garden trellis guides a flowering vine's growth, regular mindfulness practices support our authentic development. In the sixth century, St. Benedict developed a "rule of life" – "rule" meaning supporting trellis or practices maintaining authenticity and growth (Gray, 2023). We, too, will benefit from the support of mindful practices in our lives.

Mindful Practices: Somatic Breathing, Creative, and Reflection

The following mindfulness practices provide a starting point for developing your personal trellis or framework. Categorized into somatic breathing, creative, and reflection practices, these approaches have effectively supported my clients in rediscovering authentic identity and purpose.

Somatic Breathing Practice

As we seek to remember who we are, we begin by pausing habitual thinking through mindful awareness, preparing ourselves to new ways of thinking.

Locating Practice

Identify a specific physical place to do inner work; a space that will enable you to sit quietly without interruption, a space comfortable and free of distractions and interruptions. If you live with others, it may also be helpful to let those with whom you live know of your desire for quiet reflection when you are in this space.

Mindful Slowing Practice

Engage in the practice of slowing. This practice enables you to move from the busy world that often envelops you into a slower place of contemplation. As you sit quietly with your hands and feet in a comfortable position, notice and experience your breath. Notice the feeling of gently inhaling and exhaling. Some people find it helpful to identify a focus word to gently repeat in your mind. Do this to relax and to slow the body, mind, and spirit from their fast pace to one of calmness.

Embodied Leadership Breathing

Standing in a grounded position, inhale while slowly raising arms to shoulder height. Hold breath briefly while visualizing energy filling your leadership presence. Exhale while lowering arms, releasing tension and unhelpful leadership patterns. Practice for 2–4 minutes before important meetings or decisions.

Mindful Contemplation Practice

Sit quietly, focusing on deep breathing while emptying your mind of active thoughts. When thoughts arise, gently release them and return to silence. If anxious, take three deep breaths to reorient. Practice for 2–4 minutes daily, gradually increasing duration.

Creative Practices

Creative practices serve to recenter, bringing disparate perspectives to mindful integration. This recentering is rooted in Thomas Keating's (1997) work, which calls us to loosen from the false self to create space for authentic essence.

Leadership Vision Mapping

Create a non-linear map of your leadership journey. Include images, symbols, colors, and words that represent pivotal moments of your identity formation. Identify patterns, recurring themes, and transformative experiences. Display this map where you can see it regularly to reinforce your leadership identity.

Metaphor Exploration

Identify a metaphor that currently describes your leadership (e.g., conductor, coach, architect). Create a picture of the metaphor using images, drawing, or writing. Experiment with alternative metaphors that might better serve your leadership identity. Practice consciously shifting between metaphors depending on the leadership context.

Reflective Practices

The Examen

This practice is attributed to a 16th-century priest, Ignatius of Loyola. It is a practice of setting aside time daily and weekly to contemplatively reflect on the events of the day or week to recognize important insights, make meaning of them, and to look forward into the new week with these insights as a guide (Wolpert, 2003).

Daily Practice:

Morning:

- Express gratitude for your life, your leadership, and the day that is to come.
- Reflect on what the day holds in terms of action, decisions, and relationships.
- Set your intention for how you want to show up today.

Noon: Reflect on how your actions, decisions, and interactions reflect the intention set in the morning. What happened? What changes or adjustments are necessary?

Evening:

- Express gratitude for your day.
- Reflect on how your actions, decisions, and interactions reflect the intention set in the morning and adjustments made at noon. What happened? What changes or adjustments are necessary.
- What do you have to look forward to tomorrow? Consider how you might set your intention and attention for the coming day.

Weekly Practice:

> *Weeks 1–3:* Reflect on your positive core. Observe strengths, values expressed, and interests that engaged you. Assess when you felt most alive and what you anticipate in the coming week.

> *Weeks 4–6:* Mindfully reflect on needs within your sphere of influence that draw your attention or passion. Notice what excited, concerned, or upset you. Consider contributors to these responses and actions needed.

Weeks 7–9: Examine alignment between your positive core and leadership context. Consider how your authentic strengths serve observed needs. Explore where alignment provides greatest energy and purpose.

Leadership Legacy Reflection

Set aside 20 minutes to mindfully consider your leadership legacy. Ask: What do you want others to say about your leadership? What values do you want to exemplify? What do you want to be known for? Create a visual or written representation of this vision. Use the examen to highlight alignment between desired legacy and daily actions. Identify one specific action strengthening this alignment.

The Practice of Conversing with Your Higher Power

Engaging your higher power (however conceived) supports discernment of authentic self and purpose. Remember that mindful listening is as important as speaking. Share insights from your examen practice.

Noticing in Stillness

We often become so busy that we fail to notice the obvious. When stuck in traffic or waiting in line, mindfully activate observation. Step out of thoughts to notice sights, sounds, smells, and textures. Pay attention to people around you – their expressions, energy, and behaviors. Journal about what you noticed and how this mindful practice engaged your whole being.

Summary

"You have forgotten who you are ... look inside yourself, Simba. You are more than what you have become. You must take your place in the circle of life ... Remember who you are" (Allers & Minkoff, 1994). Mufasa's words offer profound guidance for today's leaders. The lightning speed of modern life, coupled with our propensity for mindless automation, disconnects us from authentic identity. Like Simba, we need encouragement to remember who we are through mindful awareness.

Our leadership identity, meaning-making, and purpose are intricately interconnected through mindful attention. Exploring and adapting our leadership identity through mindfulness practices enhances well-being for ourselves, our followers, and our organizations.

Mindfulness and contemplative practices hold the key for slowing down, becoming present, and remembering the impactful leader you are designed to be.

References

Allers, R., & Minkoff, R. (Directors). (1994). *The Lion King* [Film]. Walt Disney Feature Animation.

Bocheliuk, V., Zavatska, N., Bokhonkova, Y., Toba, M., & Panov, N. (2020). Emotional burnout: Prevalence rate and symptoms in different socio-professional groups. *Journal of Intellectual Disability – Diagnosis and Treatment, 8,* 33–40. https://doi.org/10.6000/2292-2598.2020.08.01.5

Brooks, P. J., Ripoll, P., Sánchez, C., & Torres, M. (2023). Coaching leaders toward favorable trajectories of burnout and engagement. *Frontiers in Psychology, 14,* Article 1259672. https://doi.org/10.3389/fpsyg.2023.1259672

Brown, K. W., & Ryan, R. M. (2003). The benefits of being present: Mindfulness and its role in psychological well-being. *Journal of Personality and Social Psychology, 84*(4), 822–848. https://doi.org/10.1037/0022-3514.84.4.822

Burns, J. (1978). *Leadership.* Harper Torchbooks.

Campbell, M., & Gavett, G. (2021). What covid-19 has done to our well-being, in 12 charts. *Harvard Business Review.* https://hbr.org/2021/02/what-covid-19-has-done-to-our-well-being-in-12-charts

Cardona, P., Rey, C., & Craig, N. (2019). Purpose-driven leadership. In C. Rey, M. Bastons, & P. Sotok (Eds.). *Purpose-driven organizations* (pp. 55–71). Palgrave Macmillan. https://doi.org/10.1007/978-3-030-17674-7_5

Chu, S. T. W., & Mak, W. (2020). How mindfulness enhances meaning in life: A meta-analysis of correlational studies and randomized controlled trials. *Mindfulness, 11,* 177–193. https://doi.org/10.1007/s12671-019-01258-9

Davidson, B. D. (2019). *Finding chazown: The role of coaching in the discernment of calling* (Order No. 22582679). ProQuest Dissertations & Theses Global: The Humanities and Social Sciences Collection.

DeGreeff, B. L., Burnett, A., & Cooley, D. (2010). Communicating and philosophizing about authenticity or inauthenticity in a fast-paced world. *Journal of Happiness Studies, 11*(4), 395–408. https://doi.org/10.1007/s10902-009-9147-4

Frankl, V. E. (1992). *Man's search for meaning: An introduction to logotherapy* (4th ed.). Beacon Press.

Frankl, V. E. (2014). *Viktor Frankl – Finding meaning in pain* [Video recording]. https://www.youtube.com/watch?v=fhA3mEkzLLQ

Future Forum. (2022). Executives feel the strain of leading in the 'new normal': New data shows employee sentiment and experience scores dropping among the C-suite. *Future Forum Pulse.* https://futureforum.com/research/pulse-report-fall-2022-executives-feel-strain-leading-in-new-normal/

Goleman, D. (2011). *Leadership: The power of emotional intelligence.* More Than Sound.

Gray, B. (2023). *Rule of life: A trellis for growth.* Denver Institute for Faith & Work. https://www.denverinstitute.org/rule-of-life/

Hickman, G. R., & Sorenson, G. J. (2013). *The power of invisible leadership: How a compelling common purpose inspires exceptional leadership.* Sage Publications.

Ivtzan, I., Lomas, T., Hefferon, K., & Worth, P. (2016). *Second wave positive psychology: Embracing the dark side of life.* Routledge.

John, A., Bouillon-Minois, J. B., Bagheri, R., Pélissier, C., Charbotel, B., Llorca, P. M., Zak, M., Ugbolue, U. C., Baker, J. S., & Dutheil, F. (2024). The influence of burnout on cardiovascular disease: A systematic review and meta-analysis. *Frontiers in Psychiatry, 15,* Article 1326745. https://doi.org/10.3389/fpsyt.2024.1326745

Keating, T. (1997). *Centering prayer in daily life and ministry.* Bloomsbury.

Leka, S., Jain, A., & World Health Organization. (2010). *Health impact of psychosocial hazards at work: An overview.* World Health Organization. https://iris.who.int/handle/10665/44428

Levey, J., & Levey, M. (2019). Mindful leadership for personal and organisational resilience. *Clinical Radiology*, *74*(10), 739–745. https://doi.org/10.1016/j.crad.2019.06.026

Mead, G. W. (1910). Social consciousness and the consciousness of meaning. *Psychological Bulletin*, *7*, 397–405. https://doi.org/10.1037/h0074293

Microsoft. (2022). *Hybrid work is just work. Are we doing it wrong?* (Work Trend Index). Microsoft. https://shorturl.at/P6lAT

Mols, I., Van Den Hoven, E., & Eggen, B. (2016). Informing design for reflection: An overview of current everyday practices. In S. Björk, E. Eriksson, M. Fjeld, S. Bødker, W. Barendregt, & M. Obaid (Eds.), *Proceedings of the 9th Nordic Conference on Human-Computer Interaction* (pp. 1–10). Association for Computing Machinery. https://doi.org/10.1145/2971485.2971494

Munusamy, V., Ruderman, M., & Eckert, R. (2010). Leader development and social identity. In E. Van Velsor, C. D. McCauley, & M. N. Ruderman (Eds.), *The Center for Creative Leadership handbook of leadership development* (3rd ed., pp. 147–175). Jossey-Bass.

Nader, T., & Maheshwari, A.K. (2023). Consciousness as the source of purposeful leadership. In A. K. Maheshwari (Ed.), *Consciousness-based leadership and management: Vedic and other philosophical approaches to oneness and flourishing* (Vol. 1, pp. 27–44). Palgrave Macmillan. https://doi.org/10.1007/978-3-031-06234-6_2

New International Version. (2011). *Mark 6*. Biblica Inc. (Original work published 1973) https://www.biblegateway.com/passage/?search=mark%206&version=NIV

Northouse, P. (2021). *Leadership: Theory and practice* (9th ed.). Sage Publications.

Nouwen, H. (1972). *The wounded healer: Ministry in contemporary society*. Crown Publishing.

Nyberg, D., & Sveningsson, S. (2014). Paradoxes of authentic leadership: Leader identity struggles. *Leadership*, *10*(4), 437–455. https://doi.org/10.1177/1742715013504425

Omrane, A., Kammoun, A., & Seaman, C. (2018). Entrepreneurial burnout: Causes, consequences and way out. *Multinational Business Review*, *7*, 28–42. https://doi.org/10.1177/2319714518767805

Palmer, P. (2000). *Let your life speak: Listening for the voice of vocation*. Jossey-Bass.

Parent-Lamarche, A., & Biron, C. (2022). When bosses are burned out: Psychosocial safety climate and its effect on managerial quality. *International Journal of Stress Management*, *29*(3), 219–228. https://doi.org/10.1037/str0000252

Sinclair, A. (2011). Being leaders: Identity work in leadership. In A. Bryman, D. Collinson, K. Grint, B. Jackson, & M. Uhl-Bien (Eds.), *The Sage handbook of leadership* (pp. 508–517). Sage Publications.

Southwick, S., Wisneski, L., & Starck, P. (2021). Rediscovering meaning and purpose: An approach to burnout in the time of COVID-19 and beyond. *The American Journal of Medicine*, *134*(9), 1065–1067. https://doi.org/10.1016/j.amjmed.2021.04.020

Tan, N., Peters, E. K., & Reb, J. (2023). Effects of a mindfulness-based leadership training on leadership behaviors and effectiveness. *Mindfulness*, *14*(9), 2181–2194. https://doi.org/10.1007/s12671-023-02209-1

TED^{X}Manhattan. (2012). Can a simple piece of paper change the way we eat? *Kavita Shukla* [Video]. YouTube. https://www.youtube.com/watch?v=UrqRudIUPWs

Thoits, P. (2012). Role-identity salience, purpose and meaning in life, and well-being among volunteers. *Social Psychology Quarterly*, *75*(4), 360–384. https://doi.org/10.1177/0190272512459662

van Dick, R., & Schuh, S. (2010). My boss' group is my group: Experimental evidence for the leader-follower identity transfer. *Leadership & Organization Development Journal*, *31*, 551–563. https://doi.org/10.1108/01437731011070032

Wolpert, D. (2003). *Creating a life with God: The call of ancient prayer practices.* Upper Room Books.

Zhang, J., Song, L., Ni, D., & Zheng, X. (2020). Follower mindfulness and well-being: The mediating role of perceived authentic leadership and the moderating role of leader mindfulness. *Frontiers in Psychology, 11,* Article 879. https://doi.org/10.3389/fpsyg.2020.00879

Zu, L. (2019). Purpose-driven leadership for sustainable business: From the perspective of Taoism. *International Journal of Corporate Social Responsibility, 4*(3), 1–31. https://doi.org/10.1186/s40991-019-0041-z

Part 1

Poetic Response – RETREAT: A Moment of Silence

Danny Smith

Racing and panting and cursing and ranting,
This world spins too fast for a slow drummer like me.

My pace is steady in a world that's not ready
To wait in slumber for what it needs.
The seeds from the harvest feed the soul of the artist,
Starving for the darkest and wisest days –
When the trees undress and the queen bees rest
And the bears teach best, how to tuck away.

Come winter,
Obey the silence and gentle guidance
our grandmothers laid in the wake of the rush.
Hush. the jitters, the day world critters
That flitter and swarm and heedlessly crush the trust
between me and I.

Come winter,
The work is undone
is undoing from beneath,
from within.
And when nightfall stretches and daylight catches wind
of the season,
of the meaning of inertia:
Come home.

Part 2

Recenter

> We must be willing to get rid of the life we've planned, so as to have the life that is waiting for us. The old skin has to be shed before the new one can come. (Campbell & Osbon, 1995)

When making pottery, centering is the process a potter uses to align the lump of clay so that the shape is balanced on the potter's wheel. This process creates alignment through actively using the hands to push the hands towards the center. For Potter Richards (1964), centering is a way to "bring the universe into a personal wholeness," a way of contemplation. She asserts that, "life leads us at a certain moment to step beyond the dualisms to which we have been educated: primitive and civilized, chaos and order, abnormal and normal, private and public, verbal and non-verbal, conventional and far-out, good and bad." Through centering, we "resolve the oppositions," stepping towards new ways of seeing, thinking, and being.

Recentering explores the transformative power of aligning leadership practices with core values, creativity, and collaboration. Rooted in the metaphor of the potter's wheel, recentering emphasizes the necessity of shedding dualistic paradigms and stepping into wholeness. Drawing inspiration from Joseph Campbell's wisdom on embracing life's possibilities, Part 2 highlights how leaders can refine their identity and purpose through creative practice, narrative power, and inclusive collaboration. Each chapter invites leaders to recognize their inherent potential for growth and innovation, discovering new ways of being and thinking that are both transformative and sustainable.

References

Campbell, J., & Osbon, D. K. (Eds.). (1995). *Reflections on the art of living: A Joseph Campbell Companion*. HarperCollins.

Richards, M. C. (1964). *Centering in pottery, poetry, and the person*. Wesleyan University Press.

Chapter 7

The Artful Leader: Exploring Creativity, Esthetic Sensibility, and Inclusive Practice in Leadership

Alicia D. Crumpton in Conversation with Catherine Etmanski

Alicia D. Crumpton

Kaleidoventure LLC, USA

Abstract

This chapter presents a dialogue between two scholars exploring the intersection of art, esthetics, and leadership. The conversation examines how creativity, inspiration, and esthetic sensibility influence leadership practice and interrogates systemic biases in the valuation of both art and leadership. Parallels are drawn between artistic creation and leadership innovation, highlighting how historically marginalized approaches, often associated with feminine or non-Western perspectives, have been undervalued in leadership discourse. Through an exploration of concepts including hermeneutical spirals, flow states, and awe experiences, the chapter advocates for a more inclusive understanding of leadership that recognizes diverse expressions of creativity. It is concluded that artful leadership involves creating spaces where collective creativity can flourish, diverse voices are valued, and leaders remain open to inspiration that emerges when recognizing themselves as part of something larger. Practical somatic breathing, creative, and reflective exercises designed to help leaders develop their capacity for artful leadership are included.

Keywords: Esthetic sensibility; creativity; innovation; inspiration; gender bias; valuation

Artful Leadership: Retreat, Recenter, and Rewild, 77–88

Copyright © 2026 by Alicia D. Crumpton

Published under exclusive licence by Emerald Publishing Limited

doi:10.1108/S2058-880120250000010008

Introduction

Today, organizations often tout creativity as essential for effective leadership. Although leaders may declare that they aren't creative or say *it just came to me* when asked about the sources of their innovations, they know that creativity is vital to leadership success. Added to the complexity of understanding leadership creativity are esthetic valuations, including what constitutes artful leadership, beautiful organizational design, or ugly management practices. Although esthetic experience and valuation in leadership may seem subjective and influenced by a myriad of factors, they are profoundly influential in shaping organizational culture and outcomes. The purpose of this conversation is to explore the nature and sources of leadership creativity, including esthetic experience and valuation in leadership contexts.

Catherine Etmanski and I met through our involvement with the International Leadership Association. Her passion for incorporating creative elements into and using arts-based approaches within her research, leadership, and teaching contributed to my wanting to learn more about her thoughts about creativity, inspiration, and esthetic sensibility as they apply to leadership practice. What follows is our conversation.

Defining Artful Leadership

Alicia: Thank you for talking with me although I suspect we could talk for days about these topics! To begin, I'd like to hear what's bubbling up for you as you consider the terms creativity, inspiration, and esthetic sensibility in relation to leadership.

Catherine: Thank you for this opportunity, it's so good to have this dialogue about topics we share a passion about.

Alicia: My initial question preceded these terms in wanting to understand what constitutes artful leadership, who decides, and to what effect? Leo Tolstoy (2020), for example, asked the question "what is art?" and then critiqued valuations of beauty as too subjective and limiting:

> This science of esthetics consists in first acknowledging a certain set of productions to be art (because they please us), and then framing such a theory of art that all those productions which please a certain circle of people should fit into it.

Similarly, declaring something as *good leadership* carries additional valuations and boundaries as to who is recognized as a leader and whose leadership approach is accepted by the valuators. Philosopher Alva Noë (2015) addressed this specifically in relation to esthetic judgment, which we can apply to leadership: "aesthetic evaluation to be genuinely aesthetic, it must be an impartial response, one that is indifferent to who owns the work, or who made it, etc." (p. 203). Yet in leadership, we rarely apply such impartial evaluation. I love Noë, who (2015) also highlighted how "aesthetic disagreement is never really about the art thing itself; it is about our response to the thing" (p. 203). It seems that valuation might be rife with bias and prejudice when evaluating whether something is effective leadership or whether it's beautiful leadership.

Systemic Bias in Art Valuation and Leadership Recognition

Catherine: Yes, there are so many who critique perceived bias and prejudice within the art world:

- Art historian Linda Nochlin (2015) critiqued gender bias in her article entitled: *Why have there been no great women artists?* Specifically, she explored how institutional barriers kept women from achieving recognition in the art world.
- Activists The Guerrilla Girls (n.d.) use "disruptive headlines, outrageous visuals and killer statistics to expose gender and ethnic bias and corruption in art, film, politics and pop culture … by revealing the understory, the subtext, the overlooked, and the downright unfair."
- Social critic, author and feminist bell hooks (1995), speaking of her lived experience, observed how white men in the art world are "have been canonized in such a way that their standards and esthetic visions are used instrumentally to devalue the works of new rebels in the art work, especially artists from marginal groups" (pp. xi–xii).
- Art critic and activist Lucy Lippard (1995) brought feminist perspectives to art criticism in the 1970s, highlighting how women artists are largely overlooked by mainstream criticism.

One's vantage point, including underlying biases and assumptions, shapes what art is, including its valuation. Similarly, valuations about leadership occur all the time, as evidenced by whose voices are heard, promotions, hirings, etc. Potential leadership from marginal groups is excluded by some valuative criteria that exclude their participation in the conversation and decision making. One's vantage point, including underlying biases and assumptions, shapes what leadership is, including its valuation.

Alicia: Isn't this idea of vantage point what John Berger (1972) was illustrating in his book *Ways of Seeing* that could apply to leadership as well? Specifically, he noted that "when an image is presented as a work of art, the way people look at it is affected by a whole series of [their learned] assumptions about art" (Berger, 1972, p. 11). Similarly, when someone is presented as a leader, the way people perceive their leadership is affected by a whole series of learned assumptions about what leadership should look and sound like.

Historical Gender Dynamics in Leadership

Catherine: Our human tendency to apply categories within our interpretation certainly shapes how creative works are evaluated. For example, the distinction between arts and crafts wherein crafts were seen as *women's work* and their value denigrated accordingly. Women's artistic contributions were often overlooked historically.

Alicia: An example of this is the story of Hilma af Klint's work. She created more than 1,500 pieces and compiled over 26,000 pages of notes and sketches and prior to her death she assigned caretaking of her works to her nephew with a proviso that her works could not be revealed for 20 years.

Catherine: Oh yes, I saw an exhibit of her works in New York a few years back. When the works were finally revealed, it was discovered that she was a contemporary of abstract expressionists Piet Mondrian and Wassily Kandinsky, maybe even creating prior to them. This find created quite a stir in the art community because, in part, there was resistance to rewriting art history. Another part of it, might have been a rejection of her methods. Hilma af Klint was a member of *The Five*, a group of women who held seances and then painted what was channeled to them. This intersection of spiritual influences and notions of where inspiration comes from may have played a part. In *Beyond the Visible* (Dyrschka, 2019), a documentary about her life, when her works were first discovered, there was a real resistance to her work and contribution because it meant a necessity to rewrite history.

The same challenges emerge when we consider how leadership is evaluated. For example, the distinction between so-called, *hard* and *soft* leadership skills, wherein soft skills were and continue to be often seen as women's work and their value denigrated accordingly. Women's leadership contributions were often overlooked historically because they didn't fit the dominant great man or heroic leadership model. Yet relational skills like communication, collaboration, community-building, diplomacy, and so on are essential to leadership.

Alicia: I agree, these leadership approaches have historically been undervalued compared to more directive, individual-focused approaches. Many women leaders, like Mary Parker Follett, offered revolutionary leadership ideas but weren't recognized as leadership theorists in their time.

Catherine: Yes, and when their work was finally recognized and valued, there was resistance to rewriting leadership history. Although this is changing, in some organizational contexts, there's still resistance to more relational and collaborative approaches to leadership despite their effectiveness, because these approaches challenge traditional power structures. Just listen to any news broadcast today and you'll hear talk of tough or strong leadership. That's what we're talking about, right? These powers come into play. And if you're all about power, and have access to power through your social positioning, then you want to protect and maintain boundaries around what constitutes real art or real leadership.

Art and Leadership Interpretation

Alicia: As I think about it, art and I'm using the term art to represent many forms (visual, written, theater, film, dance, music, etc.), art includes many constituents, the creator, the viewer, the work itself, and the context with each having an interpretive role.

Catherine: Yes, one of my colleagues, Carey Newman, refers to his own process of transformation when creating art as becoming both the maker and the material (Newman & Etmanski, 2022).

Alicia: Right. And it strikes me how there's a hermeneutical spiral, a dialogical co-creative process where the artist's intention, the artwork's intrinsic qualities, the viewer's subjective experience, and the broader cultural context continuously inform and transform each other.

Catherine: Yes, the artist creates a work emerging from inspiration and imagination, personal experiences, and cultural background. Even the materials used contribute to what's possible. Then, as the viewer encounters the artwork, they bring their own complex web of personal histories, emotions, biases, and assumptions that interact with the artwork's material and symbolic elements generating meanings that may diverge significantly from the artist's original conception. This interpretive encounter is not linear but spiral-like, where each engagement recursively reshapes understanding. The viewer's perception alters the artwork's significance, while the artwork's complexity continually challenges and expands the viewer's perceptual and conceptual boundaries. All of this occurs while being situated within and reflecting broader historical, social, and esthetic contexts that are themselves in perpetual flux. There's interpretation, valuation, power, and the control of who gets to say what constitutes art and who gets to say what constitutes esthetics.

Alicia: This applies also to leadership, a dialogical co-creation where people, the culture, and the place continuously inform and transform each other.

Catherine: Yes, the interpretive possibility is similar to art. The leader enacts leadership emerging from inspiration and imagination, personal experiences, and cultural background. As others encounter leadership, they bring their own complex web of personal histories, emotions, biases, and assumptions that interact with the leadership approach, generating meanings that may diverge significantly from the leader's original conception. This interpretive encounter is not linear but spiral-like, where each engagement recursively reshapes understanding. People's perceptions alter leadership's significance, while the leadership complexity continually challenges and expands perceptual and conceptual boundaries. All of this occurs while being situated within and reflecting broader historical, social, and organizational contexts that are themselves in perpetual flux. There's interpretation, valuation, power and the control of who gets to say what constitutes leadership and more specifically what constitutes effective leadership.

Nature Versus Nurture in Leadership

Alicia: An age-old question within leadership is whether a person's ability or leadership is nature versus nurture. What are your thoughts?

Catherine: As a leadership educator, I believe whole-heartedly that leadership can be taught. However, the Great Man theory of leadership (Carlyle, 1841) has certainly advanced the popular belief that certain people, largely white males, are imbued with certain heroic traits and abilities at birth. We still hear this kind of thinking in popular discourse. Leadership greatness often centers on the person rather than leadership practices. A centering on the leader's mythos versus the leadership practices or outcomes serves to exclude anyone not considered to possess those innate qualities. Moreover, it disregards any familial, social, or cultural socialization toward dominance, which is often mistaken for leadership.

The idea of "genius" is certainly at play here. Similarly, within the arts, artistic greatness often centers on the person rather than the artworks. To denote someone as artistic imbues them with a sort of aura and seemingly supernatural ability. Likewise, to denote someone as a *born leader* elevates their standing and abilities. In contrast, in many Indigenous cultures around the world, art is considered part of living. Art is not solely a personal or commercial *product*, instead, there's an idea of singing the world into being. Dances and songs are ways of communicating. Art is integrated into everyday life in so many cultures around the world, just as leadership is expressed when someone is able to manifest their gifts. An alternative to the heroic view of leadership is to consider one's capacity for relationship, dialogue, shared wisdom, and interconnection.

Alicia: Isn't it fascinating how, historically, masculinity is often associated with rationality, whereas femininity is associated with inspiration and intuition which is considered suspect. But when it comes to art, men's work has been valued more. One has to wonder how binary thinking and a tendency toward objectification are at play.

Catherine: A challenge with genius or great man thinking in leadership is how people with real leadership talent naturally negate their abilities: *Oh, I'm not a leader, I'm not innovative*, or *I couldn't lead that initiative*, or even, *It was nothing*. These self-limiting statements often stem from deeply internalized societal narratives that creativity and leadership are rare, innate gifts bestowed only on a select few, rather than skills that can be developed through practice, curiosity, and persistent effort.

Creativity Versus Innovation in Leadership

Alicia: Terms like creativity and innovation get tossed around in leadership discourse, what do these terms mean?

Catherine: Creativity is a complex term often used to describe individual inspiration and imagination, the process of creating including the medium and its capabilities and restraints, the actual creative output (poem, music, art, play, etc.) and the environment including the viewer and the context. This is a broader definition than how creativity was defined by Amabile (1988, 1996) and Amabile and Pratt (2016) who focused on creativity in terms of "production and useful ideas" emphasized utility and the either/or of individual and group creativity. Furthermore, Amabile distinguished innovation from creativity as "successful implementation."

Alicia: What is the leader's role in fostering creativity?

Catherine: Hill et al. (2014) explored the leader's role in fostering creativity and innovative thinking. Their research found that leaders could not demand or compel innovation, instead, leaders create space for creativity to occur, "a place, a context, an environment, where people are willing and able to do the hard work that innovative problem solving requires" (p. 3). The term *innovation ecosystem* was used to describe a robust space, infrastructure, processes and tools that facilitate communication, collaboration, and innovation. These spaces are conducive to fostering creativity. Note also how this definition alters the role of a leader from a directive to a support role. The leader becomes an architect of creative spaces rather than the source of all creativity.

Leadership Inspiration Versus Creative Practice

Alicia: Discussions of leadership creativity seem to sidestep inspiration and imagination. How might you talk about inspiration in leadership contexts?

Catherine: I once heard David Whyte describe poets as being the yogis of Ireland. I appreciated this idea because it speaks to attuning ourselves to the world around us. Leadership inspiration can sometimes appear to be mysterious or extend beyond the rational. Here I don't mean decisions that others perceive to be irrational. I'm talking about leaders tuning into a greater vision for what is possible in that specific moment in time.

Alicia: Yes, another example is poet Octavio Paz (1973), who described poets as those who travel to the other shore and bring forth a poem. Through poetry, a poet speaks with a "strange voice, his voice and his word are the strange ones" (Paz, 1973), because the poem comes from a different world. This is an important aspect of Paz's ideas – that a poem is not bound by this world or language, it is beyond this world, comes from a different world known as the other shore, the transcendent. Similarly, truly transformative leaders often speak with a "strange voice" – one that articulates a vision others cannot yet see but resonates deeply with followers. Paz (1973) reminded, "We are in a world that is, another world" where the poet experiences the supernatural.

Catherine: Another view comes from Mihaly Csikszentmihalyi's (1990) who used the word *flow* to describe how, for example, a painter might enter flow while creating a complex artwork, losing track of time and feeling a profound connection to their creative process. In this sense, inspiration is not a passive activity but an active engagement.

I used to teach a class on cultural leadership and social learning through the arts where I had leadership students, who didn't necessarily consider themselves artists, creating weekly artistic expressions, and facilitating (and participating in one another's) arts-based workshops. As part of my feedback process, in addition to providing written commentary, I would often offer my own creative response: their original creation inspired further creation in me and we continued this creative dialogue throughout the class. There's no question that I experienced a flow state while teaching that class. The weekly engagement through the arts inspired increasing levels of creativity.

Alicia: What I hear you saying is that leadership, like artistic inspiration, is not purely passive, but is a complex phenomenon and interplay between conscious effort and unconscious processes.

Catherine: Inspiration is something experienced through curiosity, openness, practice, and receptivity to the world. There are many practices that can open a person to this sort of receptivity to organizational and social needs. For example, being in nature, somatic breathing, meditation, physical practices, like asana or some rhythmic sports, etc. These sorts of practices open up a greater attunement to the world and potential for inspiration. When I taught arts-based practices, within those classes I felt a shift into that other realm and then creativity begets more creativity. Likewise, I encourage leaders to develop a personal leadership practice, something that allows them to feel a little more comfort in the discomfort of hanging out in the void of uncertainty. Leaders, too, often report feeling a shift into that other realm of possibility, and then creativity begets more creativity in their leadership approach.

Alicia: Just thinking about how one of the most difficult parts of strategic planning for consultants is what I call moving from technical decision making to foresight and imagination. You look at the current situation, and yes, there's analysis involved but at some point, you have to imagine a new future. People tied to rationality, can have trouble going there because foresight thinking requires part expertise and experience – I know these kinds of things work or don't work; and intuition and inspiration – here's what we could look like in the future. My experience suggests those tied solely to rationality tend to design more incremental changes rather than transformative changes that really innovate the organization. Artful leaders, on the other hand, blend analysis with creative visioning.

Conclusion: The Artful Leader

Alicia: Catherine, thank you again for agreeing to this conversation. What final thoughts might you offer about artful leadership?

Catherine: So many more topics to discuss! For all our attempts to understand leadership creativity and inspiration, there remains a mystery, something we don't quite understand. Dacher Keltner wrote a wonderful book about awe, a term he used to describe those moments where we are so moved that our sense of time and place are temporarily transcended. Keltner (2022) said, "Awe is the emotion we experience when we encounter vast mysteries that we don't understand." Our experience of awe conveys a sense of vastness, shifting our orientation from the "sense that we are solely in charge of our own fate and striving against others to feeling we are part of a community, sharing essential qualities, interdependent and collaborating" (Keltner, 2022, p. 40).

Through his examination of the research, Keltner created a taxonomy of awe-inducing experiences that cut across cultures: moral beauty, collective effervescence, nature, music, visual design, spiritual and religious awe, life and death, and epiphanies. The artful leader, I believe, is one who creates these awe-inspiring moments within their own practice and within organizational contexts – moments that transcend the everyday connecting to a larger vision and purpose. Keltner's conclusion was inspiring and applies directly to leadership:

> Awe integrates us into the systems of life – communities, collectives, the natural environment, and forms of culture, such as music, art, religion, and our mind's efforts to make sense of all its webs of ideas … In awe we understand we are part of many things that are much larger than the self. (p. 249)

This conversation serves as a reminder that creativity exists not in isolation but in relationship – to others, to traditions, to contexts, and to the mysterious sources of inspiration that transcend our complete understanding. As leaders and artists navigate increasingly complex environments, perhaps our greatest opportunity lies not in claiming individual leadership genius but in fostering the conditions where collective creativity can flourish, where diverse voices are valued, and where we remain open to the awe-inspiring potential that emerges when we recognize ourselves as part of something larger than ourselves. This is what it means to be an artful leader – not merely to create art, but to approach leadership itself as an art form, with all the mystery, beauty, practice, and inspiration that entails.

Somatic Breathing, Creative and Reflection Practices

These exercises are designed to help you develop your capacity for artful leadership as described in the conversation between Alicia and Catherine. By engaging with somatic breathing, creative practice, and reflective inquiry, you'll cultivate greater receptivity to inspiration, enhance your creative leadership capabilities, and develop a more nuanced understanding of your leadership esthetic.

Somatic Breathing Practice

360° Awareness Breathing

The purpose of this exercise is to expand your perceptual field and develop greater sensitivity to organizational dynamics.

1. Stand in a comfortable position.
2. Begin breathing deeply and evenly.
3. As you inhale, imagine you're drawing in information and awareness from all directions.
4. As you exhale, imagine you're expanding your presence in all directions.
5. Continue for 3–5 minutes, gradually expanding your awareness to include:
   ○ Your immediate physical space
   ○ People in your organization
   ○ The broader community or stakeholders
   ○ The larger systems your organization operates within
6. Notice what insights or impressions emerge as you practice this expanded awareness.

Creative Practices for Leadership Innovation

Visual Metaphor Mapping

The purpose of this exercise is to access non-rational ways of understanding organizational challenges.

Instructions:

1. Choose a leadership challenge you're currently facing.
2. Without planning or analyzing, begin to draw images, symbols, or shapes that represent different aspects of the situation.
3. Ask yourself: "If this challenge were a landscape, what would it look like? What creatures would inhabit it? What weather patterns would exist?"
4. Continue adding to your visual map for 15–20 minutes.
5. Step back and observe what you've created:
    o What stands out?
    o What surprising connections have emerged?
    o What does this visual metaphor reveal about potential approaches?
6. What can serve as a physical reminder of each quality?

Weekly Creative Dialogue

The purpose of this exercise is to develop creative receptivity through regular artistic practice, inspired by Catherine's teaching approach. Set aside 30–45 minutes each week for creative expression. Rotate through different mediums: writing, drawing, movement, sound, etc. Create in response to a leadership question or challenge. The following week, begin by reviewing your previous creation and then respond to it with a new creation in a different medium. Notice how this ongoing creative dialogue develops over time and what insights emerge.

Reflective Practices for Esthetic Leadership Development

Leadership Esthetics Journal

The purpose of this exercise is to develop awareness of your leadership Esthetic preferences and their impact.

1. Create a dedicated journal for exploring your leadership esthetics.
2. Each week, respond to one of the following prompts:
    o When have I experienced leadership that felt *beautiful* to me? What qualities made it beautiful?
    o How do my cultural background and personal history shape what I consider *good* leadership?
    o What leadership approaches do I find *ugly* or distasteful? What might this reveal about my biases?
    o How might different stakeholders experience my leadership esthetically?
    o What artists or artistic traditions inspire my leadership approach?

Awe Practice

The purpose of this exercise is to cultivate experiences of awe that expand leadership perspective, as described by Keltner.

1. Schedule 20–30 minutes each week to intentionally seek out awe-inducing experiences from Keltner's taxonomy mentioned in the article:
   o Moral beauty
   o Collective effervescence
   o Nature
   o Music
   o Visual design
   o Spiritual experience
   o Life and death contemplation
   o Epiphanies
2. During the experience, practice deep presence and receptivity.
3. Afterward, reflect on:
   o How did this experience change my sense of self and connection to something larger?
   o What leadership insights emerged from this state of awe?
   o How might I bring elements of this experience into my organizational context?

Leadership Hermeneutics

The purpose of this exercise is to explore the dialogical co-creation of leadership meaning.

1. Select a recent leadership situation.
2. Analyze it through the hermeneutical spiral described in the article by considering:
   o Your intentions as a leader (artist)
   o The intrinsic qualities of your leadership approach (artwork)
   o Others' subjective experiences of your leadership (viewers)
   o The broader organizational and cultural context
3. Identify gaps between your intentions and others' experiences.
4. Consider how this understanding might transform your future leadership approach.

Integration Practice: Creating Your Leadership Practice

Based on your exploration of these exercises, design a personalized daily or weekly leadership practice that combines elements of somatic awareness, creative exploration, and reflective inquiry. As Catherine suggests in the article, this practice should "allow you to feel a little more comfort in the discomfort of hanging out in the void of uncertainty."

Your practice might include:

- A brief morning breathing ritual
- A weekly creative exploration
- Regular moments of seeking awe
- Evening reflection on leadership esthetics.

Document your practice and notice how it evolves over time, allowing creativity to beget more creativity in your leadership approach.

References

Amabile, T. M. (1988). A model of creativity and innovation in organizations. *Research in Organizational Behavior, 10,* 123–167.

Amabile, T. M. (1996). *Creativity in context.* Westview Press.

Amabile, T. M., & Pratt, M. G. (2016). The dynamic componential model of creativity and innovation in organizations: Making progress, making meaning. *Research in Organizational Behavior, 36,* 157–183. http://dx.doi.org/10.1016/j.riob.2016.10.001

Berger, J. (Ed.). (1972). *Ways of seeing.* British Broadcasting Corporation and Penguin.

Carlyle, T. (1841). *On heroes, hero-worship, & the heroic in history.* James Fraser.

Csikszentmihalyi, M. (1990). *Flow: The psychology of optimal experience.* Harper & Row.

Dyrschka, H. (Director). (2019). *Beyond the visible* (1:34:00) [Film]. Zeitgeist Films.

Hill, L. A., Brandeau, G., Truelove, E., & Lineback, K. (2014). *Collective genius: The art and practice of leading innovation.* Harvard Business Review Press.

hooks, b. (1995). *Art on my mind: Visual politics.* New Press.

Keltner, D. (2022). *Awe: The new science of everyday wonder and how it can transform your life.* Penguin Press.

Lippard, L. R. (1995). *The pink glass swan: Selected essays on feminist art.* New Press.

Newman, C., & Etmanski, C. (2022). The witness blanket: Responsibility through an ongoing journey of transformation. In A. Nicolaides, S. Eschenbacher, P. Buergelt, Y. Gilpin-Jackson, M. Welch, M. Misawa, & A. Lim (Eds.), *The Palgrave handbook of learning for transformation* (pp. 503–519). Palgrave Macmillan. https://doi.org/10.1007/978-3-030-84694-7_28

Nochlin, L. (2015). Why have there been no great women artists? In M. Reilly (Ed.). *Women artists: The Linda Nochlin reader* (pp. 42–68). Thames & Hudson. (Original work published 1971)

Noë, A. (2015). *Strange tools: Art and human nature.* Hill and Wang.

Paz, O. (1973). *The bow and the lyre: The poem, the poetic revelation, poetry and history* (R. L. C. Simms, Trans.). University of Texas Press.

The Guerrilla Girls. (n.d.). *Our story.* https://www.guerrillagirls.com/our-story

Tolstoy, L. (2020). *What is art?* Digireads.com Publishing. (Original work published 1897)

Chapter 8

Narrative Power: The Artful Leader's Responsibility in Reality Shaping

Aaron Monts

Eastside Academy, USA

Abstract

This chapter explores the profound role of narratives in shaping individual and collective reality, and the ethical responsibility leaders bear in wielding narrative power. Leaders engage in sensemaking by organizing disparate events into coherent frameworks that help individuals discover meaning in their experiences. Through the process of re-storying – reinterpreting past experiences through new perspectives – leaders can reshape both personal and cultural narratives. The chapter examines how narrative power operates within cultural complexes, revealing how dominant narratives can either unite or fragment communities, inspire or manipulate. Drawing on historical examples of leaders who effectively harnessed narrative power for positive change – including Ida B. Wells, Martin Luther King Jr., César Chávez, Dolores Huerta, and Bryan Stevenson – the chapter demonstrates how ethical leadership requires acknowledging one's biases, understanding the fluid nature of power, and committing to using narrative force responsibly. Practical exercises are provided to help leaders develop greater narrative awareness and transform their leadership approach through somatic breathing, creative practices, and reflective journaling.

Keywords: Narrative power; sensemaking; cultural complexes; re-storying; social fabric; implicit bias; dominant narratives; cultural transformation; narrative identity

Artful Leadership: Retreat, Recenter, and Rewild, 89–103
Copyright © 2026 by Aaron Monts
Published under exclusive licence by Emerald Publishing Limited
doi:10.1108/S2058-880120250000010009

Introduction

We are all striving to make sense of the world, searching for insight into why things are the way they are, longing to piece together enough understanding to grasp as the ground shifts beneath our feet. We are a people searching for meaning, working to uncover our purpose, and dreaming of how we can artfully forge a new path forward. This is the burden of the artful leader. It, too, is their great hope.

Leaders carry an inherent burden for sensemaking. They grapple with the turmoil of an ever-changing world and organize disparate events of life into a common understanding or framework that helps individuals discover the meaning and purpose of their experiences. Sensemaking creates connection points for our personal stories within our larger world experience. However, sensemaking is not an impartial process; instead, requiring leaders to acknowledge their biases and cultural narratives. While narratives provide a structure for meaning, they also hold the power to create or destroy, to unite or fragment, and to inspire or manipulate. Ethical leadership demands a commitment to using narrative power responsibly, ensuring that it fosters truth, justice, and collective empowerment rather than division or oppression.

The work of sensemaking begins by grounding a leader's identity in something beyond mere progress. It requires reflective inner work of connecting with and recentering a leader's personal narrative. The process of re-storying, whereby we define our earlier experiences through the lens of later experiences, allows narrative's meaning to shift over time (Connelly & Clandinin, 1990, p. 9). This re-storying experience enables leaders to explore old territory with new meaning. Reintegrating new meaning into old narratives creates texture for present sensemaking frameworks. Ultimately, this process reconstructs an integrated structure where re-storied narratives bring order from chaos and guide people toward altered understandings of reality (Ricoeur, 1995).

Inherent in the process of sensemaking, a leader possesses substantial power. A leader's ability to redefine frameworks can create and destroy, generate new possibilities, or devolve into chaos; to make and remake worlds, reframe reality, or set the world ablaze. It is a power the artful leader should not take lightly, wield carefully, and remember that "with great power, there must also come–great responsibility" (Ditko & Lee, 1962, p. 13).

Artful leaders forge new paths to meet deep needs, inspiring others to journey alongside. By re-storying their personal narrative, creating deep connections to their identity, and reshaping their understanding through sensemaking, an artful leader can inspire the changes necessary to meet needs and multiply goodness in this world.

Narrative Formation of Identity, Culture, and Meaning

Stories are the foundation of our reality (Bruner, 1991) forming the framework for how we understand the world (Nelson, 2003). Narratives create meaning and structure through which we understand and experience our lived reality

(Lyotard, 1984). Narratives are our way of knowing, without which life could not be understood (Davenport, 2012). Narratives form the basis for relationships, directing our interactions with and understanding of one another.

The stories we tell ourselves are a "critical key to our identity" (Sheldrake, 2001, p. 19). Stories help answer the ultimate question of "who I am" while providing an interpretive lens for our experiences. These stories are highly curated. Through creative choice, we build our stories through embellishment and exaggeration, removing, adding, and even altering details to shape others' perceptions. We selectively render narratives to form subjective interpretations of reality.

This subjective rendering creates a singular world known only to an individual providing a unique account of events believed to represent their lived reality (Fludernik, 2009). A phenomenon known as the *Rashomon effect* was derived from the Japanese film *Rashomon* (Kurosawa, 1950), which explores the subjective relationship of truth and perception through the perspectives of four different characters. Each person's account is dramatically different, shaped by each character's motivations, biases, and emotions. No one sees what you see, even if they see it too.

This individualized rendering colors the lens through which we process the world, directly influencing how we perceive others' reality (Kimbles, 2014). We view experiences through frameworks that extract meaning singular to our needs, reinforcing preexisting structures while discarding aberrant information (Singer, 2006).

While we inhabit singular realities, humans "do not exist in a vacuum" (Schechtman, 1996, p. 95). Our identity is inherently shaped and connects to placing ourselves in larger cultural narratives; it is our search for connection and belonging. Our need to be rooted in community is "perhaps the most important and least recognized need of the human soul" (Weil, 1949/2001, p. 40). Identity construction relies upon our interpretation and contribution to societal narratives. Through reciprocal, cooperative trust, individuals construct narratives in partnership with others, creating common societal narratives.

These communal connections generate aligned realities forming the foundation of culture and history (Lyotard, 1984). "Stories make meaning," as Bruner (1997, p. 265) noted, carrying the weight of an entire community. Cultural narratives pass down collective views and unique understandings of reality. By connecting stories across generations, narratives work to create belonging and interconnectivity, resulting in culture through "an historically transmitted pattern of meaning embodied in symbols ... by which men communicate, perpetuate, and develop their knowledge about and attitudes towards life" (Sheldrake, 2001, p. 3). Narratives bind culture but are never singular or singularly understood.

Subjective Reality and Shared Cultural Narratives

The singularity of our personal, subjective reality and the shared formation of our cultural narratives can at first glance stand at odds with one another. If as the Rashomon Effect suggests individuals perceive and construct reality differently based on their personal experiences, motivations, and biases (Heider, 1988), then how do collective cultural narratives emerge and exert influence over the individual?

Humans are wired for communal sensemaking, seeking connection and belonging through shared stories, myths, and beliefs (Sheldrake, 2001). While individual narratives are inherently subjective, they do not exist in isolation. Cultural narratives form through a dynamic process of negotiation, where dominant perspectives gain traction through repetition, institutional endorsement, and social reinforcement (Bruner, 1991). This dynamic process explains how certain narratives achieve cultural dominance while others are marginalized.

Rather than viewing subjective reality and cultural narratives as mutually exclusive, they should be understood as interactive forces. Individual stories contribute to cultural narratives, and cultural narratives, in turn, shape how individuals perceive and articulate their lived experiences. This reciprocal relationship creates cycles of influence and reinforcement, highlighting the responsibility of leaders to guide this process ethically.

Narrative Power

Narratives are never neutral. Narratives are binding, contributive to a culture's social fabric, exemplified by mutuality, trust, and agreed-upon moral standards (Teymoori et al., 2017). While creating cohesion necessary for communities, narratives can create separation through their subjective rendering of narrative reality. Narrative power can strengthen or weaken the social fabric, build bridges, or foment separation between perspectives within society.

Narratives' lack of neutrality creates separation that weakens social fabric by creating power imbalances among groups with divergent realities. As competing narratives wrestle for narrative superiority, one ultimately emerges as the dominant cultural narrative, the remaining relegated to a subordinate status (Singer, 2007). These subordinate narratives, diverged from accepted cultural narratives, become perceived as deviant, weakening social fabric. One must then choose to accept the dominant narrative or associate with the perceived deviance of subordinated narratives. This creates insider/outsider identity dynamics formulating a new power dynamic (Bruner, 1997).

This insider/outsider identity revealed by the dominant and subordinated cultural narratives has been present throughout United States history (Monts, 2021). For example, Du Bois (1903) illustrated the narrative struggle present within Black consciousness:

> The Negro ... born with a veil, and gifted with second-sight in this American world, – a world which yields him no true self-consciousness, but only lets him see himself through the relation of the other world. It is a peculiar sensation, this double-consciousness, this sense of always looking at one's self through the eyes of others. (p. 7)

The "warring ideals" illustrate how narratives function as "structures of meaning [and] structures of power" (Bruner, 1997, p. 269). Narratives can be weaponized against subordinate cultural narratives.

This weaponization of narrative power serves to weaken the social fabric in pursuit of cultural dominance. While dominant narratives hold power, Collins (2002) maintained that subordinated (or marginalized) individuals and groups are not powerless. Termed the "outsider-within" (Collins, 2002, p. 12), the subordinated can provide alternative narratives revealing unique lived experience within societal systems and their impact on the marginalized. This perspectival narrative as narrative vehicle can create cracks in the dominant cultural narrative and its hold on power. These acts of narrative warfare, instigated by a power struggle between the dominant and the subordinated cultural narratives, are a battle for narrative supremacy and the privilege of constructing an alternate reality. In the hands of the leader, narratives become a tool of power employed in re-storying reality, constructed through the narrator's own experiential lens, observations, prejudices, and biases.

Manipulating Cultural Complexes for Narrative Power

Individuals harbor biases within their psyche, developed through personal and communal narratives. Carl Jung (1970) termed these phenomena cultural complexes: biases formed by lived experiences and their retelling. Jung's complex theory illuminated how these biases control our psyche.

These complexes affect both individual and cultural levels. Created through subconscious groupthink, cultural complexes form symbiotic relationships that reinforce biases by aligning personal experience with group expectations (Kimbles, 2014). Cultural complexes provide ways of "narrating relationship to the group" (Kimbles, 2014, p. 6) and creating bonds for belonging. They weave subjective interpretations, emotional responses, and psychohistorical understanding into deeply held core beliefs used to interpret the world (Abramovitch, 2007).

Cultural complexes can be manipulated through narrative vehicles that harness cultural and individual psyche through re-storying. Narratives can activate what Kimbles (2014) called "nucleating centers" (p. 14) of the psyche. This realm stores experiences and ideologies formed through personal experience. By accessing nucleating centers, core beliefs become susceptible to new narrative frameworks.

By activating narrative power against outsider groups, narrators can validate biases with confirmation that affirms "simplistic points of view [replacing] everyday ambiguity and uncertainty with fixed, often self-righteous attitudes" (Singer, 2006, p. 203). Narratives need not be true to activate nucleating centers. Rather, they need only create connections, no matter how thin. Narratives can validate biases by replacing uncertainty with fixed viewpoints. These narratives need only create tenuous connections to activate "nucleating centers" of prejudice. Examples illustrating this:

Plessy v. Ferguson, Separate but Equal

This Supreme Court case demonstrates how thin connections can validate biases. In the wake of the Civil War, a new, more insidious "racial apartheid" (Golub, 2005, p. 564) was inaugurated through the codification of Black Codes (i.e., Jim Crow laws). Deftly constructed with narrative force, *Plessy* v. *Ferguson* rendered the Black person as a "subordinate and inferior class of being .... so inferior and degraded that they cannot be allowed to sit in public coaches by white citizens" (*Plessy v. Ferguson*, 1896, pp. 559, 560). Despite Homer Plessy being visually indistinguishable from white people (seven of his eight great-grandparents were of European descent), prosecutor John Ferguson argued that race could be determined by smell rather than sight. Utilizing a thin connection of their lived experience and prejudice, Ferguson's narrative power, activated against the subordinated cultural group, redefined and re-storied the construct of race into the collective psyche, codifying another 70 years of legalized racial apartheid in the United States.

Haitian Immigrants in Springfield, Ohio

During the 2024 US Presidential election, a Facebook post about a neighbor's missing cat morphed through a game of telephone or re-storying, transforming the initial story into a malicious rumor that Haitian immigrants in Springfield were abducting their neighbor's pets and eating them (Williams, 2024). Though officials discredited these claims (Hsu, 2024), Donald Trump weaponized this narrative during a televised presidential debate:

> A lot of towns don't want to talk about it because they're embarrassed by it,' he said. 'In Springfield, they're eating the dogs. The people that came in, they're eating the cats. They're eating – they're eating the pets of the people that live there. (Ulloa, 2024)

These events illustrate the weaponization of narrative power. Narrative force preys upon fear and manipulation and is deployed from positions of power against subordinated groups. Their effect is to alter reality perception for the dominant cultural narrative entrenching biases even when based on falsehoods. According to Maan (2018), "You can more effectively control people with a story than with an army" (p. 50).

The weaponization of narrative power is an oppressive tactic deployed against the subordinated cultural narrative from a position of power. Every narrative has embedded strategic aims. By connecting a series of events (including random and unrelated events) in specific ways, altering timelines, withholding details, or fabricating stories from twisted truths, narrators communicate their ideological positions as a natural and obvious reflection of the world, even if very little of the present reality reflects their stance (Maan, 2018). Truthfulness is not required for narrative force to be effective. The ultimate purpose is to realign others' understanding with the narrator's perspective, creating a communal narrative that forges a shared identity. As such, the weaponization of narrative power further entrenches the ill-conceived biases and prejudices of the dominant cultural narrative, embedding those complexes deeper into the communal psyche. Even if they're created through "individual or collective hallucinations" (Abraham & Torok, 1994, p. 171) or have been proven false, they still alter perceptions toward subordinated groups and individuals. These weaponized narratives can "severely restrict our capabilities to be human to each other" (Kimbles, 2014, p. 33), unleashing waves of generational trauma, transforming the lived reality of groups of individuals within the subordinated cultural narrative. The weaponization of biases can lead to the basis and justification for human suffering and the perpetuation of violence through actions of "gender discrimination, racism, and genocidal violence" (Singer, 2006, p. 203).

Identifying Our Cultural Complexes

While our cultural complexes can be manipulated, they can also be identified and brought out from the recesses of our psyche into the forefront of our consciousness. This allows us to examine the unconscious biases and prejudices that control our nature and work to re-story our own cultural complexes, recentering our personal narrative on what is right and good.

In order to create a pathway for our cultural complexes to emerge from the recesses of our psyche, Jung (1973) developed an experimental procedure that utilized word association and its inherent patterns. These word association tests examined participants' reaction times to words as a way of identifying emerging patterns and exposing unconscious biases (complexes) that emanate from the nucleating centers of an individual's psyche. Jung (1973) argued that we would be able to identify how these complexes shape our perceptions and decisions while understanding how they influence or control our actions and reactions to different stimuli in various situations. Jung's (1973) Word Association Test (WAT) would become the foundational model for the modern equivalent Implicit Association Test (IAT) developed by Project Implicit.

While both aim to uncover unconscious processes and implicit biases, their methodology differs. Jung's WAT aimed to explore unconscious thoughts and emotions by analyzing reaction times and emotional responses to specific words offered to an individual subject. Conversely, the IAT uses reaction times to assess the strength of automatic associations between concepts (e.g., race, gender, and ethnicity) and attributes (e.g., good/bad) which allow the deeply held complexes to emerge from the nucleating center of the psyche. This modern adaptation of the WAT for contemporary psychological research is an important tool for the artful leader to understand and confront the biases and prejudices that shape their decisions.

Harnessing the Power of Narratives

Confronting the complexes that shape one's understanding of the world is only the beginning of the recentering journey. This individualized confrontation requires an artful reshaping of one's personal narrative arc and harnessing narrative power to connect with the larger cultural narrative to bring forth goodness and beauty in the world. The power to forge a new reality filled with goodness and beauty lies inherent in one's ability to harness the power of a narrative, maneuver it through the present narrative landscape, and connect with the nucleating centers of the cultural psyche. Fortunately, history is rich with examples of leaders who have artfully harnessed narrative power to both forge enduring connections and cultivate goodness and beauty. In the United States alone, there are numerous strong instances of these leaders such as Ida B. Wells, Reverend Martin Luther King, Jr., César Chávez, Dolores Huerta, and Bryan Stevenson.

Ida B. Wells

Ida B. Wells launched the anti-lynching movement, exposing the racial terror of lynching and changing the public narrative of lynching, particularly in Northern states. Fueled by the lynching of her close friend Thomas Moss in Memphis in 1892, she transformed her personal tragedy into a compelling narrative that exposed the systemic racial terror of lynching. Using investigative journalism, pamphlets, books, speeches, and eyewitness accounts, she used the narrative vehicle to frame lynching as a national crisis.

Traveling across the Southern United States, Wells documented the human stories of lynching firsthand and broadly shared her interviews with witnesses, survivors, and families to the broader nation. Weaving her interviews with detailed accounts of lynchings from local papers, Wells brought the evils of lynching into the light, naming the victims, and humanizing their stories. Using narrative power, Wells evoked national outrage depicting how each individual was shot, mutilated, and burned alive in the streets while white mobs cheered (Wells-Barnett, 1892). Using the narrative vehicle, Wells laid the foundation for the anti-lynching campaign launched by the National Association for the Advancement of Colored People (NAACP) and civil rights activists and created international pressure from British leaders condemning American racial policies (Wells, 1991).

Reverend Dr Martin Luther King Jr.

Through sermons, speeches, writings, televised interviews, and radio programs, Martin Luther King, Jr. harnessed the power of narrative to frame the US Civil Rights Movement as a moral issue. Utilizing biblical imagery and the Exodus story, King painted a vivid picture of racial injustice juxtaposed with a hopeful vision for the future (King, 1968). The narrative King expressed was more than a fight for civil rights, it was an epic struggle for freedom bolstered by a mandate for divine justice. In connecting the narrative frame of the Israelites with that of Black Americans, King aligned Black churches and White religious allies in a modern retelling of the biblical narrative that re-storied policy as a moral dilemma. King insisted upon more than mere laws could achieve, his was a demand for divine justice and the healing of a nation he pursued.

Beyond the narrative power of faith, King connected his personal experiences to show how oppression affected his children. In his *Letter from Birmingham Jail*,

King (1963, August) shared the personal connection of his children and the realities of segregation with an urgency that demanded present action, writing:

> When you suddenly find your tongue twisted and your speech stammering as you seek to explain to your six-year-old daughter why she can't go to the public amusement park, then you will understand why we find it difficult to wait.

Utilizing narrative power, King made the racial injustice experienced by his children relatable to mothers and fathers across racial lines by juxtaposing his personal narrative with the narrative force imposed through Jim Crow laws.

César Chávez and Dolores Huerta

The personal narratives shared by Chávez and Huerta of farmworkers' sufferings, personal hunger strikes, and the slogan ¡Sí Se Puede! (*translated,* Yes We Can!, used to great effect by Barack Obama during the 2008 Presidential campaign) helped mobilize the United Farm Workers union and the passage of labor protections for agricultural workers in California. By comparing the exploitation of farmworkers to slavery by using narrative power, Chávez and Huerta elevated the sufferings of local farmworkers outside of their local context and imbuing the issue with national significance.

The exercise of narrative power opened new avenues of connection and involvement for individuals around the country. No longer an issue solely for the farmworkers in California, their fight was your fight; their cause was your cause. "La Causa" (*translated,* 'The Cause") moved the issue of farmworkers' rights beyond the negotiating table of agricultural growers (large landowners and agribusiness) re-storying it as a people-centered movement for justice.

With narrative power, together, Chávez and Huerta transformed a labor dispute into a human rights cause, creating inclusive and relatable pathways for nonfarmworkers to understand and connect with the core of the struggle. While Chávez personally suffered through a hunger strike, Huerta shared the personal stories of women and children in the fields who were suffering under untenable conditions. Huerta gave voice to the voiceless and ignored Latina workers. Together, they recentered the narrative on people. Even today, inscribed on the César Chávez National Monument is the central narrative of "La Causa," "The fight is never about grapes or lettuce. It is always about people" (César E. Chávez National Monument, n.d.).

Bryan Stevenson

As the founder of the Equal Justice Initiative, Bryan Stevenson harnessed narrative power as a tool for social change, advocating for criminal justice reform. With narrative power, Stevenson meets narrative force by humanizing incarcerated individuals and exposing the systemic injustices present within the US legal system. Stevenson's book *Just Mercy* (2014) exemplifies the battle he waged between narrative power and narrative force in his work.

Walter McMillian, a Black man and Stevenson's client, was arrested for the murder of Ronda Morrison, a white woman. Despite multiple alibi witnesses and no prior criminal history, McMillian was convicted and sentenced to death for a crime he did not commit. In the lead-up to the trial, police and prosecutors engaged in narrative force, crafting and manipulating a story that would ensure McMillian's conviction despite overwhelming evidence of his innocence.

Before the trial began, McMillian was illegally transferred to death row, where he was held for 15 months, crafting a perception of guilt before a trial could be conducted. During the trial, prosecutors and police presented manipulated evidence, ignored exculpatory evidence, and coerced a convicted felon to fabricate testimony, which ultimately led to McMillian's conviction. Walter McMillian served six years on death row for a crime he did not commit before Stevenson was able to secure his exoneration and release.

Meeting narrative force with narrative power, Stevenson confronted the prejudicial biases and complexes that shaped the cultural narrative in Alabama, humanizing its victims through compassionate storytelling. By recognizing that narrative force is an oppressive tactic deployed against the subordinated cultural narrative from a position of power, Stevenson (2014) reflected, "Walter's case taught me that fear and anger are a threat to justice; they can infect a community, a state, or a nation and make us blind, irrational, and dangerous" (p. 313). It is fear and anger that serve as the core features of narrative force and are employed in activating the complexes within our nucleating centers (Singer, 2006). These emotions, tied to narrative force, perpetuate social suffering and our worst human instincts.

In a promise made to his grandmother, Stevenson (2012) committed to "always do the right thing, even when the right thing is the hard thing." This promise embodies the essence of narrative power. Harnessing the intrinsic power within the narrative and transforming the elements of fear and anger into goodness and beauty represents the profound work of an artful leader.

Understanding the Nature of Power

Wells, King, Chávez, Huerta, and Stevenson understood power's dynamic nature. Power does not reside solely in the hands of a few or only in the dominant cultural narrative, it does not maintain a static existence. Rather, power is "produced from one moment to the next, at every point, or rather in every relation from one point to another" (Foucault, 1978, p. 93). Power is an omnipresent vehicle for change (Foucault, 1978).

The locus of power, as Foucault (1978) suggested, resides in the bonds of relationship; for power is ultimately a dynamic force produced through networks of social relations. However, for narrative power to evolve into a transformative catalyst, networks of social relations must evolve into bonded networks of mutuality where equal and symmetrical power dynamics are present. The dynamic nature of power within networks of mutuality allows for power to increase as relational bonds are strengthened and expanded. As the social fabric grows more tightly woven through the strengthening of relational bonds, so too does the potency of power.

The Civil Rights Movement was driven by the theory of change that power gains potency through solidarity, transforming social bonds into catalysts for change. Even within dominant narratives, the subordinated are not powerless; as their mutuality strengthens, so too does their potential for power. For anywhere there are people, there is power (Alk, 1969). Rightly understood, power is "the ability to achieve a purpose. It is the strength required to bring about social, political, and economic change. In this sense, power is not only desirable but necessary to implement the demands of love and justice" (King, 1967/1991, p. 247). Power, therefore, is an active catalyst exercised through resistance driven by the goal of collective liberation.

The Fluidity of Power: Reconciling Structural Dominance and Narrative Power

Foucault (1978) argued that power is not fixed but rather a dynamic force produced through relationships and social structures. While the notion that dominant cultural narratives establish an entrenched hierarchy where power is static and insurmountable, the reality is more complex. Dominant cultural narratives are sustained through institutional and social reinforcement (Monts, 2021), yet they are also constantly challenged by competing narratives that seek to reshape the collective understanding of reality (Foucault, 1978).

As the dominant cultural narrative of Black inferiority further entrenched itself within the collective American psyche through constitutional mandates, legal rulings, and social structures, leaders like Ida B. Wells and Martin Luther King, Jr. actively resisted this dominant narrative by reframing the Black experience through moral, religious, and constitutional narratives. While power can be concentrated, it is never unassailable. Understanding the fluid nature of power allows for the possibility of change. Leaders who recognize the dynamic nature of power can strategically harness narrative power to disrupt oppressive structures and catalyze movements of change and liberation.

The Artful Leader's Responsibility

Narrative power is a catalyzing agent of change, forging our individual and communal understanding of the world we inhabit. Leaders must recognize this power and wield it with great care and responsibility, recognizing its dual potential to heal and to harm. Narrative power, when used responsibly, can dismantle systems of injustice and build pathways toward a more just and compassionate society. The responsibility of the artful leader is to harness the power of storytelling in ways that elevate truth, cultivate connection, and inspire ethical action. As King (1967/1991) reminded us, power is not inherently oppressive – it is "the ability to achieve a purpose .... Power at its best is love implementing the demands of justice, and justice at its best is power corrective everything that stands against love" (p. 247).

Commit to Try: Understanding and Re-Storying Your Personal Narrative

Before leaders can ethically shape the narrative of others, they must first examine and refine their own. Calling people into a greater story first requires strong self-awareness. This deeply reflective work delves into the core of one's narrative identity, revealing a profound sense of purpose and meaning. The process of re-storying allows leaders to explore past experiences through a new lens, reveal implicit biases and prejudices that may exist, and shape their narrative with intention and care. This journey should be undertaken with mindfulness, honesty, and hope. Here are some somatic breathing, creative practices, and reflective practices to enhance your engagement with the concepts contained herein.

Somatic Breathing

Somatic breathing can help leaders connect with their bodies and create space for deeper narrative awareness:

Narrative Awareness Breath

Take 5 minutes daily to sit quietly. Breathe deeply into your belly for four counts, hold for two, and exhale for six. During each exhale, notice what narratives you're carrying in your body – where do you feel tension when thinking about your leadership stories?

Cultural Complex Release

Breathe deeply while scanning your body for physical reactions when confronting your biases. Where do you feel tightness or discomfort? Direct breath to these areas, creating space for new understanding.

Creative Practices

Creative exercises can help leaders develop their narrative capabilities:

Narrative Mapping

Draw a visual map of the dominant narratives in your organization or community. Use different colors to represent competing stories and identify where your own story intersects or diverges from these narratives.

Perspective-Shifting Writing

Write about a challenging situation from three different perspectives – yours, someone who disagrees with you, and an objective observer. This practice develops the ability to see beyond one's subjective reality.

Reflective Practices

Reflection helps leaders integrate the chapter's concepts into their leadership approach:

Narrative Power Journal

Keep a weekly journal addressing these questions: (a) What narratives did I amplify this week? (b) Whose stories did I silence or ignore? (c) How did I use my narrative power? (d) Where could I have created more space for counter-narratives?

IAT Reflection

Take the Test: Visit Harvard's IAT site (https://implicit.harvard.edu/implicit/takeatest.html). Choose 1–2 tests that interest you. Take the test(s) and write down your results.

Reflect on Your Results: Find a quiet space where you won't be interrupted. Consider what your results reveal about your unconscious biases. Write down 3–5 specific life experiences that might have shaped these biases. Note your emotional reaction to discovering these biases.

Connect to Your Life Story

List 15 significant moments from your life (both positive and negative). Sort these into *highlights* and *lowlights*. Rank each moment by importance (10 = most significant). Create a simple timeline with highlights above a center line and lowlights below. Label each moment with 1–3 words.

Find Patterns and Insights

Look for recurring themes, people, or situations. Notice how your IAT results connect to your life experiences. Identify 2–3 key insights about how your personal narrative shapes your leadership.

Apply What You've Learned

Identify one bias or narrative pattern you want to change. Write down how this awareness will affect your leadership actions. Create a simple reminder to help you notice when this bias appears in your work. This exercise helps you understand how your life experiences have shaped unconscious biases that may influence how you use narrative power as a leader.

These practices create a holistic approach to embodying the chapter's concepts – connecting mind, body, and spirit to the important work of artful narrative leadership. By integrating these practices regularly, leaders can develop greater awareness of their narrative power and wield it more responsibly.

References

Abraham, N., & Torok, M. (1994). *The shell and the kernel: Renewals of psychoanalysis.* University of Chicago Press.

Abramovitch, H. (2007). The cultural complex: Linking psyche and society [review of *the cultural complex: Contemporary Jungian perspectives on psyche and society; Analytical psychology: Contemporary perspectives in Jungian analysis*]. *Jung Journal: Culture & Psyche, 1*(1), 49–52. https://doi.org/10.1525/jung.2007.1.1.49

Alk, H. (Director). (1969). *The murder of Fred Hampton* [Film]. F. Group; Chicago Film Archives. https://collections.chicagofilmarchives.org/Detail/objects/3500

Bruner, E. M. (1997). Ethnography as narrative. In L. P. H. Hinchman & K. Sandra (Eds.), *Memory, identity, community: The idea of narrative in the human sciences* (pp. 264–280). State University of New York.

Bruner, J. (1991). The narrative construction of reality. *Critical Inquiry, 18*(1), 1–21. https://doi.org/10.1086/448619

César E. Chávez National Monument. (n.d.). *In national park service: U.S. Department of the Interior.* https://www.nps.gov/cech/index.htm

Collins, P. H. (2002). *Black feminist thought: Knowledge, consciousness, and the politics of empowerment.* Taylor & Francis.

Connelly, F. M., & Clandinin, D. J. (1990). Stories of experience and narrative inquiry. *Educational Researcher, 19*(5), 2–14. https://doi.org/10.2307/1176100

Davenport, J. J. (2012). *Narrative identity, autonomy, and morality: From Frankfurt and MacIntyre to Kierkegaard.* Routledge.

Ditko, S., & Lee, S. (1962). *Spider-man. Amazing fantasy* (Vol. 15) [Comic book]. Marvel.

Du Bois, W. E. B. (1903). *The souls of black folk.* A. C. McClurg & Co.

Fludernik, M. (2009). *An introduction to narratology.* Routledge.

Foucault, M. (1978). *The history of sexuality, Volume 1: An introduction* (R. Hurley, Trans.). Pantheon Books.

Golub, M. (2005). Plessy as "passing": Judicial responses to ambiguously raced bodies in *Plessy v. Ferguson. Law & Society Review, 39*(3), 563–600. http://www.jstor.org/stable/3557606

Heider, K. G. (1988). The Rashomon effect: When ethnographers disagree. *American Anthropologist, 90*(1), 73–81. https://doi.org/10.1525/aa.1988.90.1.02a00050

Hsu, T. (2024). Why debunked falsehoods about Haitian migrants gained traction. *The New York Times.* https://www.nytimes.com/2024/09/24/us/politics/haitian-migrants-disinformation.html

Jung, C. G. (1970). A review of the complex theory. In R. Hull (Ed.), *Collected Works of C. G. Jung* (Vol. 8; pp. 92–104). Princeton University Press. https://doi.org/10.1515/9781400850952.92

Jung, C. G. (1973). Studies in word association (R. F. C. Hull, Trans.). In G. Adler, M. Fordham, & H. Read (Eds.), *Experimental researches* (p. 662). Routledge. https://doi.org/10.4324/9781315727653

Kimbles, S. L. (2014). *Phantom narratives: The unseen contributions of culture to psyche.* Rowman & Littlefield.

King, M. L. (1963, August). *Letter from Birmingham jail.* https://www.csuchico.edu/iege/_assets/documents/susi-letter-from-birmingham-jail.pdf

King, M. L. (1968). *I've been to the mountaintop.* The Martin Luther King, Jr. Research and Education Institute. https://kinginstitute.stanford.edu/ive-been-mountaintop

King, M. L. (1991). Where do we go from here? In J. M. Washington (Ed.), *A testament of hope: The essential writings of Martin Luther King, Jr.* (pp. 245–252). HarperOne. (Original work published 1967)

Kurosawa, A. (1950). *Rashomon* [Film]. Daiei Film.

Lyotard, J.-F. (1984). *The post-modern condition: A report on knowledge* (G. M. Bennington, Brian, Trans.). University of Minnesota Press.

Maan, A. (2018). *Narrative warfare*. CreateSpace Publishing.

Monts, A. J. (2021). *Racial narratives: A sociohistorical analysis of Michael Brown and Ferguson, Missouri* (Publication Number 28721903) [Doctoral Dissertation, Johnson University]. ProQuest Dissertation Publishing.

Nelson, K. (2003). Narrative and the emergence of a consciousness of self. In G. D. M. Fireman, T. E., & O. J. Flanagan (Eds.), *Narrative and consciousness: Literature, psychology, and the brain* (pp. 17–36). Oxford University Press. https://doi.org/10.1093/acprof:oso/9780195140057.003.0002

Plessy v. *Ferguson* (Supreme Court of the United States 1896). https://www.law.cornell.edu/wex/plessy_v_ferguson_(1896)

Ricoeur, P. (1995). *Introduction*. In M. Wallace (Ed.), *Figuring the sacred: Religious, narrative and imagination* (pp. 1–32). Fortress Press.

Schechtman, M. (1996). *The constitution of selves*. Cornell University Press.

Sheldrake, P. (2001). *Spaces for the sacred: Place, memory, and identity*. The Johns Hopkins University Press.

Singer, T. (2006). The cultural complex: A statement of the theory and its application. *Psychotherapy and Politics International*, *4*(3), 197–212. https://doi.org/10.1002/ppi.110

Singer, T. (2007). Unconscious forces shaping international conflict: Archetypal defenses of the group spirit from revolutionary America to confrontation in the middle east. *Psychotherapy and Politics International*, *5*(1), 45–61. https://doi.org/10.1002/ppi.125

Stevenson, B. (2012). *We need to talk about an injustice* [Video]. TED Conferences. https://www.ted.com/talks/bryan_stevenson_we_need_to_talk_about_an_injustice

Stevenson, B. (2014). *Just Mercy: A story of justice and redemption*. Spiegel & Grau.

Teymoori, A., Bastian, B., & Jetten, J. (2017). Towards a psychological analysis of anomie. *Political Psychology*, *38*(6), 1009–1023. https://doi.org/10.1111/pops.12377

Ulloa, J. (2024). 'They're eating the cats': Trump repeats false claim about immigrants. *The New York Times*. https://www.nytimes.com/2024/09/10/us/politics/trump-debate-immigrants-pets.html

Weil, S. (2001). *The need for roots: Prelude to a declaration of duties toward mankind*. Routledge. (Original work published 1949)

Wells, I. B. (1991). *Crusade for justice: The autobiography of Ida B. Wells* (A. M. Dunster, Ed.). University of Chicago Press.

Wells-Barnett, I. B. (1892). *South* [Pamphlet]. https://awpc.cattcenter.iastate.edu/2020/09/21/southern-horrors-lynch-law-in-all-its-phases-oct-5-1892/

Williams, K. (2024). Ohio woman says she regrets sharing false rumor about Haitians on Facebook. *The New York Times*. https://www.nytimes.com/2024/09/17/us/springfield-haitians-pets-facebook-rumor.html

Chapter 9

Beyond the Image: Recentering Leadership Identity Through Creative Practice

Sarah Andreas

Artist, USA

Abstract

This chapter explores the relationship between leadership identity, image, and creative practice. Drawing on theories of transformational leadership, personal narrative, and identity development, the author examines how leaders can realign their internal values with their external presence through creative engagement and critical reflection. The chapter begins by establishing the theoretical foundations of leadership identity formation, examining how worldviews, frames of reference, and personal narratives shape a leader's sense of self. It then contrasts transactional and transformational leadership approaches, arguing that transformational leadership fosters greater personal growth and creative development. The author shares personal experiences transitioning between leadership styles and discusses how creative practices – from visual arts to movement-based activities – can help leaders recenter their identity, prevent burnout, and develop resilience. The chapter concludes with practical exercises incorporating somatic breathing, creative expression, photo elicitation, and reflective writing to support leaders in developing authentic presence and aligning their internal narrative with their projected image. This work contributes to leadership studies by highlighting the importance of creative engagement in fostering leadership development and preventing identity-image dissonance.

Keywords: Leadership identity; transformational leadership; creative practice; personal narrative; image management; leadership development; worldview; frames of reference

Artful Leadership: Retreat, Recenter, and Rewild, 105–121
Copyright © 2026 by Sarah Andreas
Published under exclusive licence by Emerald Publishing Limited
doi:10.1108/S2058-880120250000010010

Introduction

When I was invited to write this Chapter, I was thrilled by the opportunity to combine my experiences in business, artistry, coaching, and leadership studies. These perspectives have taught me that leadership is deeply influenced by the interplay between the stories we tell ourselves and the images we project to others. Freeman (1997) described identity as the "fabric of our self" (p. 27), woven from personal narratives that shape how we see ourselves.

Leadership, like life, often requires shedding outdated narratives, images, and assumptions, our "old skin," to embrace an authentic identity waiting to emerge. This transformation mirrors the process of recentering, where leaders align their internal values with their external purpose, achieving balance and authenticity. Narratives reflect internal stories of identity and purpose, while images shape external perceptions (Freeman, 1997; Gardner et al., 2005). Aligning these elements fosters trust and authenticity in leadership.

Coaching others led me to unexpected personal growth. Drawing on this experience, I examine how identity, image, and creative practices strengthen leadership. I offer reflection exercises to help leaders reconnect with their core purpose. By aligning personal narratives with projected image, leaders can develop authenticity and intentional influence. Our stories shape both our actions and impact, making alignment between identity and image crucial for effective leadership.

Foundations of Leadership Identity: Worldviews and Frames of Reference

Personal narratives, shaped by worldviews and frames of reference, guide leadership authenticity by aligning internal beliefs with external actions (Howard, 2000; Kegan, 2000; Komives et al., 2005; Montero et al., 2008). While narratives form the internal framework of our identity, shaping how we see ourselves, image refers to the external expression of that identity – the perception others hold of us. The interplay between these concepts is central to leadership, as leaders must align their internal narrative with the image they project to cultivate authenticity and trust. Gardner et al. (2005) emphasized the importance of authentic leadership, which involves aligning internal narratives with external images to build trust. Similarly, Freeman (1997) highlights the power of personal narratives in shaping identity, and Komives et al. (2005) connect these narratives to leadership identity development.

Worldview as Leadership Lens

A worldview serves as the lens through which we interpret and understand the world, encompassing the beliefs, values, attitudes, and assumptions that guide our interactions with others and our environment (Cooling, 2020). This layered identity is essential to authentic leadership, as it shapes both our inner sense of self and the image we present to the world, aligning our purpose with the way we lead. Similarly, frames of reference are the mental models we use to process and evaluate information. These cognitive structures are influenced by our past experiences, cultural background, and personal beliefs, all of which shape how we perceive and respond to situations (Cranton & Taylor, 2012).

Worldviews serve as foundational lenses through which we interpret our environment. They encompass our beliefs, values, and assumptions, guiding not only our personal understanding of the world but also our leadership choices (Cooling, 2020). These deeply held perspectives influence how we engage with others, make decisions, and react to challenges, often operating beneath the surface of conscious thought. For leaders, recognizing the role their worldview plays in shaping their actions is critical, as it allows for greater self-awareness and alignment between personal values and leadership practice.

Frames of Reference and Leadership Perception

Frames of reference, shaped by cultural and personal experiences, guide how we evaluate situations (Cranton & Taylor, 2012). These deeply held frames influence how we engage with others, make decisions, and react to challenges, often operating beneath the surface of conscious thought. While these frames provide structure to our thinking, they can also limit our ability to see beyond familiar perspectives. In leadership, this becomes particularly important, as leaders must navigate complex and diverse environments that often challenge their existing frames of reference.

By engaging in reflective practices and embracing transformative learning, leaders can critically assess and adjust these mental models, opening themselves to new perspectives and ideas. This ability to reassess and reshape frames of reference not only enhances personal growth but also fosters a leadership style that is adaptable, empathetic, and inclusive.

Narrative Construction in Leadership Identity

As Freeman (1997) noted, our identity is woven from the stories we tell. These narratives are not simply accounts of what has happened but are also acts of meaning-making. In leadership, consciously shaping these stories becomes a powerful tool for personal and professional development. As we reflect on our past, we can reinterpret our experiences, allowing us to grow and adapt our leadership identity.

Freeman's (2010) concept of hindsight is particularly relevant for leaders who seek to understand how their experiences have influenced their leadership style and identity. By looking back on key moments with the benefit of reflection, leaders can identify patterns, lessons, and shifts in perspective. This reflective process allows them to consciously reshape their leadership narrative, aligning it with their evolving values and goals. For instance, a leader might reinterpret a past failure as a pivotal learning experience, reframing it in a way that reinforces resilience and growth in their personal narrative.

Our experiences, worldviews, perspectives, and frames of reference play a critical role in shaping our identity as leaders (Andreas, 2019; Mezirow, 1991, 2000;

Podolny et al., 2010; Yukl, 2014/2011). The challenge lies in the fact that many of these identities and frames of reference were formed before we were even consciously aware of our own identity (Carden et al., 2022). As we grow and develop, it becomes crucial to reassess these frames of reference and worldviews, ensuring they align with the identity we wish to cultivate and the way we want to be perceived as leaders (Andreas, 2019; Grashow et al., 2009; Mezirow, 2000).

Transactional and Transformational Approaches to Leadership

Leadership is one area where it is essential to reassess our beliefs about ourselves. To illustrate this, I'd like to share a personal story. My journey into leadership began at a Harley-Davidson dealership, an industry that, in my experience, practices transactional leadership. Transactional leadership is a style where compliance is achieved through rewards and punishments, with a focus on routine tasks, clear structures, and expectations (Choi et al., 2020).

At a Harley-Davidson dealership, transactional leadership focused on structured goals and incentives, reflecting a compliance-driven approach. The structure is simple: if a salesperson exceeds the target, they are rewarded with a bonus or exclusive perks such as premium shifts or branded merchandise and a bigger commission check. Conversely, if they fail to meet the goal, they might face reduced commissions or less favorable sales opportunities.

The manager reinforces these expectations during regular team meetings, ensuring that the focus remains on consistent performance and adherence to dealership protocols. As I embraced this style, I was leveraging my strengths in alignment with its principles. For me, transactional leadership came naturally.

While transactional leadership is effective in structured, goal-oriented settings, it often limits personal growth and creativity. In contrast, transformational leadership emphasizes inspiring and empowering others, focusing on long-term development rather than short-term results. This distinction between transactional and transformational styles reveals how different approaches to leadership can either constrain or expand a leader's influence and the growth of their team.

Transformation Through Reflection and Creative Practice

Through my Ph.D. studies in leadership studies and my exploration of personal growth through coaching and creative mindful practices, I realized that my definition of success had been narrow, primarily focused on financial achievements, titles, and external recognition. As I began reassessing my perspectives and frames of reference, I questioned why I was pursuing goals that didn't bring me genuine fulfillment, both personally and as a leader.

The pandemic offered a pause for reflection, allowing me to embrace creative practices that reshaped my leadership approach. During this time, I explored creative mindful practices, including painting, which expanded my worldview and helped me approach leadership from a fresh perspective. I found that this creativity, combined with internal reflection, increased my ability to view leadership through different lenses and opened the door to personal transformation.

Creative practices like vision boards and storytelling help leaders align their identity with their leadership image. Vision boards, for instance, allow leaders to curate images, symbols, and words that resonate with their goals and guiding principles, forming a visual representation of their leadership vision. Similarly, storytelling exercises – whether through writing, art, or spoken narrative – enable leaders to articulate and shape their personal journey, clarifying how they wish to be perceived and the impact they want to make.

Embracing Transformational Leadership

Transformational leaders focus on fostering positive change in others by empowering them to grow and take ownership of their work (Bass & Riggio, 2006; Choi et al., 2020). In a sales organization, a transformational leader might focus not just on achieving monthly sales targets but on developing the long-term potential of their team. This approach emphasizes mentoring and inspiring team members to grow beyond short-term goals.

In this environment, the leader leads by example, showing commitment to personal growth and fostering a culture where team members feel valued not just for their performance but for their potential. This approach nurtures an atmosphere of innovation, creativity, and ownership – key elements of transformational leadership. By prioritizing the development of others, the leader inspires their team to go beyond transactional exchanges and strive for personal excellence and deeper fulfillment in their roles.

While I began to see the value in this approach, I also recognized that different leadership styles are effective in different contexts. Transactional leadership, with its emphasis on structure, rewards, and clear expectations, is essential for achieving certain organizational goals and maintaining efficiency. However, as I went through my own process of transformative learning, I realized that I wanted to focus more on cultivating personal growth in others. This led me to model my leadership more closely on transformational principles – leading by example and creating an environment that encourages innovation and personal development.

The shift was not immediate or easy; it required deep self-examination and a willingness to unlearn old habits that no longer aligned with the leader I aspired to be. I also had to rethink my image or personal brand. For years, I projected the image of a results-driven, transactional leader, but I am now working to transform that image into one that reflects a leader focused on growth, both my own and that of others.

Image and Branding in Leadership

Our image is the perception others have of us, while our identity is our internal self-perception (Howard, 2000; Kegan, 2000; Kunrath et al., 2019; Price et al., 2024). Changing how others perceive our image can be a complex and challenging process (Roberts, 2005).

Consider a photograph: it captures a visual moment in time, but the meaning of that image is not inherent or fixed. Instead, meaning is constructed by the viewer, shaped by their experiences, culture, and knowledge (Berger, 1972). While the photograph itself is just a snapshot, its interpretation is influenced by the context in which it is viewed, as well as by the creator's intent and the subject's positioning (Berger, 1972; Davison, 2010).

Similarly, a leader's image – how they are perceived by others – is shaped by a complex interaction between the leader, their followers, and the environment in which they operate (Day & Dragoni, 2015; Day et al., 2009; Marion et al., 2007).

Visual imagery has a profound impact on us, often more than we consciously realize, affecting us both intellectually and emotionally (Barry & Meisiek, 2010; Davison, 2010). Photographs, for example, are not simply objective representations of reality; they are interpretations subject to the often ambiguous relationship between art and truth. Even seemingly straightforward images, like newspaper photographs, are shaped by choices in scale, cropping, and retouching – a process made even easier with digital technology.

These images are thin slices of time and space, heavily reliant on context and open to alteration. Like all forms of communication, they are received within a framework of symbols, carrying both literal and symbolic meanings that are shaped by the viewer's perception (Davison, 2010). Just as photographers and artists carefully craft images to convey a certain message, influential people have mastered the art of curating their personas. They shape public opinion by meticulously crafting the image they want their followers to see (Abidin & Ots, 2015; Kaplan & Haenlein, 2010). Similarly, leaders who understand the power of image and branding can strategically manage their personal leadership brand (Kaplan & Haenlein, 2010; Pearson, 2022).

A leader's ability to "understand and consciously influence the symbolic/metaphorical dimensions of self and others that are linked to specific values, mindsets, and worldviews" (Pearson, 2022, p. 167) is crucial for authentic leadership, as it helps leaders manage their image and effectively shape how they are perceived by others (Gardner et al., 2005). However, Harter (2023) cautioned that these images and stories can "serve as surface representations of a far more complicated depth" (Harter, 2023, p. 8).

Case Studies in Leadership Image

Leaders across various industries have long understood the importance of shaping their image to align with their leadership goals and the expectations of their followers. For instance, Steve Jobs, the co-founder of Apple, was renowned for meticulously managing his public image. By consistently presenting himself as a visionary, Jobs cultivated an image of innovation and creativity, which became central to Apple's brand. His signature style – black turtlenecks, jeans, and minimalist product presentations – helped reinforce his persona as a focused, forward-thinking leader. His image became synonymous with Apple's identity, aligning his personal brand with the company's values of simplicity and innovation (Isaacson, 2011).

Equally, leaders can also struggle with managing their image effectively. A notable example is Tony Hayward, the former CEO of BP, during the Deepwater

Horizon oil spill crisis in 2010. Hayward's attempt to downplay the severity of the disaster by stating "I'd like my life back" (Strawser, 2022) was seen as insensitive and tone-deaf. His failure to manage his image as a compassionate and responsible leader during the crisis severely damaged both his reputation and BP's public image. This example highlights how a leader's inability to align their image with the expectations of their stakeholders can lead to negative perceptions and long-term reputational damage.

The Risk of Image-Identity Dissonance

This complexity is one reason leaders often experience burnout, leaving colleagues and loved ones surprised when they step away from roles they've held for years (Kruse & Edge, 2023; Markgren & Miles, 2022). In the pursuit of climbing the corporate ladder, many leaders create images that exclude and abandon the creative and recreational practices that once refueled and refreshed them, believing they are too busy to make time for these activities. As they focus on projecting an image of tirelessness and composure, they may neglect the very things that sustain their inner well-being (Lin et al., 2019).

Over time, this disconnection from their creative outlets leads to a sense of depletion, even as they outwardly maintain an appearance of strength (Sonnentag, 2001, 2003). This dissonance between the external image and internal reality is further exacerbated by the "fake it until you make it" mentality, where leaders believe that by projecting confidence, they will eventually embody it. However, without nurturing their true identity through creative and restorative practices, leaders risk becoming disconnected from themselves, leading to deep dissatisfaction and eventual burnout.

The Impact of Environment on Perceptions and Reactions to Images

The environment or location where we encounter an image significantly influences how we perceive and react to it. This applies not only to physical images, such as artwork or photographs, but also to the personal image we project to others. The context in which an image is situated can alter its meaning, affect our emotional response, and shape our judgments and behavior.

Contextual framing refers to the idea that the environment or context in which an image, message, or object is presented can influence how it is perceived and interpreted by an audience (Leder et al., 2004). Physical images are often subject to varied interpretations depending on where they are located. For instance, an artwork displayed in a prestigious gallery might be perceived as more valuable or esthetically pleasing than the same piece shown in a casual setting. The same image might evoke different thoughts, emotions, or judgments depending on the setting or situation in which it is viewed. For example, a photograph of a family enjoying a picnic might be seen as cheerful and warm in the context of a family photo album, but the same image could feel out of place and provoke different feelings if displayed in a war-torn country's news coverage.

Research in visual perception, including work by Leder et al. (2004), showed that contextual framing affects both cognitive and emotional responses to stimuli by shaping the lens through which the audience processes information. Understanding contextual framing provides valuable insight into how our environment influences perception, not only of physical images but also of the personas we project.

Just as the context in which an image is viewed can shift its meaning, the social and physical settings in which individuals present themselves can impact how their projected image is received (Andreas et al., 2015). This leads to an important consideration for leaders: the environment in which they operate plays a crucial role in shaping others' perceptions of their authority, competence, and approachability.

Impact on Projected Images

Just as the environment influences our perceptions of physical images, it also impacts how we perceive and react to the image that individuals project to others. The social context in which a person presents themselves plays a critical role in shaping how their image is received (Roberts, 2005). For instance, a leader projecting an image of authority and competence may be perceived differently in a corporate boardroom compared to a casual social setting. The formal environment of a boardroom, with its structured and hierarchical cues, can reinforce the leader's image as authoritative, whereas a casual setting might dilute this perception, making the leader seem more approachable but less commanding (Gardner et al., 2005).

The location can also affect how individuals tailor their image. People often adjust their behavior, attire, and communication style depending on the setting to align with expected social norms and to elicit desired reactions from others (Goffman, 1959). This process of impression management highlights how the environment serves as a backdrop that can either enhance or detract from the image a person wishes to project.

Impression management (Goffman, 1959) refers to the process by which individuals attempt to control or influence the perceptions others have of them. It involves consciously shaping one's behavior, appearance, and communication to project a desired image. For example, in a professional setting, a leader might dress formally, speak confidently, and emphasize achievements to convey competence and authority.

The environment not only affects how images are perceived but also interacts with our internal sense of identity. The situational context can either affirm or challenge our self-perception. For example, someone who sees themselves as a leader may feel their identity reinforced when they are in a leadership-oriented environment, such as at a conference or during a formal presentation. Conversely, in an unfamiliar or informal setting, they may struggle to maintain the same sense of identity, leading to potential shifts in how they project themselves.

Creativity and Transformational Leadership

Transformational leadership is inherently connected to creativity, cultivating an environment where innovation and creative problem-solving are not just encouraged but are fundamental to success (Bass & Riggio, 2006). Unlike transactional leadership, which often depends on established routines and predictable outcomes, transformational leadership thrives on new ideas and innovative approaches.

The Creative Dimension of Leadership

This leadership style challenges individuals to think beyond conventional boundaries, encouraging them to explore uncharted territories and develop novel solutions to complex problems (Hoxha, 2019). Creativity in transformational leadership extends beyond intellectual exercise; it encompasses a leader's ability to inspire and mobilize their team through visionary thinking and emotional engagement (Cengiz Ucar et al., 2021).

Creativity in transformational leadership is also not confined to strategic thinking alone. Engaging in creative activities such as art, cooking, or other forms of physical creation can significantly enhance a leader's capacity to lead. Incorporating creative activities into leadership not only enhances strategic thinking but also fosters the critical reflection necessary for transformative learning (Mezirow, 2000).

These activities offer leaders the mental space to challenge established patterns of thinking, leading to personal and professional transformation. They enable leaders to tap into different modes of thinking, breaking free from conventional patterns and fostering a mindset open to new possibilities (Kaplan & Haenlein, 2010).

Expanding Leadership Perspective Through Creativity

Harter (2023) underscored the importance of accumulating images and stories – descriptive imagery – to broaden our view of leadership and inspire a unique leadership perspective. He warned that possessing only a single image of leadership can reduce our ability to adapt, stating, "If all we possess is a single image of leadership, then we will be like the guy with only a hammer to whom everything is a nail" (Harter, 2023, p. 3).

Harter further explained, "It follows logically that presuming to lead means that you are projecting yourself onto the imagination of others [...]" (Harter, 2023, p. 4). We unconsciously gather fragments of information that contribute to our imaginative storehouse, shaping how we perceive and engage with the world around us.

As leaders, we influence and are influenced by those around us through interactions, whether intentional or not (Hall & Lord, 2005; Harter, 2023; Komives et al., 2005; Parks Daloz, 2000; Vygotsky, 1978). Leadership is a deliberate attempt to impact others' imagination, creativity (Harter, 2023), identity (Hall & Lord, 2005; Komives et al., 2005), and self-perception (Parks Daloz, 2000).

However, as Harter (2023) noted, an image or story intended to represent an underlying reality may persist long after that reality has changed. He compares it to an outdated map – once accurate and useful, but no longer relevant (Harter, 2023, p. 9). In social psychology, this concept is reflected in how we treat people based on who we imagine them to be (Harter, 2023, p. 51). Our creativity can influence our identity and how others perceive our image (Beghetto & Karwowski, 2019; Koh et al., 2019).

While creativity is often associated with artistic pursuits, it's important to recognize that creativity comes in many forms and is not limited to traditional art forms. Leaders who feel they are "not creative" can cultivate their creativity by reframing their understanding of what creativity looks like in their daily work. Creativity in leadership might involve project design, problem-solving, strategic thinking, or finding innovative approaches.

Cultivating Creative Practices for Leadership Resilience

When I began this journey, I read *The Artist's Way* by Julia Cameron (2002) to explore my beliefs about myself as a wife, mother, artist, and leader. To sustain long-term effectiveness, leaders must cultivate creative practices that reconnect them with their inner selves, rejuvenate energy, and foster innovation. Creativity extends beyond artistic expression; it is essential for adaptability, resilience, and leadership.

Integrating creative practices into daily life provides space to process challenges, generate ideas, and prevent burnout. I encourage you to explore activities that bring you joy and schedule time for them. As Laura Vanderkam (2016) noted in her TED Talk on time management, when we say we don't have time, it simply means it's not a priority.

Engaging in the arts – such as painting, music, or writing – enhances mindfulness and creates a state of *flow*, where full immersion leads to heightened focus and enjoyment (Csikszentmihalyi, 2008/1990). This deep concentration allows leaders to step outside habitual thought patterns, leading to breakthroughs in problem-solving and self-awareness (Sawyer, 2012).

Leaders who invest in creative pursuits nurture their emotional well-being, fostering confidence and authenticity that positively influence how they are perceived by others (Gardner et al., 2005; Koh et al., 2019).

Movement-based creativity, such as dance, yoga, or mindful walking, helps leaders clear mental clutter and enhance clarity. These activities regulate emotions, promoting a balanced self-image and healthier interactions with others (Lin et al., 2019). Likewise, culinary creativity offers a tactile, sensory experience that fosters mindfulness and self-care, allowing leaders to recharge while deepening their presence in daily tasks (Eisenberg et al., 2019; King, 2023).

Creativity in leadership is not limited to the arts. Many leaders mistakenly believe they are "not creative," when in reality, creativity is evident in problem-solving, strategic thinking, and innovative approaches to leadership challenges. Small steps, such as brainstorming unconventional solutions or engaging in reflective practices like journaling, can help leaders develop their creativity. By reframing their understanding of creativity, leaders can integrate it into their work, driving both personal and organizational growth (Beghetto & Karwowski, 2019; Mezirow, 2000).

Prioritizing creative activities – whether artistic, physical, or reflective – restores mental and emotional energy, allowing leaders to return to their roles with a broader perspective. Leaders who nurture their creativity tend to project a more authentic, positive image, fostering stronger engagement with those around them. Ultimately, creativity is a critical component of effective leadership, shaping both identity and influence (Belawati et al., 2019).

Somatic Breathing, Creative and Reflection Practices

Leadership transformation begins not just in the mind, but in the body, imagination, and reflective capacity. The practices that follow are designed to complement the journey of leadership identity exploration described throughout this chapter.

Somatic Breathing Exercises

Somatic breathing practices help you physically embody the changes you seek, anchoring new leadership qualities in bodily experience.

Leadership Presence Breathing

- Sit comfortably with your spine straight
- Breathe deeply into your abdomen for four counts
- Hold for two counts
- Exhale slowly for six counts, imagining releasing limiting beliefs
- As you inhale, visualize embodying your authentic leadership qualities
- Practice for 3–5 minutes before important meetings or decisions

Narrative Reset Breathing

- Lie down with one hand on chest, one on abdomen
- Breathe deeply into your abdomen, noticing how your hands rise and fall
- With each exhale, mentally release one self-limiting story or belief
- With each inhale, introduce a new empowering narrative
- Continue for 5–10 minutes, noting sensations throughout your body

Creative Practices

Creative exercises bypass rational thought to access deeper insights about your leadership narrative and image. In my own journey, I experimented with multiple creative activities before finding fulfillment in mixed media oil painting and cooking. These practices not only enriched my personal life but also strengthened my ability to generate new ideas and approaches as a leader. Creativity is a muscle, and the more you engage in the act of creating, the more natural you will find opportunities to innovate in all areas of your life.

Leadership Collage Making

- Collect magazines, photos, fabric scraps, and other materials.
- Create two collages: one representing your current leadership image, another depicting your aspirational leadership identity.
- Note the differences in colors, shapes, and symbols between the two.
- Display where you'll see them regularly as visual reminders.

Leadership Soundtrack Creation

- Create a playlist of songs that represent different aspects of your leadership.
- Include music that energizes, centers, inspires, and challenges you.
- Write brief reflections on why each piece resonates with your leadership identity.
- Use different selections for various leadership contexts (decision-making, conflict resolution, innovation).

Photo Elicitation and Visual Storytelling

Photos serve as powerful prompts that bypass rational thinking and access emotional and intuitive knowledge about your leadership journey, revealing patterns, values, and aspirations that may remain unexpressed in daily leadership practice.

1. Preparation: Gather 10–15 photographs that span your life journey. Include:

- Photos from different life stages and roles.
- Images where you are leading or influencing others.
- Pictures that evoke strong emotions (positive or negative).
- Photos that represent significant transitions or milestones.
- Images that feel meaningful but you're not sure why.

Find a quiet space where you won't be interrupted and spread the photos in front of you.

Exploration: Without overthinking, select the three images that most strongly resonate with how you see yourself as a leader right now. For each selected image, answer these questions:

- What draws you to this image?
- What emotions arise when you look at it?
- What does this photo reveal about your leadership values or style?
- What story does this image tell about who you are as a leader?
- Is there a tension between this image and how you present yourself professionally?

Pattern Recognition: Now look at all your photos together:

- What themes or patterns do you notice across the images?
- Which aspects of yourself are prominently represented?

- What seems to be missing or underrepresented?
- How do these images compare to the leadership image you project professionally?

Integration: Select one photo that represents an aspect of your authentic leadership that you want to strengthen or express more fully. Write a brief narrative (1–2 paragraphs) describing:

- What this image represents about your leadership identity.
- How this aspect of yourself could enhance your leadership effectiveness.
- One specific action you can take this week to integrate this quality into your leadership practice.

Reflective Practices

Reflective practices bridge the gap between theory and lived experience, helping you consciously reshape your leadership identity.

Leadership Narrative Exercise

This exercise explores how your life experiences shape your leadership identity and create a vision for your future self. The stories we tell ourselves serve as the foundation of our personal and professional presence, guiding our decisions, interactions, and the image we project to the world.
Step 1 Current Self: Write briefly about who you are today:

- Who you are as a leader?
- Who you are as a person?
- What you are achieving right now?

Step 2 Reflection: Once your story is complete, revisit it with a critical eye. Highlight (a) what feels authentic, (b) what no longer fits who you are, (c) consider what you need to let go of. Ask yourself: What am I holding onto that no longer serves me? How can I release these outdated aspects of my identity?
Step 3 Future Vision: Imagine yourself one year from now, living your dream:

- What are my thoughts and actions?
- What are my focus areas?
- How am I taking care of myself?
- Who is in my circle?
- What is my big dream?
- What questions guide me?

Step 4 Visual: Create a vision board using images that represent your aspirations. Collect images, symbols, or photos that represent your aspirations. These visuals can serve as inspiration and clarity for the future you are building.

Step 5 Action Plan: Identify 1–3 specific actions to move toward your future self, with clear deadlines. By combining reflection with purposeful action, you can reshape your leadership narrative and bring your vision to life.

Delving into your narrative is an essential step toward embracing your potential as a creative and authentic leader. Engaging in creativity offers a powerful pathway to uncover and explore the layers of your story.

By engaging your breath, creative expression, and reflective awareness, these exercises create multiple pathways toward authentic leadership presence. Together, these approaches support the integration of internal narrative with external image, fostering the alignment so essential to transformational leadership. We invite you to approach these practices with curiosity and compassion, recognizing that leadership development is both an art and a practice that unfolds over time.

Conclusion

Leadership is personal, connecting identity, image, and creativity. Leaders must carefully shape their public image while staying true to themselves. External perceptions are influenced by context and social interactions, but misalignment between image and identity leads to disconnection, exhaustion, and burnout.

Self-care improves both self-perception and how others view you, projecting authenticity and confidence. Creative practices in all their forms, whether arts, physical movement, cooking, etc., serve as vital tools for leaders to cultivate resilience, clarity, and emotional balance. By taking care of yourself in creative ways, leaders not only improve their self-perception but also influence how others perceive and interact with them. As leaders become more in tune with their own well-being, they project authenticity and confidence, fostering stronger connections with those they lead (Lin et al., 2019; Sonnentag, 2001, 2003).

Leadership is about more than just the roles we play; it is about the narratives we construct and how they shape our identity. As Freeman (1997) noted, this identity is the "fabric of our self" (p. 27) constantly woven and rewoven through the stories we tell. By embracing creativity and reflection, leaders can ensure that their identity remains authentic and aligned with their true purpose.

To be effective, leaders must attend to inner needs through creativity that fuels passion and energy. This balance between image and identity ensures authentic leadership driven by self-connection and vision. The practices in this chapter help leaders align internal self-perception with external image, empowering authentic purpose and more effective inspiration. In so doing, their passions are fueled and energy sustained. Leaders can recenter their leadership identity by harmonizing their internal self-perception with the image they project to the world.

References

Abidin, C., & Ots, M. (2015, August 6–9). *The influencer's dilemma: The shaping of new brand professions between credibility and commerce* [Paper presentation]. AEJMC 2015, Annual Conference, San Francisco, CA, USA. https://urn.kb.se/resolve?urn=urn:nbn:se:hj:diva-27812

Andreas, S. (2019). *Exploring leadership development experiences of leadership Tuscarawas alumni* (Order No. 13807023). Available from ProQuest Dissertations & Theses Global: The Humanities and Social Sciences Collection; Publicly Available Content Database. (2195471308).

Andreas, G., Nicolas, K., & Helmut, L. (2015). The effects of visual context and individual differences on perception and evaluation of modern art and graffiti art. *Acta Psychologica, 156*, 64–76. https://doi.org/10.1016/j.actpsy.2015.01.005

Barry, D., & Meisiek, S. (2010). Seeing more and seeing differently: Sensemaking, mindfulness, and the workarts. *Organization Studies, 31*(11), 1505–1530. https://doi.org/10.1177/0170840610380802

Bass, B. M., & Riggio, R. E. (2006). *Transformational leadership* (2nd ed.). Lawrence Erlbaum Associates.

Beghetto, R. A., & Karwowski, M. (2019). Unfreezing creativity: A dynamic micro-longitudinal approach. In R. A. Beghetto, & G. E. Corazza (Eds.), *Dynamic perspectives on creativity: Creativity theory and action in education* (Vol. 4, pp. 7–25). Springer. https://doi.org/10.1007/978-3-319-99163-4_2

Belawati, F. E., Setyadi, D., & Hendri, M. I. (2019). Effect of transformational leadership style and knowledge management on organizational innovation through empowerment, member creativity and learning. *Journal of Arts and Humanities, 8*(8), 1–16. https://doi.org/10.18533/journal.v8i8.1699

Berger, J. (Ed.). (1972). *Ways of seeing*. British Broadcasting Corporation; Penguin.

Cameron, J. (2002). *The artist's way: A spiritual path to higher creativity* (10th anniversary ed.). Putnam.

Carden, J., Jones, R. J., & Passmore, J. (2022). Defining self-awareness in the context of adult development: A systematic literature review. *Journal of Management Education, 46*(1), 140–177. https://doi.org/10.1177/1052562921990065

Cengiz Ucar, A., Alpkan, L., & Elci, M. (2021). The effect of servant and transformational leadership styles on employee creative behavior: The moderating role of authentic leadership. *Journal of Organizational Leadership, 10*, 99–119. https://doi.org/10.33844/ijol.2021.60538

Choi, C. H., Agus Purwanto, I. B., Asbari, M., & Laksmi, M. W. (2020). Effect of transformational and transactional leadership style on public health center performance. *International Journal of Humanities and Social Science, 8*, 46–58. https://doi.org/10.13140/RG.2.2.33517.13283.

Cooling, T. (2020). Worldview in religious education: Autobiographical reflections on the commission on religious education in England final report. *British Journal of Religious Education, 42*(4), 403–414. https://doi.org/10.1080/01416200.2020.1764497

Cranton, P., & Taylor, E. W. (2012). Transformative learning theory: Seeking a more unified theory. In P. Cranton & E. W. Taylor (Eds.), *The handbook of transformative learning: Theory, research, and practice* (pp. 3–20). Jossey-Bass.

Csikszentmihalyi, M. (2008). *Flow: The psychology of optimal experience*. Harper Perennial Modern Classics. (Original work published 1990)

Day, D. V., & Dragoni, L. (2015). Leadership development: An outcome-oriented review based on time and levels of analyses. *The Annual Review of Organizational Psychology and Organizational Behavior, 2*(1), 133–156. https://doi.org/10:1146/annurev-orgpsych-032414-11328

Day, D. V., Halpin, S., & Harrison, M. M. (2009). *An integrative approach to leader development: Connecting adult development, identity, and expertise*. Routledge.

Davison, J. (2010). [In]visible [in]tangibles: Visual portraits of the business élite. *Accounting, Organizations and Society, 35*(2), 165–183. https://doi.org/10.1016/j.aos.2009.03.003

Eisenberg, D. M., Willett, W. C., Massa, J., Righter, A. C., Matthews, B., & Zhang, W. (2019). Feasibility pilot study of a teaching kitchen and self-care curriculum in a workplace setting. *American Journal of Lifestyle Medicine, 13*(3), 319–330. https://doi.org/10.1177/1559827617709757

Freeman, M. (1997). *Rewriting the self: History, memory, narrative.* Routledge.

Freeman, M. P. (2010). *Hindsight: The promise and peril of looking backward.* Oxford University Press.

Gardner, W. L., Avolio, B. J., Luthans, F., May, D. R., & Walumbwa, F. (2005). 'Can you see the real me?' A self-based model of authentic leader and follower development. *The Leadership Quarterly, 16*(3), 343–372. https://doi.org/10.1016/j.leaqua.2005.03.003

Goffman, E. (1959). *The presentation of self in everyday life.* Doubleday.

Grashow, A., Heifetz, R. A., & Linsky, M. (2009). *The practice of adaptive leadership: Tools and tactics for changing your organization and the world.* Harvard.

Hall, R. J., & Lord, R. G. (2005). Identity, deep structure and the development of leadership skill. *The Leadership Quarterly, 16*(4), 591–615. https://doi.org/10.1016/j.leaqua.2005.06.003

Harter, N. W. (2023). *The role of imagination in understanding leadership: The forgotten dimension.* Taylor & Francis.

Howard, J. A. (2000). Social psychology of identities. *Annual Review of Sociology, 26*(1), 367–393. https://doi.org/10.1146/annurev.soc.26.1.367

Hoxha, A. (2019). Transformational and transactional leadership styles on employee performance. *International Journal of Humanities and Social Science Invention, 8*(11), 46–58. https://www.ijhssi.org/papers/vol8(11)/Series-3/G0811034658.pdf

Isaacson, W. (2011). *Steve Jobs.* Simon & Schuster.

Kaplan, A. M., & Haenlein, M. (2010). Users of the world, unite! The challenges and opportunities of social media. *Business Horizons, 53*(1), 59–68. https://doi.org/10.1016/j.bushor.2009.09.003

Kegan, R. (2000). What 'form' transforms? A constructive-development approach to transformational learning. In J. Mezirow & Associates (Eds.), *Learning as transformation: Critical perspectives on a theory in progress* (pp. 35–70). Jossey-Bass.

King, D. (2023). Mindfulness and meditation—Self-care and being digital in the arts. In Z. Adil (Ed.), *A focus on pedagogy: Teaching, learning and researching in the modern academy* (pp. 8–13). AMPS (Architecture, Media, Politics, Society) Proceeding Series 28.1. University of Kassel, Ball State University, Beaconhouse National University and the University of Pretoria. 20-22 April, 2022. https://tinyurl.com/bdzaedxw

Koh, D., Lee, K., & Joshi, K. (2019). Transformational leadership and creativity: A meta-analytic review and identification of an integrated model. *Journal of Organizational Behavior, 40*(6), 625–650. https://doi.org/10.1002/job.2355

Komives, S. R., Longerbeam, S. D., Mainella, F. C., Osteen, L., & Owen, J. E. (2005). Developing a leadership identity: A grounded theory. *Journal of College Student Development, 46*(6), 593–611. https://doi.org/10.1353/csd.2005.0061

Kruse, S., & Edge, K. (2023). Is it just me? The organizational implications of individual and collective burnout in schools. *Journal of Educational Administration, 61*(3), 272–286. https://doi.org/10.1108/JEA-10-2022-0187

Kunrath, K., Cash, P., & Kleinsmann, M. (2019). Social- and self-perception of designers' professional identity. *Journal of Engineering Design, 31*(2), 100–126. https://doi.org/10.1080/09544828.2019.1676883

Leder, H., Belke, B., Oeberst, A., & Augustin, D. (2004). A model of aesthetic appreciation and aesthetic judgments. *British Journal of Psychology, 95*(4), 489–508. https://doi.org/10.1348/0007126042369811

Lin, S., Matta, F., & Scott, B. (2019). The dark side of transformational leader behaviors for leaders themselves: A conservation of resources perspective. *Academy of Management Journal, 62*(5), 1556–1582. https://doi.org/10.5465/amj.2016.1255

Markgren, S., & Miles, L. (2022). Combating burnout: Positive/transformational leadership and organizational culture. In S. Holm, A. Guimaraes & N. Marcano (Eds.),

Combating burnout: Positive/transformational leadership and organizational culture (pp. 305–321). Association of College & Research Libraries. https://doi.org/10.17613/sdnn-c183

Marion, R., McKelvey, B., & Uhl-Bien, M. (2007). Complexity leadership theory: Shifting leadership from the industrial age to the knowledge era. *The Leadership Quarterly, 18*(4), 298–318. https://doi.org/10.1016/j.leaqua.2007.04.002

Mezirow, J. (1991). *Transformative dimensions of adult learning.* Jossey-Bass.

Mezirow, J. (2000). Learning to think like an adult: Core concepts of transformational learning. In J. Mezirow & Associates (Eds.), *Learning as transformation: Critical perspectives on a theory in progress* (pp. 3–34). Jossey-Bass.

Montero, R., Quintana, S. M., & Scull, N. C. (2008). Identity development. In F. T. L. Leong, E. M. Altmaier, & B. D. Johnson (Eds.), *Encyclopedia of counseling* (Vol. 3, pp. 1163–1168). Sage.

Parks Daloz, L. (2000). Transformative learning for the common good. In J. Mezirow & Associates (Eds.), *Learning as transformation: Critical perspectives on a theory in progress* (pp. 103–124). Jossey-Bass.

Pearson, K. (2022). Imaginative leadership: A conceptual frame for the design and facilitation of creative methods and generative engagement. In A. Franklin (Ed.), *Cocreativity and engaged scholarship: Transformative methods in social sustainability research* (pp. 165–204). Palgrave Macmillan.

Podolny, J. M., Khurana, R., & Besharov, M. L. (2010). Revisiting the meaning of leadership. In N. Nohria & R. Khurana (Eds.), *Handbook of leadership theory and practice* (pp. 65–106). Harvard Business Press.

Price, A. A., Leavitt, C. E., Gibby, A. L., & Holmes, E. K. (2024). What do you think of me? How externalized self-perception and sense of self are associated with emotional intimacy. *Contemporary Family Therapy: An International Journal, 46*(1), 52–62. https://doi.org/10.1007/s10591-023-09673-w

Roberts, L. M. (2005). Changing faces: Professional image construction in diverse organizational settings. *Academy of Management Review, 30*(4), 685–711. https://doi.org/10.2307/20159163

Sawyer, K. (2012). *Explaining creativity: The science of human innovation* (2nd ed.). Oxford University Press.

Sonnentag, S. (2001). Work, recovery activities, and individual well-being: A diary study. *Journal of Occupational Health Psychology, 6*(3), 196–210. https://doi.org/10.1037/1076-8998.6.3.196

Sonnentag, S. (2003). Recovery, work engagement, and proactive behavior: A new look at the interface between nonwork and work. *The Journal of Applied Psychology, 88*(3), 518–528. https://doi.org/10.1037/0021-9010.88.3.518

Strawser, B. (2022). *Crisis communication strategies in the media: BP's failure during the deepwater horizon oil spill.* https://bryghtpath.com/deepwater-horizon-case-study/

Vanderkam, L. (2016). *How to gain control of your free time* [Video]. TEDWomen. https://www.ted.com/talks/laura_vanderkam_how_to_gain_control_of_your_free_time?subtitle=en

Yukl, G. (2014). Contingency theories of effective leadership. In A. Bryman, D. Collinson, K. Grint, B. Jackson, & M. Uhl-Bien (Eds.), *Sage handbook of leadership* (pp. 286–289). Sage. (Original work published 2011)

Chapter 10

The Muse, Dialogue, and Collaboration: Agential Realism in Practice

Kevin D. Collins

Independent Scholar, USA

Abstract

This chapter explores the dynamics of creative inspiration through the lens of Barad's agential realism, examining how the classical concept of the muse, dialogical interaction, and collaborative processes intertwine to form a holistic understanding of creativity. Using an arts-based research methodology, the paper presents a fictional radio interview between a host and an academic discussing the historical development of the muse concept from ancient Greece to contemporary revisioning, Bakhtin's notion of dialogism, and collaborative creative processes across various disciplines. Barad's agential realism challenges traditional subject/object dichotomies, suggesting that creativity emerges not from individual inspiration but through intra-active processes of becoming. This framework offers a transformative approach to creative leadership and decision-making that de-objectifies others, emphasizes process over product, and re-centers human experience within a collective creative discourse. Practical exercises are included for experiencing this intra-relational creativity, providing a pathway for readers to engage with these concepts experientially rather than abstractly.

Keywords: Muse; dialogue; collaboration; agential realism; recentering

Introduction

This chapter approaches the dynamics of creative inspiration and the process of re-centering. I begin by reviewing the historical development of the idea of a muse, or the muses as ideal figures of inspiration, from Greek mythology to

Artful Leadership: Retreat, Recenter, and Rewild, 123–138
Copyright © 2026 by Kevin D. Collins
Published under exclusive licence by Emerald Publishing Limited
doi:10.1108/S2058-880120250000010011

21st-century revisioning (Millington, 2022a). As a condition of muse activity, I then approach the idea of dialogue philosophically, overviewing Bakhtin's (1981, 1929/1984) notion of dialogism. From Bakhtin, I move to a topical discussion of creative collaboration, tying the muse to the dialogic process. Although much has already been written about these topics, I analyze them holistically through Barad's (2007) conceptualization of the intra-action of matter and of agential realism, a philosophical turn based on quantum physics. Through this lens, the muse, dialogue, and collaboration are examined to derive a sense of how creative inspiration may tie us all together.

The method used herein, fiction-based research, has previously been implemented by writing novels, plays, or interviews (Banks, 2008; Leavy, 2015, 2018). I have created an ostensible radio interview between a renowned author and a host intending to blend the conceptual with the accessible. Conversational voices are employed to ask questions and explain the sometimes ponderous content. This method should help readers explore ideas and hear the interview voices as secondary reinforcements to reading the material.

With these thoughts in mind, please tune in as we listen:

Interview

Glennis: Good morning. I'm Glennis Farquharson and you're listening to *Frontispiece*. Today we're honored to have Dr. Rounce Aberwick, distinguished Professor of Aesthetical Change at Östenaar University and author of the recent nonfiction best seller, *Creating Creativity: Behind and Beyond Creating*. We are so glad to have you with us today Dr. Aberwick.

Rounce: Thank you, Glennis, for having me, and please call me Rounce.

Introduction

Glennis: OK, Rounce. Let's dive right in. For those of us who haven't read your book, can you give us a brief overview?

Rounce: Sure, Glennis. In *Creating Creativity*, I tried to approach the process of creativity descriptively, essentially basing it in the language of physics through Barad's (2007) philosophical agential realism. I first examined the idea of the muse or the muses, traditionally a source of creative inspiration. Then, I looked at some of the notions of dialogue and its creative variances giving particular attention to Bakhtin's (1981, 1929/1984) dialogism. Tied into both subjects is the sense of collaboration and I pulled them together through its discussion. These three concepts give some background, some of the "behind" of creativity.

Glennis: That covers the first part of the book. Where do you take it from there?

Rounce: Part II was where I went both behind the Part I discussions and beyond them. I went behind because I tried to show how the universe is in a constant state of flux, continually creating and we as human participants in that creating, tap into the processes of becoming ourselves. I went beyond in the use of the language and concepts of quantum physics as a descriptive way to show how we may pass beyond the first quarter of the 21st century.

Muse

Glennis: It sounds complicated yet fascinating. Can we take it slowly and start with the idea of the muses?

Rounce: Sure. First some background. The idea of muse is primarily a Greco-Western concept (Millington, 2022a). It seems to have its source in the appearance of the nine muses of Greek mythology, each of whom sponsored a particular field of creativity, Erato for lyric poetry, Clio for history, Calliope for epic poetry, and so forth (*Muse*, 2024). The muses seemed to validate human creative endeavors and through these endeavors, advance humanity along the civilized path (Volpone, 2024). Prior to the advent of the muses, we were considered to be uncivilized and barbarian – at least from the point of view of postmuse commentators. Just let it be said that the presence of the idea of the muses permitted the Greek world to engage in presumedly higher cultural activities, that is, activities not necessary for basic survival.

Glennis: How did the muses work? Or what evidence do we have of their influence?

Rounce: Consider the Greek writers Homer and Hesiod (Franek, 2018). They admonished the muses for inspiration – within the scope of their works, usually at the beginning, as if asking for a blessing. The muses were inspirational, personified, external to the poet, revered almost to the extent of deification (Millington, 2022a). The writers were dependent on the muses, but not just for inspiration. The muses served as social validation and were sources of power and authority, legitimizing the writers' authenticity. In a nutshell, Greek writers depended on the muses for their inspiration and social standing.

Glennis: How has this ideal changed through the centuries?

Rounce: By and during the Renaissance, two things happened. First, the representations of the muse became more sexualized as well as idealized as the epitome of female beauty (Millington, 2022a). The second trend was that artists and writers began moving away from the mythological muses and began using real people for inspiration (Millington, 2022b).

Glennis: Has this type of idealization continued?

Rounce: Yes and no. What happened was the objectification of the idealized and sexualized muses (Millington, 2022b; Xuan, 2023). Artists, almost exclusively male, assumed a role of the great male artist who possessed their muse. Even if their bonds were close, there were "patronizing, sexist and pejorative connotations" (Millington, 2022a, p. 6) inherent in the relationship. This patriarchal narrative viewed the muse as a powerless object and opened the door to exploitation (Millington, 2022a).

Glennis: Can you give some examples of this objectification?

Rounce: Consider the relationship between T. S. Eliot and Emily Hale (Scudeler, 2023). Eliot seemed to depend on Hale for inspiration as his muse, a transcendental imagining of her as an object. He also wanted her as her flesh and blood person and while Hale was willing in the latter, she resisted the former. The poet Ernest Dowson auditioned or courted young girls to be his literary muses (Stark, 2023). Just a couple of examples which demonstrate the popular patriarchal viewpoint as well as the unwillingness of a muse to be objectified – when we realize that the muse may also have a voice and a point of view.

Glennis: Just curious. Are females always the object of being a muse?

Rounce: No, it's just the most common and prevalent in popular culture (Franek, 2018). Cultural context may be considered a muse as can an environmental context. Alexander Blok idealized his memory of Old (Tsarist) Russia in contrast to post-World War I Russia (Harmash, 2024). Robert Louis Stevenson used the American landscape as a muse (Rieger, 2024). Sometimes a muse has been male also. The singer Madonna stated that David Bowie was her muse – until she realized how patriarchal the music industry was (Lawson, 2023). Schlesinger served as a male muse to the male painter Hockney (Millington, 2022b). A muse hasn't always been female; yet because the predominant narrative has been written and promulgated by patriarchal culture, the female has been the typical object of the muse (Millington, 2022a).

Glennis: This objectification of the other seems to be a recurrent theme as well as being inherent to the idea of a muse. How do you think this issue may be rectified?

Rounce: There are two or three trends afoot which have begun to address it in different ways, and which broadly relate to our topic. First, there is some discussion in legal circles about de-objectifying plants and animals (van Laarhoven & Claerhoudt, 2024). In other words, both plants and animals may have legal rights and status due to their acknowledged sentience. If plants and animals can be subjectified, then surely, we can work through de-objectifying the muse concept.

Glennis: I'll have to think about that a little more.

Rounce: A trend closer to our topic is that of drawing female cartoon characters in a less sexualized manner (de Liz, 2016). Especially in heroine characters, female features have often been exaggerated to appease a patriarchal cartoon culture. The prevailing assumption seems to be that sexualized characters are more marketable. However, the characters can be drawn to retain their female characteristics without being blatantly sexualized.

The idea of female gaze has also cropped up in the film and television industries (Xuan & Yi, 2022). These industries have overtly sexualized many of their female characters – introducing some of them with a leggy walk up an aisle or ignoring the character's talents and skills beyond mere sexuality. These effects are part of the predominant male gaze rooted in a toxic masculinity leading to stock stereotypes which take away female agency and treats them only as pretty objects.

Glennis: I'd never quite thought of those things in such strong terms although I have been maybe subconsciously offended by such portrayals and the seeming need, even of heroines, for a significant male counterpart and/or protector. It seems then that a 21st-century muse may be characterized differently. How would you respond to that statement?

Rounce: This begins to get to the heart of the conversation, an effort to unpack the real idea and function of a muse. Whereas in the past, they have been "fetishized, mute and submissive" (Xuan, 2023, para. 15), more recent work has emphasized the mutuality of the influence of muses on artists as performers (Millington, 2022a, 2022b; Xuan, 2023). In other words, in the *process* of creating – whether art or anything else – and not focusing entirely on the product, the *process* of creation requires mutual participation between performer and muse.

Glennis: We haven't heard of these critical roles because…?

Rounce: I'll answer the question with a question. Who has written about or promoted artists and performers? We return to a patriarchal society which has emphasized great men (Carlyle, 1846), to a predominate narrative written by males about males whose intent has been to produce products effectively (McDonough & Harrison, 1978). A close look, again at process rather than product, shows that "muses have played a pivotal role and … left an indelible mark" (Millington, 2022b, para. 28). In fact, muses have exercised considerable power: "They have inspired, bringing emotional support, intellectual energy, career-changing creativity and practical help" (Millington, 2022b, para. 28). A case in point among many others: Dora Maar acted as Pablo Picasso's muse for several years (Millington, 2022a). She taught him certain photographic processes which he then used to produce portraits of her. She influenced him with her leftist political views to the extent of influencing his dramatic anti-war painting, *Guernica* (Pound, 2019). She was a Surrealist photographer in her own right but only recently achieved significant name recognition.

Glennis: Should we then discard the notion of muse altogether and speak of inspiration differently?

Rounce: That's what a feminist critique of the idea has suggested as being fraught with the baggage of patriarchalism (Millington, 2022a). Millington (2022a) proposed a postfeminist reappropriation of the concept, acknowledging the baggage but expanding it through collaborations like Maar and Picasso, reclaiming a broader view of the muse.

Dialogue

Glennis: Rounce, doesn't this conversation about mutual inspiration segue into the second idea in your book, dialogue?

Rounce: Perfect timing, Glennis. Again, we're going to hearken back to Ancient Greece – Socratic dialogue as recorded by Plato featured Socrates as a presumably nescient interlocutor to various purported experts (Kraut, 2024). Through dialogic questioning, Socrates explicated his philosophical point. In fact, we're engaged in a Socratic dialogue in which you interrogate me in my ostensible knowledge.

Glennis: Just for the record, I haven't claimed to be completely clueless – I have read your book.

Rounce: I know. I'm making a point that dialogue is a familiar form of communication from philosophy to literature to everyday life. This interposition into everything helps us understand how important an understanding of it is.

Glennis: Dialogue is pervasive. Given. How do we then talk about it?

Rounce: Dialogue emphasizes the plurality of society, that it is a listening to the other, that it is an "inter-relationship between subjectivities [where people] create and recreate their world" (Martins, 2023, p. 4). There is agency. There is inter-relationality. There is creativity.

Glennis: I can support that definition. But earlier you mentioned Bakhtinian dialogue.

Rounce: That is correct because Bakhtin (Brandist, n.d.; Walker, 1992) has been considered a foremost theorist of dialogue or dialogism. I'll just summarize some key Bakhtinian points.

Bakhtin (1981) was primarily concerned with language, dialogue and with "verbal discourse [as] a social phenomenon" (p. 259). While he did acknowledge that other forms of art could be discursive, his interests lay in literature, especially the novel (Mambrol, 2018). For us, we should understand his focus on the social nature of language, that is, language does not exist in an individual vacuum but is mediated, a dialogic encounter with an other. There must be some type of relationality between parties before dialogue may occur. This relationality requires a recognition of the other and the spaces and boundaries occupied by the one and the other. Language mediates the boundaries between different parties.

For Bakhtin (1981, 1929/1984), language lay "on the borderline between oneself and the other" (Bakhtin, 1981, p. 293). Speakers populated language with their own intentions, intentions being the way that consciousness transcends itself (Zahavi, 2019). With this intentionality, a speaker declared ownership of its use (Mambrol, 2018). Thus language, although liminally existing on the boundaries, was never neutral; it was packed with intentions and thus, with meanings. Dialogue was the social process of linguistic interaction.

Bakhtin also recognized that language did not have singular characteristics (Mambrol, 2018). There is a multiplicity of language variances and nuances active in dialogue, the differences of which must be mediated and sometimes overcome (Bakhtin, 1929/1984). Consider the use of jargon and how meanings may differ, or regional issues in which terms differ from one area to another. Or think about linguistic evolutions such as British English and American English. When we're trying to understand discourse, all of these layers must be considered.

Glennis: Isn't this just a complicated way of saying, "We're talking back and forth?"

Rounce: Superficially, yes, we're having a conversation. But it becomes a "no" when you approach it phenomenologically, that is, when you start trying to describe the "experience *of experience*" (Engelland, 2020, p. 2). This dialogic interaction can represent a search for truth in which "truth … is born between people collectively searching" (Bakhtin, 1929/1984, p. 110) for it.

Bakhtin also had a political edge to his discursive search for truth (Walker, 1992). He was searching for a singular way to describe the effect of dialogue as a creative element in social change distinguishing between poetics and novelistics (Brandist, n.d.). The poetic discourse upheld the existing social structures, exercising a hegemonic voice over social inequities, seeking to maintain those inequalities through language. It was monologic, reinforcing one dominant authoritative narrative. In contrast, novelistic discourse was dialogic, attempting to disturb narrative hegemony. It was social, integrating a multiplicity of narratives. It referred to "the character of a genre, multi-accented artistic discourse, *and* [italics mine] an anti-authoritarian relationship between discourses" (Brandist, n.d., sect. 4, para. 4). The ruling class, or the power holders, or the social structures, tried to establish a single discourse, the poetic, while the underclass, the oppressed, the dispossessed tried to disrupt their grasp through novelistic discourse (Brandist, n.d.).

Glennis: How does this overview relate to creativity and the muse and collaboration?

Rounce: The next step I took was to analyze the concept of the muse in Bakhtinian terms. The Greeks created their narrative of civilized and creative activity through the muses (Volpone, 2024). They assigned them the role of inspirer, which created an artistic dependency from poets, writers, and artists. This dependency created a power differential in which the muses dominated subservient artists, and their power seemed to grow over time almost achieving deification (Millington, 2022a). So, the Greeks established a monologic narrative which has endured for millennia. For Bakhtin, this monologic nature of the concept dominated social structures and prevented people from realizing truth and meaning (Brandist, n.d.). Dialogue, however, must rise from the masses to subvert the static structures represented by the muses.

This point is where feminist critique (Parker & Pollock, 1991) and revisionists like Millington (2022a) have made inroads. In their work of raising the status of muse to partnership, they have reassessed those partnerships showing mutual inspiration, balancing the contributions of both parties. Recent centuries have brought a dialogic movement to the creative world allowing meaningful relationality to blossom (Coghlan & Brydon-Miller, 2014). Public discourse has begun achieving this dialogic character, subverting established patriarchal narratives and allowing for multiple voices to create meaning.

Glennis: Wow. I think that's a powerful statement of the creative power of dialogue.

Rounce: Further, dialogue is a continual process rather than a static statement of being (Moate & Vass, 2023). It could even be seen dialectically, that is, dialogue occurs and is synthesized into a narrative at which point dialogue resumes. For Bakhtin, "the self is in an unceasing, receptive-responsive dialogue with its physical, social, or cultural environment" (Moate & Vass, 2023, p. A55), a dialectic between self and other. I find this idea to be inherently transformational – that creation happens through a continual dialogical discourse.

Collaboration

Glennis: It seems from your review of the muse and dialogism that agents – artists, creators, and so forth – do not act alone or perhaps never act alone regardless of reputed eccentricities. In other words, creation and/or art seems to be collaborative and only successful through an interrelated mutuality.

Rounce: Exactly what researchers seem to have said. Thus, we come to the third level. We're saying that collaboration is the essence of creativity. While we're primarily looking at creativity in the arts, in fact, creativity is essential to everyday life (Runco, 2004). In our workaday lives, "creativity drives innovation and evolution … but [it] is also a reaction to the challenges of life" (Runco, p. 679). That is, to live our lives, we must provide either proactive or reactive solutions to our daily existence which require a creative process which is inherently social and thus collaborative (John-Steiner, 2000). As Pera (2013) noted, "significant creations are almost always the result of complex collaboration" (pp. 208–209) in which dialogue plays a critical part. Because our lives intersect with events, other people, and environments unpredictably, creativity has the quality of improvisation (Rusu, 2019). Here again, we see a process, a social phenomenon, rather than a burst of inspiration. This process is creativity, is collaboration, as opposed to instrumentalism in which an object is produced, an othered thing. This view of creativity shows "the process [to be] the product" (Rusu, p. 275).

Glennis: You mention several examples of collaborative creation in your book. Do you have any favorites you could share with us?

Rounce: I've mentioned Maar and Picasso, and I particularly like the fact that Maar's photographic surrealism directly influenced *Guernica* (Millington, 2022a). However, at another point in his life, Picasso collaborated closely with Braque, the French painter (John-Steiner, 2000). Picasso and Braque would visit each other's studios almost daily to critique and converse about their work (Richardson, 1991, 1996). They relied on each other's approval before a work was complete. In their dialogue, their collaboration, they developed techniques that changed not only the art world but the world in toto.

The partnership between Simone de Beauvoir and Jean Paul Sartre, philosophers and writers, also bears mention due to the proximity of their shared lives (Madsen, 1979). De Beauvoir (1968) claimed that their conversations and collaborations became so close that they even thought alike, partly through the influence of common background experiences but also through dialogic interaction. While they never actively wrote together, "they jointly established a philosophy that governed their writings" (John-Steiner, 2000, p. 15). In these collaborations, it was necessary to have both mutual respect and mutual support (John-Steiner, 2000; Mehta & Henriksen, 2019).

Marie and Pierre Curie provide an example of close collaboration in the sciences (John-Steiner, 2000). They worked closely together, achieving joint success in their radiation research. Even though Pierre worked more conceptually and Marie more pragmatically, their multi- and trans-disciplinary approach complemented each other's efforts (John-Steiner, 2000; Mehta & Henriksen, 2019).

Successful collaborations are also noncompetitive (John-Steiner, 2000). They thrive on mutual respect in pursuit of co-creation (Mehta & Henriksen, 2019). Because collaborators don't necessarily have to think alike, this sense of noncompetition allows them to act complementarily, where "cooperation displaces hypercompetitiveness" (Boje, 2014, p. 357) based on areas of "expertise, disciplinary knowledge, roles, and temperament" (Collins, 2016, p. 111).

Glennis: How would you tie these three ideas together then, succinctly?

Rounce: Succinctly? We're talking about creativity. Creativity occurs through social interaction, collaboratively through dialogue generated by mutual inspiration. Did that cover it?

Glennis: I think so. Before we continue our discussion with Dr. Rounce Aberwick on his current book, *Creating Creativity*, we're going to take a quick sponsor break.

Announcer: *Frontispiece* has been thoughtfully and carefully provided to you, our listening audience, by Emerald Publishing, your place to publish for academic excellence.

Agential Realism

Glennis: We're back on the air. Where does the discussion of *Creating Creativity* go from here?

Rounce: Phenomenologically, we're going to try to describe the "experience *of experience*" (Engelland, 2020, p. 2). Or we're going to return to where we've been, and re-turn, that is, turn over repeatedly, what we've already said (Barad, 2014). We've asserted that a muse interacts inspirationally between multiple entities which may be considered dialogic action, and through this dialogue, exemplifies collaborative processes. We need to turn these ideas over and work on reframing the discussion in a more accurate – at least to my mind – version of the substance of reality. To do this, I'm going to rely on the work of Barad (2007), a quantum physicist, feminist, and philosopher, who in turn, relied on quantum physicist and philosopher, Niels Bohr, in her development of agential realism.

Glennis: Wait. Is this going to be intelligible or am I going to get lost in the ether trying to track physics and philosophy?

Rounce: I don't think it's appropriate to oversimplify conceptually, but I will try to present them coherently. Fair?

Glennis: That'll work.

Rounce: First, let me issue a caveat about quantum language. Rovelli (2020/2021) has castigated the world for calling every little thing quantum without understanding the concepts, misapplying concepts, and thinking that quantum mechanics has disciplinary universality. I agree with him that quantumness has been overused. However, he continued by positing the indirect universal influence of quantum thought in that "the discovery of quanta changes the terms of our questions" (Rovelli, 2020/2021, p. 162). Through quanta, the world has become a world of relationality rather than a determinate world of objects, challenging Newtonian physics and subject/object, matter/spirit dualities (Rovelli, 2020/2021; Wendt, 2015). While not everyone may be able to follow the math and physics of quantum mechanics, it is possible to understand the philosophical ramifications, because in fact, not just in theory, "everything is quantum" (Carroll, 2019, p. 311).

First, though, we'll return to Greece with Leucippus and Democritus who taught us about atomization, that is, every thing may be broken down until we reach the smallest possible component (Barad, 2007). Notice that the agent of the process is external to the process, that is, human agents act on other objects. This concept has endured millennia, acting as the foundation of Newtonian physics, and purportedly becoming pure common sense. Quantum physics displaces atomism and Newtonian physics (Rovelli, 2020/2021).

Barad (2007) took processes of quantum physics and applied them to philosophical questions on the nature of agency, causality, and representation to develop what she called agential realism. I'll discuss a few of her key points.

To start with, reality is a continual process of becoming (Barad, 2007). It is never completely static being and never completely instrumental doing. It is becoming. Agential reality dispenses with the subject/object or knower/known divide. In classical definitions, there is an inherent boundedness, a preconceived determination to the definitions of one and the other as the subject and the object. Agential reality relinquishes this boundedness as incompatible with how the world works quantumly. In the quantum description, boundaries only become evident when a portion of reality acts or reacts to apparatuses within its range of activity.

To understand this better, Barad (2007) used the well-known experiments on the physical nature of light (cf. Wendt, 2015). When we define light, is it waves or is it particulate? The results are contingent on the apparatus by which it is measured, that is, one apparatus gives wave results and another gives particles. Yet what is light? It is both when it interacts with something, but it is neither until it interacts. If we say it is either, we have presupposed conclusions on the nature of light. Light, then, is included in indeterminate phenomena which are entangled with other nonconstituent inclusions until they are processed intra-actively through apparatuses. Barad (2007) claimed that this process of describing light energy is applicable to all forms of energy from which all reality is composed. Then this intra-action, in contrast to interaction which presupposes bounded entities, is the continual relationship within phenomena which, through intra-action, makes the conditions in which determinacy may occur. In other words, we are "part of the intra-active ongoing articulation of the world in its differential mattering" (Barad, 2007, p. 381). Humans *and* nonhumans are part of these phenomena and remain indeterminate until intra-active processes occur.

Secondly, Barad (2007) challenged the representationalism of words in that "language has been given too much power" (p. 132). Rather, reality is performative in its continual intra-active flux instead of determinate as per linguistic representation (Wendt, 2015). When we name something, we have represented it as an other (Barad, 2007). Representationalism supports individualism in the belief "in the ontological distinction between representations and that which they purport to represent" (Barad, p. 46). In quantum thought, however, the notion of preconceived individuality is discarded in favor of the process of indeterminate processional intra-activity, relationality rather than definition. For Barad (2007), the processes of matter, that is quanta, mattered more than predefined linguistic definitions.

Thirdly, discourse is not identical to language and supersedes dialogue (Barad, 2007). "It is that which constrains and enables what can be said" (Barad, 2007, p. 146), causal intra-actions by which parts of the world become determinate and bounded in relation to other parts. It also is part of the continuum of process as a way of establishing meanings through boundary setting without the finality of linguistic representation. Discourse is part of the performativity of reality, the "iterative intra-action" (Barad, 2007, p. 179), the continual becoming. Humans are part of this performative discourse. They continue becoming, unbounded between their selves and nonhumanity. We are not external agents or observers, nor do we have a distinct place, but we are human becomings.

Glennis: That was quite a mouthful. I think I understood most of it, although it seems to disrupt everything we've already said.

Rounce: True and that's the fascination of it. Let's re-turn the idea of the muse. The muses were a representation of what civilized people did for civilized pursuits (Volpone, 2024). Then the personifications became idealized and sexualized (Millington, 2022a). As the muse became more human and the term passed into the vernacular, shadows of its idealized representations followed the idea, retaining the sense of otherness from the artist. Recent discussions attribute inspirational mutuality between muse and artist.

Agential realism provides the next marker (Barad, 2007). By dismissing the subject/object duality, agential realism de-objectifies the deified other, the idealized other, the mutually inter-related other. The object of the artist, even in mutually mediated space, may now be understood as being embodied in the phenomena, integral in the intra-active becoming, that is, in the unbounded creating of reality. Not only does the muse become embodied as part of the agential determination which occurs, but the muse is co-equal with the artist and with the artwork in the determinative process of becoming. The essence of creativity and nature of reality is not about who or what is creating, nor who or what is being created – both of which are categorical representations, but about the process of *"agential separability"* (Barad, 2007, p. 140) through which entities become.

Glennis: Would you say this process is applicable to the discussion of dialogue as well? Bakhtin's (1981, 1929/1984) primary focus was linguistic which you seem to be suggesting must be displaced due to some erroneous assumptions.

Rounce: Bakhtin (1981, 1929/1984) can certainly be helpful after we arrive at the use of language so I'm not dismissing his work altogether. Yet, his idea of dialogue still arises from the necessity of presupposed, bounded agents, differentiated prior to the advent of any dialogue (Brandist, n.d.). For him there had to be at least two separate entities, human entities, for the use of language. Think of the implications for conversation, for politics, for everyday living, if we could see through, or beyond, or better yet, behind the separating assumptions of our differentiated humanness and our differentiated environments. If we could think of all reality as integral phenomena, as inclusive in the functioning of the material universe, then the beginning points of dialogue are not built on differences – race, language, gender, stereotypes, objects – but on the commonality of the discursive process. This discourse of becoming is a discourse of becoming rather than a monolithic statement of is.

Glennis: And collaboration then is…?

Rounce: Collaboration is the return to and the re-turning of a collective sense of becoming together. Creativity appears to be unpredictable (Lamain et al., 2024). We can go back to the improvisational nature of creativity and begin seeing evidence of agential realism at work (Pera, 2013). This improvised collaboration is not something that can be preplanned or managed.

Collaborations may kindle "joy, curiosity, creativity and meaning" (Lamain et al., 2024, p. 1). I submit that this collaborative spark becomes most effective when we approach the collaboration through an agential reality frame, beginning to understand the intra-actions between beginning-to-be-determined agencies as the source of creativity. When de Beauvoir (1968) said that she and Sartre began thinking alike, their circumstance seemed to indicate the process of co-becoming, collaborative agential realism. To collaborate means to re-turn the becoming process, that all – human, nonhuman, environmental, contextual, social – are included simultaneously in becoming and that any agency is formed in the discourse of becoming expressed through creativity.

Implications

Glennis: You've given us quite a bit to ponder. Does this discussion have any implications for decision makers, guides, managers, authority figures?

Rounce: Sure. Two things stand out. First, it should reframe the way we consider our contexts – people, places, and things around us. When we de-objectify these others, we discard the categorical representations of their otherness. When we consider constant co-creation of our reality, we begin understanding that when we act, we affect the intra-action and intra-relationality of the whole. To act, then, becomes an ethical proposition in its entirety. When we are intra-related on a discursive level, as we are continually co-determined, then each function ripples from one entity through all other aspects of reality. If what we do affects everybody and everything, then we bear the continual responsibility for the influences of our becoming. Thus, we should consider the effects of our becoming activities on the becomingness of all.

Secondly, and a correlate to the first, the framework on which we make decisions shifts. Production is no longer venerated; rather, creativity through a discursive process becomes primary. Efficiency is no longer paramount. Capital loses its stranglehold on social and environmental life. Agential realism displaces individualistic mastery with collective creativity. This transformation shifts the whole conversation about how decisions are made and the basis for making them.

And a correlate to the correlate: We're re-turning, but we're also in the process of re-centering. However, we're actually shifting where the center is – not as a locus of creativity, a defined space, but as a conceptual center of becoming. Much of what has seemed to pass as centering or re-centering seems to focus on each person in their individuality, perhaps centering on their particular wants, needs, or peculiarities. As we re-center through agential realism, we can begin to understand this intra-relationality as central – not a focal point but a locus of movement, of becoming, motively, and collectively.

Glennis: Rounce, you've given us a lot to think about. Thank you for this discussion of creatively re-centering ourselves through the muse, dialogue, and collaboration. We are out of time for today's program. We encourage our listeners to read *Creating Creativity*. For Dr. Rounce Aberwick, this has been Glennis Farquharson and *Frontispiece*.

Practicing

The following experiential practices are designed to guide leaders in exploring the concepts of agential realism, collaborative creativity, and the dissolution of subject/object boundaries. Each practice offers a designed pattern to facilitate better understanding of these concepts.

Intra-active Habitation: Placing Yourself in Becoming

Intention: to experience creativity through inhabiting your environment, integrating your context into creation through the dissolution of boundaries rather than as external inspiration

- Prepare materials of creative expression with which to participate.
- Locate yourself in a comfortable place where you can engage with your context.
- Take 10–15 minutes to consider everything in your context not for inspiration but as consideration of holistic integration.

    o   Reflect on the nature of undifferentiated reality among the differentiation in your context.

- Begin expressing through your chosen medium – writing, painting, music.
- Collaborate with your context in creating.
- Continue to a point of saturation relinquishing the compulsion to produce a finished product.
- Reflect on the following:

    o   How are you becoming in collaboration with your context?
    o   How is engaging your context through the discourse of becoming different than using your surroundings for inspiration?
    o   How are your creative efforts different by focusing on becoming rather than focusing on production?

- Release yourself from your comfortable place after reflection.

Discourse: Musing on Creative Silence and Collaboration

Intention: to discover a deeper sense of creativity centered on the physics of intra-relationality

- Self-select 4–6 individuals to participate.
- Find a room and remove all possible sources of external stimuli.
- Arrange seating for the participants – does not have to be particularly configured.
- For 20 minutes practice silent discourse; participants may take notes, draw, journal, or essay within the silence.

    o   During silence, consider creative collaboration through the dissolution of individuated boundaries.

- For 20 minutes practice collaborative discourse with co-participants sharing your creative efforts during the silence.

- For 20 minutes practice collaborative discourse with the following:

    o   How does practicing silent discourse affect your consideration of the participatory place and people?
    o   How does understanding dissolution of individuated boundaries affect your understanding of collaboration?
    o   How does becoming differ from being in this context? In your typical context? In your typical leadership role?
    o   How can an unbounded understanding of creative collaboration change leadership practices?

Conclusion

This concludes this ersatz radio interview. I have tried to add to the conversation on creativity and leadership by reviewing some trends on the idea of the muse, dialogue, and collaboration, providing some context on how to re-turn and re-center through agential realism. Through an overview of agential realism, I have provided a guide to reframing creativity in our living contexts. We are always in the continual process of becoming, intra-acting with each and every differentiated creation.

Three benefits seem to emerge from this research method. It may make difficult ideas more accessible to a wider range of readers. It may engage the reader conversationally rather than as an exterior observer. Finally, with the reader participating, the dialogue becomes a larger conversation which gives writer, reader, and actants the opportunity to intra-relate through creative discourse.

This process becomes a centering act because many of us have never centered in *this* process. Yet it is also a re-centering act, not to find a static, spatially and temporally defined locus of being where we have been before, but to discover a way of becoming that refines how we may intra-relate. This way of becoming seems to demand a change to the way we have learned to lead and dialogue. Through this discourse, we may collectively be able to transform our shared becomings, thus re-centering in mutual creativity.

References

Bakhtin, M. M. (1981). Discourse in the novel. In M. Holquist (Ed.), *The dialogic imagination* (C. Emerson & M. Holquist, Trans.; pp. 269–434). University of Texas Press. http://www.europhd.net/sites/europhd/files/images/onda_2/07/27th_lab/scientific_materials/jesuino/bakhtin_1981.pdf

Bakhtin, M. M. (1984). *Problems of Dostoevsky's poetics* (C. Emerson, Trans.). University of Michigan Press. (Original work published 1929)

Banks, S. (2008). Writing as theory: In defense of fiction. In J. G. Knowles & A. L. Cole (Eds.), *Handbook of the arts in qualitative research: Perspectives, methodologies, examples, and issues* (pp. 155–164). Sage. https://doi.org/10.4135/9781452226545

Barad, K. (2007). *Meeting the universe halfway: Quantum physics and the entanglement of matter and meaning.* Duke University Press. https://smartnightreadingroom.files.wordpress.com/2013/05/meeting-the-universe-halfway.pdf

Barad, K. (2014). Diffracting diffraction: Cutting together-apart. *Parallax, 20*(3), 168–187. https://doi.org/10.1080/13534645.2014.927623

Boje, D. M. (2014). Introduction: Part IV. In D. M. Boje & T. L. Henderson (Eds.), *Being quantum: Ontological storytelling in the age of antenarrative* (pp. 356–361). Cambridge Scholars Publishing.

Brandist, C. S. (n.d.). The Bakhtin circle. In J. Fieser & B. Dowden (Eds.), *The internet encyclopedia of philosophy*. https://iep.utm.edu/bakhtin-circle/

Carlyle, T. (1846). *On heroes, hero-worship, and the heroic in history*. Wiley and Putnam. https://books.google.com/books/about/On_Heroes_Hero_worship_the Heroic_in_ His.html?

Carroll, S. (2019). *Something deeply hidden: Quantum worlds and the emergence of space-time*. Dutton.

Coghlan, D., & Brydon-Miller, M. (Eds.). (2014). *Bakhtinian dialogism: The Sage Encyclopedia of action research* (Vols. 1–2). Sage. https://doi.org/10.4135/9781446294406.n37

Collins, D. (2016). Creative collaborative thought and puzzle canons in Renaissance music. In M. S. Barrett (Ed.), *Collaborative creative thought and practice in music* (pp. 111–126). Routledge. https://doi.org/10.4324/9781315572635-17

de Beauvoir, S. (1968). *Hard times: Force of circumstances, 1952–1962 (Autobiography of Simone de Beauvoir)*. Penguin Books.

de Liz, R. (2016, July 26). *How to de-objectify women* [Twitter feed reposted with permission by J. Marcotte] Heroic Girls. https://www.heroicgirls.com/de-objectify-women-comics-guide/

Engelland, C. (2020). *Phenomenology*. MIT Press.

Franek, J. (2018). Invocations of the muse in homer and hesiod: A cognitive approach. *Antichthon, 52*, 1–22. https://doi.org/10.1017/ann.2018.8

Harmash, L. (2024). The genesis of a poetic title: Georgy Ivanov's poetry collection *The Roses. Agathos, 15*(1), 183–198. https://doi.org/10.5281/zenodo.10968045

John-Steiner, V. (2000). *Creative collaboration*. Oxford University Press.

Kraut, R. (2024, November 13). Socratic method. In The Editors of the Encyclopedia Britannica (Eds.), *Encyclopedia Britannica*. https://www.britannica.com/topic/Socratic-method

Lamain, C., Brugman, S., Boes, M., Schoevaars, C., Tetteroo, D., Veldhuizen, M. D., Wijnen, J. P., Lakens, D., Albronda, F., Hofmann, S., Knittel, S., & Duncan, J. (2024). Finding joy, creativity and meaning through unusual interdisciplinary collaborations. *Humanities & Social Sciences Communications, 11*(1), Article 1159. https://doi.org/10.1057/s41599-024-03634-w

Lawson, F. R. S. (2023). Why can't Siri sing? Cultural narratives that constrain female singing voices in AI. *Humanities & Social Sciences Communications, 10*(1), Article 287. https://doi.org/10.1057/s41599-023-01804-w

Leavy, P. (2015). *Method meets art: Arts-based research practice* (2nd ed.). Guilford Press.

Leavy, P. (2018). Fiction-based research. In P. Leavy (Ed.), *Handbook of arts-based research* (pp. 190–207). Guilford Press.

Madsen, A. (1979). *Hearts and minds: The common journey of Simone de Beauvoir and Jean-Paul Sartre*. Morrow Quill.

Mambrol, N. (2018, January 24). *Key theories of Mikhail Bakhtin*. Literary Theory and Criticism. https://literariness.org/2018/01/24/key-theories-of-mikhail-bakhtin/

Martins, A. (2023). Christian ethics and liberation from below: A way of doing theological ethics in Brazil. *Religions, 14*(6), Article 794. https://doi.org/10.3390/rel14060794

McDonough, R., & Harrison, R. (1978). Patriarchy and relations of production. In A. Kuhn & A. Wolpe (Eds.), *Feminism and materialism: Women and modes of production* (pp. 27–57). https://doi.org/10.4324/9780203094082-8

Mehta, R., & Henriksen, D. (2019). An embodied, dialogic endeavor: Towards a posthumanizing approach to creativity with Dr. Kerry Chappell. *TechTrends, 63*(1), 6–12. https://doi.org/10.1007/s11528-018-0357-7

Millington, R. (2022a). *Muse: Uncovering the hidden figures behind art history's masterpieces.* Penguin Books.
Millington, R. (2022b, December 15). *What is an artist-muse relationship really like?* Ruth Millington. https://ruthmillington.co.uk/what-is-an-artist-muse-relationship-really-like/
Moate, J., & Vass, E. (2023). Exploring dialogical spaces of discovery. *Dialogic Pedagogy,* *11*(1), A39–A59. https://doi.org/10.5195/dpj.2023.504
Muse. (2024, November 13). In The Editors of Encyclopedia Britannica (Eds.), *Encyclopedia Britannica.* https://www.britannica.com/topic/Muse-Greek-mythology
Parker, R, & Pollock, G. (1991). *Old mistresses: Women, art and ideology.* Pandora Press.
Pera, A. (2013). The role of social factors in the creative process. *Contemporary Readings in Law and Social Justice, 5*(2), 207–212.
Pound, C. (2019, June 7). Why Dora Maar is much more than Picasso's weeping woman. *BBC.* https://www.bbc.com/culture/article/20190607-why-dora-maar-is-much-more-than-picassos-weeping-woman
Richardson, J. (1991, 1996). *The life of Picasso* (Vols. 1–2). Random House.
Rieger, C. (2024). 'Frail warrior': Stevenson as manly invalid at Saranac Lake. *Humanities, 13*(4), Article 93. https://doi.org/10.3390/h13040093
Rovelli, C. (2021). *Helgoland: Making sense of the quantum revolution* (E. Segre & S. Carnell, Trans.). Riverhead Books. (Original work published 2020)
Runco, M. A. (2004). Creativity. *Annual Review of Psychology, 55,* 657–687. https://doi.org/10.1146/annurev.psych.55.090902.141502
Rusu, M. (2019). Methods of individual creativity stimulation. *Review of Artistic Education, 18*(1), 274–285. https://doi.org/10.2478/RAE-2019-0031
Scudeler, B. (2023). *The hyacinth girl: T. S. Eliot's hidden muse.* [Review of the book *The hyacinth girl: T. S. Eliot's hidden muse* by L. Gordon]. *Christianity & Literature, 72*(3), 517–520. https://doi.org/10.1353/chy.2023.a910045
Stark, R. (2023). Project Muse: Ernest Dowson and "the right type of girl". *Victorian Poetry, 61*(1), 97–128. https://doi.org/10.1353/vp.2023.a905523
van Laarhoven, J., & Claerhoudt, R. (2024). A new leaf: Is it time to de-objectify plants in private law? *Transnational Environmental Law, 13*(2), 286–311. https://doi.org/10.1017/S204710252400013X
Volpone, A. (2024). "From out the portals of my brain": William Blake's *partus mentis* and imaginative regeneration. *Humanities, 13*(4), Article 99. https://doi.org/10.3390/h13040099
Walker, D. B. (1992). *Mikhail Bakhtin: Creation of a prosaics* [Review of the book *Mikhail Bakhtin: Creation of a prosaics* by G. S. Morson & C. Emerson]. *Philosophy and Literature, 16*(1), 180–181. https://dx.doi.org10.1353/phl.1992.0074
Wendt, A. (2015). *Quantum mind and social science: Unifying physical and social ontology.* Cambridge University Press.
Xuan, J. (2023, March 15). *Unpacking the muse: Just an inspiration or something more?* Sunway Echo Media. https://sunwayechomedia.com/2023/03/15/unpacking-the-muse-just-an-inspiration-or-something-more/
Xuan, J., & Yi, Z. (2022, July 15). *What is the female gaze in media?* Sunway Echo Media. https://sunwayechomedia.com/2022/07/15/what-is-the-female-gaze-in-media/
Zahavi, D. (2019). *Phenomenology: The basics.* Routledge.

Chapter 11

Improv as Recentering Practice: Leveraging the Art of "Yes, And" for Leadership

Eve Ridgeway

Anglican Minister, UK

Abstract

This chapter explores how principles from theatrical improvisation can serve as recentering practices for leaders facing competing demands in today's complex organizational environments. Drawing primarily on the legacy of Viola Spolin, "the grandmother of improv," and structured approaches from the Upright Citizens Brigade, core improv concepts are explored including: establishing "base reality," practicing agreement through "yes, and," working "line by line," and skillful "framing." The concepts can help leaders reconnect with their purpose while fostering collaborative creativity. Improv-inspired leadership emphasizes deep listening, presence, and trust rather than control and manipulation, enabling people to share responsibility and develop intuition. By incorporating specific improv exercises and reflective practices, leaders can create environments where creativity flourishes without sacrificing structure or accountability. This approach to leadership recognizes that recentering is not merely an individual practice but a communal one rooted in mutual discovery, where the wisdom needed already exists within the group. By approaching leadership challenges with the playful exploration characteristic of improvisation, leaders can cultivate environments where creativity flourishes, novel solutions emerge organically, and people develop a deeper sense of shared purpose and responsibility.

Keywords: Improvisation; leadership; recentering; base reality; agreement; yes-and; line-by-line thinking; framing; play; reflective practice

Artful Leadership: Retreat, Recenter, and Rewild, 139–152
Copyright © 2026 by Eve Ridgeway
Published under exclusive licence by Emerald Publishing Limited
doi:10.1108/S2058-880120250000010012

Through spontaneity we are re-formed into ourselves. (Spolin, 1999, p. 4)

Introduction

Leaders today face competing demands: they must innovate while maintaining institutional boundaries all while fostering positive team environments. This balancing act can be exhausting. What leaders need are recentering practices that both stabilize their internal purpose and enhance their ability to promote creativity and teamwork where everyone takes responsibility for their work.

Theatrical improvisation (improv) offers valuable insights for leadership. Improv, appreciated as an entertainment art form in theatre, delights crowds by inviting them to watch and discover a story (or group of scenes) that seems so inevitable that performers could have written and rehearsed in advance, but in fact was made up on the spot. Improv performers play in front of an audience, seemingly having such a good time together, riffing, building on one another's ideas, that the audience member wishes they could also somehow be part of the group feeling this synergy and delight.

Improv, while being a constant source of creativity and originality, is rooted in core rules and values that require diligence, commitment, community, and long-term training. As a team-based art form, improv is intrinsically communal, formative, and culture-setting. Thus, there is much to be drawn from this art form for life, particularly leadership.

This chapter explores how the principles of improv can be applied to leadership, particularly for those focused on innovation, transformation, and community building. While existing literature often emphasizes improv's benefits for team building and problem-solving, this chapter will specifically examine how leaders can use improv techniques to create culture, influence values, and maintain focus on priorities.

Viola Spolin, a key figure of improv history, will be discussed to show how the origins of improv align with the heart and themes of this book (retreat, recenter, and rewild). It is worth noting that Spolin is but one figure within a growing, helpful corpus of material written on Improv including its importance to leadership (Harding, 2004; Keefe, 2003; Poynton, 2022). Existing material often focuses on the benefits of improv for team building and coming up with innovative solutions to problems.

Particularly, I reflect on the leaders' role as a creator of culture and values, and on their need to frequently *re-center* both themselves and their team/s keeping the main thing the main thing in whatever context they are leading. This role, alongside the expectation of innovation (often for the sake of financial profit), can be tiring and lonely. It is into this task that some of Improv's *rules* or maxims may prove especially valuable and received as a gift within an invitation to play, discover, and re-center, rather than grind and produce. Leaders will be given an opportunity to translate the maxims of improv into their own practice, with the encouragement to play and discover what might come next.

The Origins of Improv

Theatrical improv involves performers (sometimes a solo or duo) creating and performing unrehearsed scenes or games, often incorporating audience suggestions (such as a relationship between two people, a location, or an occupation). Audience suggestions offer a starting point for performers. While short-form improv features quick games (like *Whose Line Is It Anyway?*), long-form improv creates extended scenes without scripts (such as *Middleditch & Schwartz*, 2020). Lines or actions are "offers" from players to one another, received with agreement and built upon to create a whole performance. Sometimes long form proceeds without even an audience suggestion (Besser et al., 2022, p. 8).

As theatre improv has gained increasing popularity over the past few decades, literature on its origins has increased, including stimulating and accessible oral histories such as Jeffrey Sweet's (2023) *Something Wonderful Right Away* and Mark Larsons' (2019) *Ensemble: An Oral History of Chicago Theater*. The history of modern improv traces back to *The Compass* (established in Chicago in 1955) and its successor, *Second City* (established in 1959) as the beginnings of what would become a major theatrical movement (Sweet, 2023, p. xxx). These theatre companies were the result of years of existing artistic relationships, creative experimentation, and a seemingly serendipitous meeting of imaginative minds. Their histories are worth exploration, particularly for leaders, as they include creative people breaking the status quo, trying out new ideas (and sometimes "failing"), explorations in hierarchy specifically flattened, and finding ways to generate a huge amount of new material at a rapid pace.

The oral and written histories also acknowledge that there is further back to go; if not all the way back to commedia dell'arte in Renaissance Europe, then, certainly in recognizing the "grandparents" of theatre improv as Viola Spolin in the United States, and Keith Johnstone in the UK and Canada. Both figures would be suitable to explore in this chapter; however, for the sake of space and focus, Spolin will be spotlighted because she is most linked to the Chicago theatre scene.

Viola Spolin: The Grandmother of Improv

The foundations of improv owe much to Viola Spolin, the mother of Paul Sills (one of the founders of *The Compass*), who trained as a recreational director at Hull House in Chicago during the mid-1920s under sociologist Neva Boyd. According to Sweet (2023), Boyd recognized the constructive potential of play, using traditional games to help immigrant children adjust to American society. As Sweet outlined:

> At the heart of Boyd's work was an awareness of the constructive potential of play. Boyd led inner-city and immigrant's children in traditional games to help them adjust to the new society in which they lived. Spolin's contribution was to create new games designed to create creativity, making play the catalyst for self-expression and self-realization ... [the games] were a means of dealing with theater problems in a playful spirit. (p. xvi)

Spolin found that games which had "rules" to play were more fruitful in encouraging children to act and lose their inhibitions than were prescriptive and propositional directions. Spolin (1999) pondered: "What happens if you all get on one side of the boat? It tips over" (p. 4). Spolin used this pondering to help children understand what it was to use the whole of the stage and not *bunch up* at one end.

Spolin's (1999) core text *Improvisation for the Theater*, which includes hundreds of theatre games and the play theory behind them, is not a narrative or textbook so much as a compendium of improv games and pedagogical wisdom. Spolin was adamant that her work was "not predicated on improvisational theatre" and it was only later on that she realized she had created theater games (Sweet, 2023, p. 5). Rather, her work, in collaboration with Boyd, was rooted in efforts to cultivate human flourishing through creative and resourceful pedagogy: "My years of working with the games have shown that this living, organic, non-authoritarian climate can inform the learning process and, in fact, is the only way in which artistic and intuitive freedom can grow" (Spolin, 1999, p. 3).

Spolin's work is integral not only to understanding and appreciating the improv movement that was birthed from it, but also in application, making holistic connections between improv and recentering leadership. Her approach emphasized several key values that align with recentering leadership:

- Valuing people as complete human beings.
- Using play to release creativity and spontaneity.
- Building group dynamics that foster collaboration.
- Understanding that we are all constantly improvising, even within structured plans.

Spolin (1999) herself, while supportive of her son's later efforts, was skeptical of improv as a system of training and end in itself, as it led to spontaneity being destroyed and "cleverness" fostered: "it is the enriching, restructuring and integration of [improvised] … daily life responses for use in the art form that makes up the training of the actor for scene improvisation and formal theatre" (p. 44). Spolin recognized that we are all improvising, all the time, even within our efforts to plan and prepare.

Spolin (1999) advocated games as a pedagogical device, but believed in the games as an end, not just the means to, learning. She emphasized the importance of group response in which players understand themselves as fellow peers, part of an organic whole, building trust and teamwork. She also highlighted the need for players to develop intuition through getting out of their head and into space, the actual space of the stage, of engaging with others in action (Spolin, 1999, p. iii).

Spolin's values should not be set aside when translating improv's gems into leadership and recentering practices, even if more formal training techniques are utilized. The value of people as human persons, the gift of play to release creativity and spontaneity, the adhesiveness of group dynamic in improvisation all speak to the idea of recentering. Recentering in leadership should not be a selfish endeavor at the expense of people's human dignity. Selfish endeavors, while possible, would deny the underlying values of improv and its founders.

Leadership and Improv Theater

"When it bogs down, play a game" (Spolin, 1999, p. xiii).

From the outside looking in, improv may appear to have little to say to the area of leadership, because the dynamic on stage is of a group, performers of equal status where roles such as leader are not clearly defined for the audience. However, having experience in leading an organization and in performing and practicing improv, I find many connections, with improv enabling a refinement of my definition and goals of leadership.

In improv, the director/coach role involves being a trustworthy guide experienced in the discipline of improv, teaching, and reminding the group of the rules and maxims that they are agreeing to operate within (whilst also being a player), which allows maximizes creative freedom for the whole group.

Each player carries responsibility for themselves and others, bringing focus, attention, and listening to the performance. Players will also play characters in scenes with varying status with players needing to agree with the scene's base reality (described later) allowing the flow of creativity.

In Spolin's legacy we receive the gift of play as relevant to leadership – if one is trying to build collaboration, unity, or flourishing, play is infinitely more powerful than directives. Leadership in improv mode involves being a trustworthy guide guiding people toward a common goal, centered around values (of the leader or of the organization). While there may be more concrete goals in an organization or business (e.g. profit, sales, recruitment, impact), the way to achieve these goals may be flexible, and up to the leader to determine or guide.

Leaders need not fear play as being frivolous or leading to anarchy. Play is purposeful involving deliberate enabling, creating and holding space, rules for engagement, and exploration without fear of failure. A centered leader enables people to work together toward a common goal, sharing responsibility, and feeling a sense of common purpose. Leaders aid in knowing what to do next, or what is to come, by discovery rather than repeating information or script by rote (cf. Meek, 2014 for additional thoughts on knowledge as discovery). Leaders drawing from improv seek to build a culture of collaboration over control, offer guiding maxims over micromanaging, and encourage corporate intuition over blind obedience.

Improv is rooted in the understanding that individuals are constituted through relationships with others. As Paul Sills (son of Viola Spolin) noted, drawing on philosopher Martin Buber: "You can only know you exist in an area of mutuality... A lot of people think they come out of their own heads, that they're self-created. It's not true" (as cited in Sweet, 2023, p. 25). We are aware of ourselves in the presence of others. Security in oneself comes from trust in others to pull their weight in the scene, and a release from the fear of failing, as there is no set end that must be achieved or that the scene can be judged upon.

Centered leaders recognize they are both self-aware and others-aware, building groups that share this understanding. Having a goal of profit (or something other than social justice or having communal flourishing as a goal) does not automatically exclude having an understanding of people as valuable and worthy of investment. Additionally, it is worth noting that improv has not always maintained the values of equality and diversity in its professional forms (Larson, 2019; Seham, 2001). This recognition challenges us to implement improv principles in leadership with intentional inclusivity, ensuring that our recentering practices don't perpetuate existing power imbalances but instead create truly collaborative spaces where diverse voices can contribute to organizational innovation.

Rules of Improv as Tools for Recentering

The Upright Citizens Brigade (UCB), created in Chicago in the 1990s and then reestablished in New York, developed an improv stream that is fairly structured in its training approach, and thus lends itself to application in other disciplines. The UCB's structured approach to improv training, describes an improv scene as establishing a *base reality* using agreement and *yes, and*, identifying an *unusual thing*, and then exploring this element as the *game* of the scene. This anatomy does not need to be fully grasped and inhabited as an experienced improviser in order to benefit from exploring these ideas in the realm of recentering leadership, although understanding the grammar of improv contributes to an increased appreciation for comedy since this grammar is found in sketch comedy and sitcoms as well as improv. The *unusual thing* applied to leadership might be the unique selling point of an organization representing an innovation sought within an existing discipline or product space, or the fresh center from which to expand.

The UCB's school or rules are not designed to restrict or disempower, but to enable a group of people to collaborate, agree, and create together on the spot, using "a clear set of guidelines that everyone has practiced" (Besser et al., 2022, p. 7). In exploring these maxims and rules, I focus on those particularly helpful in recentering, which align with what improvisers are doing at the start of a scene.

Base Reality

The UCB coined the term *base reality* to describe "the world of the scene. It's the who-what-where, the general situation, the context, the what's-going-on" (Besser et al., 2022, p. 13). As two or more players begin a scene, they initiate and respond with who they are in the scene, where they are, and what they're doing. This establishing of the scene, this base reality, should be truthful to the reality of the scene (even if it's an imagined or fantastical reality).

At the outset, the players are not performing for laughs, but building a reality within which unusual, funny, new things may occur. When done well, this base reality is simply accepted by the audience, where we step into the world created. Seasoned improvisers build this base reality by way of agreement, listening to what is contributed by other players and building upon it. It may seem counterintuitive to talk about a laugh-less, truthful scene in the context of improv where spontaneity and creativity is the goal, but UCB noted that it is only in the normative base reality that the "first unusual thing" is identified (Besser et al., 2022, p. 13).

Base reality is a helpful term or practice for recentering leadership, as it gives language to the reality or center that a leader is recentering around. If a leader feels disconnected, depleted, and disillusioned, then recentering involves a returning or reorienting around a center or source that brings connection, energy, and vision. Recentering involves returning to the initial purpose or calling that brought a person into leadership, or reconnecting with their organization's core values. The center for many leaders might be a sense of initial purpose or calling that brought them into their arena of leadership, or the goals or values that their organization centers around. There may be a vision statement or set of values that exist but no longer serve their purpose or have been forgotten. It is only in recognizing *what is* that leaders can then notice or discover what a new or innovative idea or goal might be, or if in fact, the fit-for-purpose center has been lost and needs to be regained, over and above pioneering new things.

Simple questions (which can be adapted for groups) exploring who I am, why I'm here, and what I'm about help leaders remember and recenter around their base reality. These questions are resonant of the who-what-where questions that when answered by improvisers, form a base reality. Base reality also recognizes the need for deep listening and agreement in establishing the context for new ideas and innovation. If in recentering, a leader discovers a deep lack of agreement in an organizational base reality, they may have to go further back and re-establish this from scratch, asking the same questions but in a generative form.

Agreement (Yes-And)

In improv, yes, and means building upon what others contribute to establish the scene. For improvisers to build a base reality in a scene, there needs to be agreement, or the practice of yes, and, in establishing the who, what and where and building upon the initiation, line by line. For example, if Player one initiates the character of a mother addressing a child, situated in a kitchen, then Player two can *agree* by taking the role of a child, acknowledge the kitchen surroundings and *add* more by clarifying if they are the son or the daughter.

Agreement doesn't mean characters must get along or agree within everything each person says. For example, in the dialogue, the players may have an argument. They can argue within a scene, but players need to seek to agreement with the situation and reality they are building together. Agreement means agreeing with the previous line of dialogue or action as a building block of the truth of the scene, and its opposite is blocking or denial.

In leadership contexts, agreement means developing an organizational culture where people trust each other and align around common purposes. Within the spirit of good-willed trust and agreement, there is clarity about roles and responsibilities while encouraging collaboration for creativity and innovation. This does not mean that people agree on every idea, suggestion, or method put forward in a group. Disagreements about specific ideas don't necessarily indicate a lack of commitment to shared goals. Instead, players practice deep listening within a commitment to build on ideas, especially ideas built around the centering base reality of the group.

A tired or de-centered leader may feel dismayed or irritated by an apparent lack of agreement, if a person disagrees with or pushes back on an idea or directive, a leader may receive the disagreement as a lack of trust and respect. But a disagreement (i.e. difference of opinion) in and of itself does not necessarily mean there is a lack of overall agreement by that person in what you are corporately trying to achieve together, or a lack of respect for the roles others have in an organization. Discernment and practice are needed in this area, and as it takes time for novice improvisers to learn agreement, it takes time for leaders and teams to grow in agreement.

Line by Line

A substantive part of learning agreement for improvisers is to learn to improvise line by line. That is, to build on the last thing spoken or acted (the *offer*), and offer the next line or action in keeping with the growing base reality. Experienced improvisers build scenes line by line, responding to each offer without trying to control the overall direction. This requires presence, trust, deep listening, and resisting the urge to *write ahead* or manipulate outcomes. For example, while listening to others, you focus on what you want to say in response, versus listening attentively.

Not writing ahead may sound obvious but when a person begins to improvise, it is surprising to learn how conditioned a person is to think ahead, write ahead, to imagine or plan in our minds what *we* think should happen in a scene, and therefore try to manipulate the scene in that (our) direction. We are used to narrative, to scripts, to wanting control over the situation, and the desire to get it right. Instead, improv is an act of being present in the moment, slowing down, and trusting your scene partner (regardless of how fast the dialogue or action is performed on stage). Listening, waiting, and responding one line at a time, without presuming what the other will say or do, but instead, attending to the person and responding in a way that makes sense of their offer. This practice also includes offering silence, or simply mirroring action.

Watching veteran improvisers such as T. J. Jagadowski and Dave Pasquesi perform is a masterclass of nonanxious, line-by-line improv rooted in deep listening and trust (Jagodowski & Pasquesi, 2024; Jagodowski et al., 2015). Improvisers find huge freedom in responding line by line, being released from the lonely responsibility to get it right, instead, being in a fully collaborative partnership where the goal is to make the other player look good, to serve the whole scene, discover together, then end the scene in a way that will, in the end, feel inevitable and right.

If one is serving the scene, the characters, and the setting, then one is free to respond in the way that is in keeping with that character in that situation at that time, to be *obvious*. Theologian Sam Wells (2018), drawing on theater improv within Christian theological ethics, said "Experienced improvisers know that if they have attained a state of relaxed awareness, they can trust themselves to be obvious" (p. 61). Wells drew from Johnstone's seminal work in which Johnstone (2018) challenged the concept of originality:

The improviser has to realise that the more obvious he is, the more original he appears… . People trying to be original always arrive at the same boring old answers. Ask people to give you an original idea and see the chaos it throws them into. If they said the first thing that came into their head, there'd be no problem. (p. 79)

Likewise, Spolin (1999) recognized the need for "players to get out of their head" and be present in the space [scene] they find themselves in, within which "the playing (energy exchange) takes place between players" (p. liii).

For leaders facilitating creative discussions, line by line means creating spaces where team members aren't bound by past scripts or fear of being wrong. It might involve structured conversations where people build on each other's ideas sequentially, trusting that solutions will emerge from collective wisdom rather than individual brilliance.

It is more than a leader's contrived attempts at allowing everyone an opportunity to speak in a meeting for the sake of fairness (although this might need to be a consideration), it is creating spaces where people are not bound by the past scripts, fear of getting it wrong, or being in competition with others.

A group operating line by line might look like a leader setting the scene at the beginning of a meeting (i.e., the issue, problem, opportunity), then, enabling a slow, thoughtful improv conversation in which people are invited to go around the table, offering one line of thought at a time, where the next person can only build on the idea or offer of the last, until a possible conclusion is reached. The building blocks of offers might initially feel obvious or simple, but this is the point, to not rush ahead and assume you know the outcome, but assume that the answer may be in the room, in the wisdom of people within the group, available only through this trusting conversation.

This could be repeated with different starting offers or centers, so that a variety of possibilities are explored. These sorts of meetings and discussions could happen regularly, so that intuition and wisdom grow as a result of this practice. There are also simple games and exercises that can be offered as a way to inhabit what it really means to go line by line, as a general approach in human interactions as well as in an organizational setting. This way of leading builds trust through real, deep listening, widens imagination, and can also bring humor and laughter into a team.

Leaders can also practice going "line-by-line" themselves, even if the other person in a conversation is not aware of it! Going line by line can greatly help a leader entering a highly anxious or emotionally charged interaction. Line by line could also be described as listening to understand, as described by medic and author Kathryn Mannix (2022):

Listen fully, and don't be distracted by wondering what to say next, how to sort this out, or any of the other thoughts that jump into your mind. Ignore your inclination to work out something consoling to say. Just listen. Trust yourself; just like feet move in rhythm to unfamiliar music, when it is time to speak words will come to you. (p. 32)

Framing

In UCB-style improv, *framing* means highlighting something unusual within the scene's base reality, essentially saying *this is interesting, let's explore it* without breaking character. Players practice this by repeating and emphasizing noteworthy details.

In long-form improv, players establish the base reality of a scene and then discover the *game* of the scene (particularly in UCB style improv – not all schools have this approach). The game is the heightening and exploring of the unusual funny thing that happens in contrast to the base reality of the scene. While we will not go further into game here, it is worth offering another technique that improvisers can learn and use to improvise line by line, to make their scene partner look good, and work together to build a great scene.

Framing means "letting your scene partner know that you feel they have said or done something unusual within the context of the base reality" (Besser et al., 2022, p. 76); it is the player expressing *oh, that's interesting, this might be the game!'* but as the character in the scene. This may look like a player's character simply reacting to the other (e.g., What?), or responding in such a way that makes clear the player is emphasizing a particular aspect or specific of the scene that could be expanded upon.

In improv training, framing can be learned and practiced by playing many different scenes through, and each time a perceived first unusual thing happens, the players repeat back and forth the line or specific detail (in their characters' dialogue) to name and frame it clearly for both players (Besser et al., 2022, pp. 98–99). Notice how improv, lauded for its spontaneity and originality, is rooted in muscle and mind memory, in *reps* and rehearsal of the communal rules for the sake of corporate freedom and collaboration in performance.

For leaders, framing helps in communication and negotiation. Centered leaders don't need constant novelty; they can draw on existing vision and values to contextualize various situations. Framing involves helping others understand parameters and clarifying what's being discussed without being restrictive or controlling. Wise and centered leaders find they do not need to have something new to say all the time, but can draw on the ideas and contributions of others, or on their existing vision and values to frame the various circumstances they find themselves in.

Leaders are often also responsible for framing or re-framing for others, as well as themselves, helping others know the parameters of the current task or project, or what is actually being said in a conversation, for example. Framing does not necessarily mean being restrictive or dictatorial, and if done through deep listening, framing will relate to the base reality and be for the good of the whole rather than the leader's preference or manipulation.

While Spolin (1999) advocated for a "side-coaching" approaching to direction and leadership, she also acknowledged the role of the side coach in maintaining the integrity of the activity and its values for the group: "a firm hand must be used, not to attack or impose one's will, but to maintain the integrity of the art form" (p. 25). There is a role for the leader in maintaining the integrity of whatever activity they are leading, and teaching and training in these adapted improv practices can aid the leader in this endeavor.

Creative and Reflection Practices

While UCB has distilled their practice into a helpful "anatomy of an improv scene," they emphasize that improv (like leadership!) cannot simply be learned by reading a book. The practices and rules must be put into practice, with others, over many, many "reps" (Besser et al., 2022, p. 8).

While improvisation omits rehearsal as such, "all good improvisers invest a lot of time doing exercises, practices, and shows so that they're comfortable with anything that comes their way" (Besser et al., 2022, p. 8). There are many resources for using improv games in settings outside the theatre. Two very simple improv games are offered here, as a starting point for play and recentering, but exploring further resources is highly recommended (cf. Poynton, 2022).

Creative Practices

One Word Story

Two or more participants build a story one word at a time, with each person contributing a single word in sequence. This teaches collaborative thinking and helps teams practice building ideas incrementally. The first person gives the first word of a story, the second person the next, and so on. Sentences are closed and begun by players intonation and physical gestures, that is, someone demonstrates they mean to end a sentence with a small nod of the head.

If people find it difficult to begin, using *Once upon a time* can help get people started, one word at a time. The story will usually find a natural ending, or the side coach can invite the group to "find an ending." While this sounds simple, it often takes people a little while for people to stop saying more than one word at a time, or feeling worried or frustrated at how the story should go. This game is a good ice breaker or starting point if a leader is looking to develop their team in thinking "line by line" together. It also provides low stakes, and a fun way of "shaking off" any embarrassment or awkwardness.

Presents

Presents or Gifts is a well-known game, outlined clearly by Robert Poynton (2022) in his short accessible volume *Do Improvise* (p. 33).

- Played in pairs, this game involves player one miming picking up a present, and offering it to player two with "I bought you a present."
- Player one indicates the size and weight of the gift by their gestures, but they do not define what the gift is.
- Player two then receives the gift, as given (i.e. the gestured weight and size – this in itself is practicing agreement), mimes unwrapping the gift and then thanks Player one while naming the gift, for example, *Thank you, it's a football*. The thanks and naming should also agree with the gestures of Player one – *obvious is good*.

While this may seem like a simple exercise (or in fact quite intimidating to many, who think it requires "acting"!) it takes time for pairs to build up trust that they are working together, before joy and laughter begin to emerge as players truly begin to play.

There are variations to this game (i.e., playing with the expectations of size and shape of gift and what the next player names it as), but the basic form teaches agreement, trust, and helps people get into their body, and out of their heads.

Reflective Practices

Just Listen

This listening exercise is structured as a personal listening development exercise. Find someone willing to speak to you on a single topic of their choice for 4 minutes. Example conversation starters follow or your volunteer can use their own!

- Describe your idea of a perfect weekend.
- Describe a person who had the biggest impact on who you've become.
- Describe your bucket list or things you want to accomplish before you die.
- Describe a book that's had an impact on your life.

While the person is talking for 4 minutes, simply listen in order to understand what they're saying. You are not allowed to say anything while they're talking – no comments, no questions. Eye contact and nodding are okay to show that you are paying attention to them. Just listen in silence and try to understand the speaker.

At the end of 4 minutes, you may speak. Paraphrase in your own words the main points that you think you heard the person say – they should remain quiet while you're paraphrasing. Use paraphrasing lead-ins such as *I think I heard you say* or *it sounds like*. Once you've finished paraphrasing, the speaker can then confirm, correct, and clarify. And you may ask follow-up questions if desired.

Debrief the experience by discussing with the speaker the following:
Speaker observations:

- What did it feel like to have your full attention?
- What did it feel like to have the freedom to speak without interruption?
- What did you observe while speaking?

Listener observations:

- Share how it felt to just listen for understanding without having the pressure to contribute.
- Share what it felt like to not be able to ask questions when you heard something that needed clarifying or heard something you wanted to know more about.
  - Discuss what happened to your internal dialogue.
  - Did you actually need to plan your response? Why? Why not?
  - Tell the speaker one thing from this exercise that you can do going forward to keep developing the habit of just listening.

Reflective Questions for a Leader

Am I aware of my base reality? (Who am I? What am I here for? What is my purpose?)

As a leader, do I instinctively seek to side-coach, or to correct and micro manage?

Am I able to discern and frame situations accurately for myself and others?

Do I feel able to play in my work/leadership, or am I concerned with "getting it right?"

Summary

The principles of theatrical improv offer valuable resources for recentering leadership. In this chapter, we have mined the riches of theatre improv (really only scratching the surface) for recentering leadership. The origins of improv provide resonance with the aims and values of many leaders today, to build teams and organizations that work together in trust, valuing the gifts of individuals while contributing to a whole, and seek to release creativity and innovation. The teaching and training of improv schools reminds leaders that healthy cultures require rules and maxims (values) guided by side-coaches who can establish and maintain a base reality, lead "line by line" and frame emerging issues and opportunities for their teams.

Improv also reminds leaders that we ourselves are also players and learners; while we hold significant responsibility, it is not all "on us" to deliver a solo performance, rather to listen, offer, and respond in "obvious" ways, being open to new and exciting outcomes.

References

Besser, M., Roberts, I., & Walsh, M. (2022). *Upright Citizens Brigade comedy improvisation manual* (2nd ed.). Upright Citizens Brigade Theater.
Harding, C. (2004). Improvisation and negotiation: Making it up as you go along. *Negotiation Journal, 20*(2), 205–212. https://doi.org/10.1111/j.1571-9979.2004.00017.x
Jagodowski, T. J., & Pasquesi, D. (2024). *TJ & Dave, theatre performance, August 27–31, 2024*. Soho Theater, Barrow Street Theatricals. https://sohotheatre.com/events/tj-
Jagodowski, T. J., Pasquesi, D., Victor, P., & Sedaris, A. (2015). *Improvisation at the speed of life: The TJ and Dave book*. Solo Roma, Inc.
Johnstone, K. (2018). *Impro: Improvisation and the theatre*. Bloomsbury Academic.
Keefe, J. A. (2003). *Improv yourself: Business spontaneity at the speed of thought*. John Wiley & Sons.
Larson, M. (2019). *Ensemble: An oral history of Chicago theater*. Agate Midway.
Mannix, K. (2022). *Listen: How to find the words for tender conversations*. William Collins.
Meek, E. L. (2014). *A little manual for knowing*. Cascade Books.
Middleditch, T., & Schwartz, B. (Creators). (2020). *Middleditch & Schwartz* [TV series]. Netflix.
Poynton, R. (2022). *Do improvise: Less push. More pause. Better results: A new approach to work (and life)*. Do Book Co.
Seham, A. E. (2001). *Whose improv is it anyway?* Beyond Second City. University Press of Mississippi.

Spolin, V. (1999). *Improvisation for the theater: A handbook of teaching and directing techniques* (P. Sills, Ed., 3rd ed.). Northwestern University Press.

Sweet, J. (2023). *Something wonderful right away: The birth of Second City—America's greatest comedy theater* (2nd ed.). Allworth Press.

Wells, S. (2018). *Improvisation: The drama of Christian ethics* (Repackaged edition). Baker Academic.

Chapter 12

Courage in Motion: Changemaking Through Art

Tracy Ferron

Life On Art, USA

Abstract

This chapter explores rewilding as a transformative approach to leadership that integrates personal healing, creative expression, and collective liberation. Through personal narrative, a leader's journey is traced from childhood trauma and familial mental illness to midlife awakening and artistic emergence. Central to this transformation is the symbolic figure of the "Walled Woman" – a dream image that became personal metaphor and collective archetype, representing the imprisonment and potential liberation of the divine feminine. This illuminates how depth psychological practices, including dreamwork, active imagination, and creative expression, facilitated the author's healing process and creative development. This personal metamorphosis eventually led to the founding of Life On Art, a nonprofit organization that develops large-scale community art projects like Unbound, which united psychiatric patients, hospital staff, and community volunteers in creating an 80-ft sculpture featuring 800 winged hearts. Through exploring connections between individual trauma recovery, depth practices, and social activism, the chapter demonstrates how leaders can cultivate resilience, creativity, and systemic awareness – fostering a leadership paradigm that embraces vulnerability, imagination, and radical inclusion to address complex social challenges.

Keywords: Rewilding, depth psychology; artistic activism; community-participated art; feminine consciousness; dreamwork; active imagination; collective healing; participatory art

Artful Leadership: Retreat, Recenter, and Rewild, 153–171
Copyright © 2026 by Tracy Ferron
Published under exclusive licence by Emerald Publishing Limited
doi:10.1108/S2058-880120250000010013

Introduction

It is two months since Donald J. Trump took the helm of the US Government for the second time and, like millions of Americans, I wake feeling trapped in a collective nightmare of societal destruction and authoritarian cruelty. In the last months, many have been shocked out of their disconnection and complacency. How can we find the compass to a new collective story while under constant siege?

We cannot effectively respond to authoritarianism if bound by personal trauma and operating from fear. We need to be resilient, fully alive, connective participants in civic life with tools and leaders to guide us. We need new stories, symbols, and ways of visualizing a more just and compassionate society. Our time calls for leaders who invite the unknown, embrace uncertainty, while dancing on the edge of consensus reality. Artists inhabit *non-rational spaces* outside of time, giving voice to the emergent through symbols and metaphors. In times of societal upheaval, artists are uniquely positioned to forge pathways to meaningful change.

This chapter explores rewilding as a transformative approach to leadership that integrates personal healing, creative expression, and collective liberation demonstrating how leaders can cultivate resilience, creativity, and systemic awareness through self-discovery, artistic engagement, and radical compassion.

Personal Foundations: From Trauma to Empowerment

My path into art and change-making began in mid-life. In my search for self through depth psychological practices and artmaking, I forged a new story by retrieving parts lost to childhood trauma, developing trust, and surrendering to improvisatory conscious and unconscious practices.

Childhood

I grew up filled with terror and isolation in a family besieged by mental illness. My two much older brothers were severely mentally ill – both of them delusional and one violent with paranoid schizophrenia. My mother struggled with depression and never connected emotionally with me. In my home, there was a constant sense of despair, heartbreak, and often pure fear. Connected to nature and writing stories from dreams. I found inventive ways to make my life not only tolerable but wondrous.

When I was 14, I had a nightmare of a child being kidnapped, dismembered with their head and heart put in a box. I wrote this into a story and, to my horror, my ninth-grade teacher read it to the class. Soon after, my brother, Bob, came to live in our basement. I knew he had committed violent crimes, including murder, when delusional. When he began acting erratically, I remember crawling under my parents' bed, praying I wouldn't be found. No one would help – the police would not do anything until he committed a crime. He finally did. Bob killed a neighborhood dog and dismembered it, putting the parts around our property. My parents and I were shocked and sadly understood that, in the depth of my brother's delusion, it could easily have been me instead of the dog.

After the incident was reported in our small-town newspaper, all eyes were on our family and me, or so I felt. My quirky imagination and inspiration became suspect. The boundaries between creativity and madness seemed porous and I began to view my imagination as dangerous. Unconsciously, to feel safe, I cut myself off from my wild flow of creativity, which had been my lifeline and source of delight and hope. I exiled my artist self for over 30 years.

Marriage and Family

It was a dream of mine to create a fun and connected family. I felt blessed to meet my husband in London, become a step-mom to his two children, and have three of our own. However, my husband's corporate job took a toll on our family. He was barely a participant, short-tempered, stressed, and rarely present.

In an attempt to save our marriage, he left his job, and we moved to California, but his behaviors worsened. He refused to seek help, I felt very confused and abandoned and was preparing to leave when he was diagnosed with stage-4 cancer. I wasn't going anywhere and felt trapped and sinking.

What we later learned was that this disconnection was largely caused by undiagnosed autism spectrum disorder (formerly called Aspergers), which presented as hyperfixation on work, difficulty with changes in routine, anxiety, and a very different way of processing the world.

I felt isolated, hopeless, and ashamed – similar to my childhood emotional environment. I desperately needed a rewilding, a connection to my true self: a new story, orientation, and remembering. When my therapist suggested a program in depth psychology and creativity, I jumped at this lifeline.

> The trees you planted in childhood have grown too heavy. You cannot bring them along. Give yourselves to the air, to what you cannot hold. (Rilke, 2019)

Transformative Space, Cohort, and Learning Approach

When in between stories, one is like a flying trapeze artist who must have the courage and trust to release one bar to reach for the next. Pacifica Graduate Institute's graduate program in *Humanities and the Creative Life with an emphasis on Depth Psychology* provided conditions for me to develop this courage: a supportive cohort of fellow seekers and professors, the nourishing study of depth psychology, and tools to explore the self by dancing with the unconscious safely.

A depth psychological approach offers a different way of being in the world, one guided by the right brain, cooperation, improvisation, surrender, wonder, patience, interconnectivity, synchronicity, and flow. While I chose this program to ignite my creativity, opening up to the pure flow of imagination and its expansive, irrational, and chaotic energies was terrifying, given my two brothers' mental illnesses. Joseph Campbell (as cited in Grof, 2000) famously said, "The [schizophrenic] drowns in the very same waters in which the mystic swims with delight." My deep need for creativity and my fear of it became the Gordian knot to unravel.

Depth Psychological Practices

Depth psychology offers frameworks to examine individual experiences in the context of all of human history through exploration of the collective unconscious and archetypes. Depth psychological practices elicit an engagement of the unconscious through explorations in dreams, myth, history, and art. These practices cultivate a *mythopoetic* orientation to the world, an approach infused with wonder, inspiration, synchronicity, interconnectedness, and deeper meaning.

As I moved through the Pacifica program, all my classes and projects took me deeper into hidden truths, as I realized there were many repressed memories, things I simply did not remember about childhood. I gradually faced and integrated trauma due to three supports: the wonder of my newly unleashed imagination, an encouraging community where I could share my individual self and be seen and the healing power of artmaking. Depth psychologists say that one of the most powerful things you can do is to locate yourself symbolically, identifying your central metaphor.

Dreamwork – The Walled Woman: A Metaphorical Journey of Liberation

A profound dream featuring a *Walled Woman* became a transformative symbol, representing systemic constraints and the potential for liberation. This metaphor evolved from personal imprisonment to a collective narrative of resilience and empowerment.

In 2016, a few months before Trump was first elected, I had what Carl Jung (2010) would call a big dream. Jung said that a big dream demands expression from the individual because the dream comes from beyond the personal sphere (pp. 77–78). Let me take you into it:

> I am standing in front of a vast, grey stone castle, which is covered in rust spots. A man is making his young son powerwash these spots but it is not working. The son refuses to continue so the father proclaims, *"There must be a sacrifice."* And suddenly we are in the basement of the castle, where the father has created a small theater set, with candles and photos on an antique dresser. A young naive woman comes in, expecting to audition. But she is the sacrifice. She is murdered and plastered into the basement wall of the castle. I can see the scattered outline of her broken body under the brick and plaster, her limbs askew like a Picasso painting. The only thing exposed is her right eye. Now I am in front of her, I am the murderer and the woman is emerging from the wall. I pull off her eye and begin stabbing her in the chest but she is unstoppable. She is coming out from the wall.

I woke up with my heart pounding but deeply happy that this walled woman was still alive. Dr Stephen Aizenstat (2017, personal communication), founding president of Pacifica Graduate Institute, said that a dream is "a letter from deep psyche, which if opened allows us to read into what is in fact our true nature and true direction." What a letter I was sent!! Through the dream, I saw clearly my stuckness and desire to emerge. Only later, I realized how childhood trauma bound me in ways I couldn't rationally access.

Dr Ginette Paris (2011) claimed that to move intractable trauma you first need to locate yourself, find your symbolic orientation, a "pin in the map" of your true state of being (p. 80). Art therapist, Dr Sally Adnams-Jones (2018) referred to this as a central metaphor (p. 43). This big dream offered this unconscious symbol that became a beacon. I was struck by this horrific image of a woman sacrificed and immured into a wall. Captivated, I began a quest to discover this walled woman: who she was, why she came, what she would teach me, and how I could free her. Finding the Walled Woman (as I affectionately call her) and freeing her was my path to liberation.

Furthermore, the *Walled Woman* appeared just before Donald Trump won the 2016 election, when women and walls would attain cultural importance. I feel she brought a message for the collective, sounding a call to activate feminine energy and examine the concept of sacrifice. It was a call to tend to our personal and societal traumas and shift our paradigm from fear and hierarchy to love, interconnection, and interdependence.

Amplifying the Dream's Symbols

Amplification explores dream images to understand symbols, myths, stories, and collective wisdoms. This research involved three key practices: (a) researching global historical and mythological contexts, (b) engaging in active imagination techniques, and (c) exploring the symbol through diverse artistic expressions. These methods revealed complex narratives of women's sacrifice, resistance, and spiritual power, providing a broader understanding of personal struggles within larger social dynamics.

Historical Context of Female Sacrifice and Immurement

Researching this obscure symbol, I found a provocative history of female sacrifice and punishment with women being built into walls or entombed in small spaces with no exit. This is called *immurement* and fell into two main categories:

1. The sacred feminine making a sacrifice to support the collective.
2. Rebel women who challenged social norms and were punished.

Global Perspectives on Foundation Sacrifice

According to religious scholar Mircea Eliade, foundation or construction sacrifice was practiced around the world, dating back to pre-historic times (as cited in Dundes, 1996). It was believed that these sacrifices would:

- Placate earth spirits.
- Transfer the woman's soul to become the structure's guardian spirit, or what Eliade (as cited in Dundes, 1966) termed an "architectonic body."

Folklorist Alan Dundes (1996) traced over 700 variants of an Indo-European folk ballad "The Walled in Wife" over 1,000 years. The ballad was typically sung by female choruses that Dundes interpreted as a symbolic metaphor for the women's sacrifices expected in marriage. The central motif focuses on building the living wife of a mason into a structure's foundation to withstand supernatural forces trying to destroy it. The Japanese created *hitobashira* (i.e., human pillars), where women were sacrificed into temple pillars as early as the 16th century. These examples show an immobilized woman as the cornerstone of culture, her innate spiritual power being the foundation.

Anchoresses: Voluntary Spiritual Immurement, Direct Relation to God

My research revealed a more empowering model of immurement in female spiritual practice: the medieval and early modern Anchoresses, known as Emparidades in Spain. These were not traditional nuns bound by conventional church hierarchies. Instead, they made a radical choice, voluntarily enclosing themselves within small cells along churches' outer walls to dedicate themselves to prayer and to counsel the community. By sacrificing their lives in the world, anchoresses were thought to be bringing life to and purifying their towns. Many often nurtured a distinctive feminine version of God with their mysticism emphasizing a direct connection to God, something that was deeply threatening to the Church's hierarchy. Their small space was often referred to as a tomb but also as a return to the womb, indicating the paradoxical liminal space held by these women in the cycle of death and rebirth in their communities.

Profound Symbolism of Sacrifice

My research into and journey with the Walled Woman was a complex emotional terrain, simultaneously revealing:

- A sense of empowerment through the divine feminine.
- Deep rage at the systemic oppression of women.
- A profound confrontation with the nature of personal and collective sacrifice.

A Pivotal Moment of Revelation

In the dream, the murderer declared: "There must be a sacrifice." This transformative statement unveiled fundamental truths about human experience. Amplification revealed how *sacrifice* stands at the core of human experience. To truly live, we must be in a state of growth, which always requires sacrifice. This journey through history and myth underlines the necessity of closely examining what or who we sacrifice, both personally and as a society. Do we make these choices consciously or unconsciously?

To move forward, it became necessary to reflect on what must be released. The journey with the Walled Woman highlighted the intimate connection between personal and collective experiences. The dream offered an opportunity to return to my teenage self and her unconscious sacrifice of wild creativity and to reclaim it.

The Jungian Approach to Dream Interpretation

The Jungian practice of amplifying dream images offered a powerful approach for exploring dream symbols through human history and myth, connecting personal experiences to broader cultural narratives. Central to this approach is *active imagination*, a technique Jung developed for bridging conscious and unconscious minds. Unlike traditional dream analysis, within active imagination you cultivate a waking dream in an inner meditative landscape, requiring surrender, patience, curiosity, and non-attachment.

The practitioner makes a gentle mental request, such as visiting a dream figure or symbol and then surrenders to the unfolding of spontaneous mental imagery and relationships. One can personify a dream symbol and animate it to enter into dialogue with it. The fundamental goal is minimal intervention, allowing this journey to emerge organically. To embrace this improvisation or spontaneous collaboration with the figures and symbols of your unconscious requires a surrender of the ego and intellectual control in this imaginal space.

For many, inviting dream figures into animated conversation might seem weird or alarming. This is particularly true for someone like me with a family history of mental illness, where the boundary between imagination and reality feels fragile. However, within the established field of depth psychology and with my supportive cohort at Pacifica, I summoned the courage to use active imagination to facilitate a return to my imagination and its inner guidance. The practice requires a leap of faith to surrender to the unconscious and seek wisdom in the non-rational.

Personal Practice and Creative Transformation

Through dedicated practice, I developed a profound relationship with emerging imaginal figures. The Walled Woman, the murderer, the Castle, and a young boy became recurring characters in an evolving narrative through which complex internal conflicts were resolved. The practice addressed a fundamental tension between creative expression and the fear of losing touch with reality. A supportive academic environment, including exposure to works like Naomi Epel's (1994) *Writers Dreaming: 26 Writers Talk About Their Creative Process* provided crucial validation and reassurance.

One transformative session occurred in an imagined art museum, where the Walled Woman appeared as an abstract, three-dimensional artwork, broken yet luminous, proud in her uniqueness. This image offered a powerful reframing:

brokenness was not a deficit but a source of extraordinary beauty. My insight: "Why mourn the naïve young woman when her new form is so extraordinary and she is so happy?" Here you see the power of the spontaneous imaginal image working to help heal and resolve the past. The brokenness of the woman was not the focus, but her beauty and uniqueness.

I emerged from these sessions inspired to create her in art. Drawing from art therapist Shaun McNiff's (2015) concept of creativity as "a force of Nature" (p. 1), my artistic process became a means of transmuting challenging personal energy. Without formal training, the creative impulse emerged as an act of radical self-love. I tended my little artist girl and carved out space for her to explore, play, wander, listen, and create. Gradually, I reintegrated my exiled artist.

The Walled Woman Art Project

I gave voice to this Walled Woman archetype through multiple art forms: 3D sculpture, staged photographs of myself bricked into different locations, a short video, a solo performance piece, and poetry. My immurement and that of the collective divine feminine merged in my art. Each art expression, a step toward liberation. In his book, *Cultural Dreams: Windows to the Future*, author John Woodcock (2018) interpreted my artwork as offering a prescient message for today: "In rendering her artistic variations on the dream, Ferron speaks to Jung's idea of artist as Mouthpiece for the Coming Guest, that is, the artist as the one who can give us hints of an unknown future approaching us" (pp. 48–49). By highlighting the sacrifice of the feminine, Woodcock claimed that the art series urges the viewer to "attend to the condition of the *foundation of our existence*," and to tend the divine feminine in the face of a brutal "masculinized civilization" (Woodcock, 2018, p. 50).

Artistic Emergence into Community

In his book *Nonrational Logic in Contemporary Society,* depth psychologist Jim Kline (2023) described my Walled Woman art journey as an archetypal possession orchestrated by the Self to heal trauma:

> There was no doubt that she was possessed by this archetypal motif which demanded that she share it with the world since it was not only an expression of her core essence, but a universal expression of the necessity to sacrifice oneself–one's old persona– in order to give birth to a new, revitalized soul-self. (p. 144)

Each creative act triggered corresponding expansion in other life domains. Opportunities emerged: juried art shows, presentations at innovative spaces like Google Headquarters and Burning Man, and speaking engagements at professional conferences.

A pivotal moment arrived through an unexpected collaborative experience. I wanted to make brick wall platforms to imprison myself and be photographed.

My husband offered to help build brick wall platforms for my photographs. Without judgment, he appeared by my side, helping me express myself symbolically. Together, we constructed a brick-lined platform for a powerful photographic metaphor of the divine feminine releasing a winged heart to the world. This symbolic metaphor represented the emerging integration in our marriage of the masculine and feminine. Despite our differences, we found a way back to each other and our bedrock of love by creating art together.

A Vision Emerges: From Personal Healing to Collective Liberation

In my personal art, I had been working with the image of a caged winged heart as a way to locate myself and acknowledge my childhood grief. It was a hauntingly beautiful yet devastating image. An evocative symbol, the winged heart holds different meanings from courage and love, to grief and freedom. Symbolically, the winged heart represents our deepest, most precious self. When creating this symbol in art, we can dance in the past, present, and future, exploring what it means to be human.

A breakthrough moment came through a collaboration with artist Ruben Guzman for the Museum of Sonoma County's *Día de Los Muertos* exhibit in 2018. Researching the exhibit's *Roots* theme, I uncovered a devastating history of medical experiments on children with cerebral palsy at Sonoma State Hospital in the late 1950s and early 1960s. Children were recruited from their family homes with the promise of the best care and then subjected to painful experiments without their parents' knowledge or consent. Many of the 1100 children died. My brother was also experimented on during his decades in state institutions. To honor these children, we created a 15-ft-high cage with dozens of paper mâché hearts flying to freedom – to both bear witness to cruelty and symbolically set the children free. The result was *Los Olvidados Liberados (The Forgotten Ones Set Free)* – a powerful installation seen by an estimated 3,500 visitors.

To make the hearts, I invited people to my house from dawn to dusk. This was autumn 2018 amid news of migrant children being separated from parents and the Kavanaugh and Christine Blasey Ford hearings. What developed was a community forum, of mostly women, where we discussed oppression while making hearts for social justice and healing. The project became about our collective suffering and trauma in our society. *Los Olvidados* showed me the healing potential for this art-making form to become a broader project and inspired my nonprofit, *Life On Art*, built in partnership with my husband.

Surrendering to Art: From Imprisonment to Liberation

My artistic journey began with a moment of profound vulnerability at Pacifica, where I was challenged to create art despite having no artistic or drawing experience. Vincent Van Gogh (as cited in Burvall, 2016) said: "I am always doing what I cannot do yet, in order to learn how to do it." As a perfectionist terrified of failure, the early years were marked by internal resistance and psychic meltdowns where my core identity and ego trembled with each new creative challenge. But I forged forward, I felt compelled.

Carl Jung identified a key requirement of artistic emergence: sacrifice: "the Self, that unconscious potential for individuation and psychic wholeness, requires the ego to sacrifice itself so that the dynamic reality of the Self can come into life" (as cited in Slater, 1996, p. 10). Over time, guided by depth practices, I learned to trust the creative process, moving my ego out of the way. I discovered the power of iteration, collaboration, and surrender and allowed my art to emerge organically.

My artistic journey took a significant turn with *Los Olvidados,* where my personal work with the cages of trauma merged with collective expression. My central metaphor had transformed dramatically:

- From a woman trapped in a wall.
- To the immobilized woman releasing a winged heart.
- To a caged winged heart.
- Finally, to 51 hearts flying free from a cage.

This symbolic progression mirrored my journey of personal liberation and new integration in outside community. In her book, *Art-Making with Refugees and Survivors*, Sally Adnams-Jones (2018) articulated how personal art can create ripples of transformation out into public life creating social change:

> The voicing of a central metaphor is, in my view, one of the most transformative elements of art... The image becomes an identity which becomes a voice, which becomes a discourse, which becomes a field, which can then create change.... We paint/stitch/carve/dance/ourselves into being and then into our communities and then into action. We bridge our interior world into the social world and into political change through art and through this act we evolve culture and awareness into deeper, more intimate, more inclusive ways of being. (p. 43)

With *Los Olvidados,* my personal work merged with the collective shifting my central metaphor from one of imprisonment to liberation. Inspired to share this work with others, I wanted to create a platform that offered people a catalytic combination of community, creativity, art, and depth. Little did I know how this vision was going to expand dramatically bringing me to full-circle healing.

Breaking the Spell: Large-Scale Artistic Statements

My art shifted to address societal injustice more directly, becoming more connective, collaborative, and activist. I was blessed to collaborate with amazing artists, craftsmen, and volunteers to help me realize my work, now drawn into a larger community, out of my former isolation, into work for the good of humanity. We brought winged hearts to social actions at San Quentin Prison, the Women's March Sacramento, and Pride and Veteran's Day Parades.

I developed a series called *Breaking the Spell*, consisting of three large inter-connected artworks:

1. *The Spell*: An 8-ft square wooden cage covered in paper money, with a coin floor and rusted bars. The cage has no top, illustrating the power of a spell or paradigm to imprison when this is NOT an immutable reality.
2. *Spellbound*: A revolving 12-ft spherical steel cage resembling a collapsing earth, containing a 15-ft winged heart. Originally conceived as a powerful statement at the US–Mexico border, it represented the current suffering of the world, where the heart is cut off from the head.
3. *Unbound*: Hundreds of winged hearts fly free from a small cage dripping with the black ooze of trauma, which pools on the floor.

Three cages tell a story of a world bound under a collective spell, where profits are put before people, where we are trained not to see or feel dehumanization and suffering. These works were designed to be displayed along with expressive arts and community justice heart-making workshops to foster dialogue, community resilience, and action through the making of paper mâché winged hearts.

Ultimately, my journey transformed from a deeply personal exploration to a collaborative platform for community healing and social change.

The Unbound Project: A Movement of Hope

A transformative opportunity emerged with the California Department of State Hospitals in Napa. In 2021, we launched the *Unbound project* – a 9-month program creating an 80-ft sculpture featuring 800 winged hearts. Partnering with 70 rehabilitation therapists, the project aimed to provide uplift during COVID, build a community-collaborated sculpture symbolizing hope, and destigmatize mental illness.

Personally, this project was significant since my brother had spent much of my childhood in similar facilities. By inviting psychiatric patients as artists to co-create a large artwork, they became essential participants in an innovative community art project that would overturn social hierarchies by illustrating that everyone matters and no one is dispensable. The patients could be elevated as invaluable co-creators.

We galvanized 1,500 people: 500 psychiatric patients, 200 hospital staff, and 800 community volunteers. *Life On Art* and *DSH-Napa* forged an innovative model of public art, combining behavioral health services, creative art therapies, and community artmaking with high-level artistic design, engineering, and craftsmanship. The model is one of radical inclusion, empathy, and commitment to creativity to build hope.

Unbound was recognized by state, national, and international organizations, awarded first place for Arts for Innovation by the *National Organization of Arts in Health* (2022) and selected as one of the top 100 Global Art and Design Projects by CODAworx (2023).

Unbound was born from my deep desire to forge human connection and healing at scale. To create a healing project of this scale behind a 16-ft razor wire fence of a California state hospital, reaching hundreds of people like my brother, offered a deep full-circle and generational healing. I held a core belief that *Unbound* must be made. The fact that I was not a trained artist or therapist and was without any non-profit experience didn't matter. The fact that others saw this project as wild, audacious, and counter-intuitive was irrelevant. Many critics questioned the viability and rationale for the project. They couldn't imagine the vision. But I could. I led with heart, compassion, curiosity, an openness to collaborate, intuition, and a tenacity focused on figuring out how to get it done while leading from that edge of not-knowing, open to the emergent. People were drawn to the vision which attracted many people who had family members struggling with mental illness. They saw this as a much-needed outlet and found understanding and healing by being part of the project.

From Personal Trauma to Collective Healing: The *Life on Art* Story

My leadership emerged from childhood trauma, forging a path of resilience and creativity. Growing up outside societal norms, I learned to create my world, finding sustenance in nature and imagination. Early experiences of isolation became the crucible for developing a profound inner life and a deep sense of interconnectedness. My childhood contributed to developing traits that influence my leadership: (a) a drive and ability to find common ground and connect with anyone; (b) a drive to collaborate; (c) a capacity for being willing to be outside of convention and do things differently; and (d) a persistence toward turning vision into reality.

The Winged Heart Project: A Dream of Unity

Imagine thousands participating in healing workshops exploring one's heart, societal values, and creating winged hearts as testaments to love and hope. The winged hearts bridge personal and collective consciousness through a model fusing healing, activism, and large-scale community-participated art experiences. This project led me to found an art nonprofit in Northern California, *Life On Art* (www.lifeonart.org).

Life On Art is a nonprofit that brings together diverse groups to create transformative public art. These collaborative experiences are healing journeys that rebuild community connections across multiple sectors. The core mission is to shift our cultural paradigm from fear to compassion. Our approach is revolutionary.

My dream is to create a blueprint for large community-participated public art that weaves together diverse people in a healing process, focusing on elevating our most trauma-impacted communities. My goal is to create awe-inspiring artwork combined with creative workshops utilizing an integrative social design to build artworks that model the culture of care we need. The artworks can become beacons for how to get there.

The impactful public displays of the winged hearts are designed to evoke awe, compassion, and to motivate others to take action to create a better world. Many have told me this is the beginning of a movement. I sense that many people want a tangible way to unite toward building a more just and compassionate world reflective of their values. Winged hearts are touchstones for our divinity, who we truly are, offering a collective path to healing and action. Making winged arts in community gathers people in service to human and earth rights, united in a creative common purpose. Building artworks of wonder and beauty together can help guide us toward a new future story.

Awe as a Catalyst for Transformation

Drawing on Dr. Dacher Keltner's research, a University of California psychology professor, I now understand awe's profound impact as an essential counterbalance to human suffering. Keltner (2023) suggested that awe expands what philosopher Peter Singer called "the circle of care," the network of people we feel kindness toward (as cited in Keltner, 2023, p. 40). Further Keltner noted:

> Awe seems to orient us to devote ourselves to things outside of our individual selves. To sacrifice and serve. To sense that the boundaries between our individual selves and others readily dissolve, that are true nature is collective. (p. 6)

When Dr. Keltner visited *Unbound*, he claimed the project was a "collective expression of transformation and redemption" (personal communication, November 26, 2024) that brought community members together to build something transcendent. What follows is an excerpt of his interview:

> One of the things I was most struck by with Unbound was you had all kinds of members of a community…. working together to build something. And that is transcendent. It's very hard to get a community involved at that scale. Truly, we've lost that art and Tracy's bringing it back. A project like Unbound and Life On Art is part of a convergence of new approaches to health and healing. Ralph Waldo Emerson, when he was standing in the forest and had this near mystical experience, he said, you know the old categories just don't make any sense anymore, that we're all sort of united in some creative spirit. And that's what Unbound does for viewer and participant alike. Brilliant. Knowing the life conditions of the people who made the art and what it represented to them and how much care they put into them and the people they worked with on them–it left me speechless. That's exactly what our culture needs.

Keltner sees the experience of awe as resourcing people to lean into courage, kindness, and collectivism. It is this collective visceral experience of our interdependence that *Life On Art* builds through workshops and large-scale participatory art experiences.

Leadership Principles

Reflecting on my story, the creation of *Life On Art*, and my experiences with community-participated art projects, I offer the following personal and collective observations about leadership.

Personal Leadership Foundations

Radical Self-Compassion: Vulnerability becomes strength when embraced. Personal challenges are transformed into opportunities for vision, creation, and connection. Leadership begins with self-acceptance and the courage to be imperfect.

Continuous Learning Mindset: Remain receptive to emerging perspectives. Cultivate curiosity and intellectual humility. Uncertainty becomes a catalyst for growth when approached with openness.

Imaginative Resilience: Creativity as a tool for navigating adversity. The creative process builds resilience that extends beyond the individual to communities.

Depth Awareness: Leadership flows from connection to inner wisdom. Develop practices such as deep listening to cultivate presence and meaningful engagement.

Transformative Vision: Leadership emerges from personal healing journeys. Visionary leadership originates from personal experience rather than formal credentials.

Collective Leadership Principles

Radical Inclusion: Honor diverse perspectives for innovative solutions. Dismantle hierarchies by elevating marginalized voices as essential co-creators.

Collaborative Transformation: Bridge diverse communities for systemic change. Design initiatives that connect different stakeholder groups through shared purpose, giving voice to all who participate.

Compassionate Action: Connect personal healing with collective transformation. Use art to bridge disparate individual experiences and broader social contexts.

Generative Imagination: Use artistic approaches for complex social challenges. Creative methodologies open possibilities that logical analysis alone cannot reveal.

Awe as Leadership Strategy: Cultivate wonder to activate deeper engagement, collective imagination, systemic change, and sustained action.

Embodied Leadership Practices: Pathways to Healing and Collective Transformation

Somatic breathing, creative, and reflective practices offer embodied pathways to deepen leadership presence and cultivate resilience. These practices serve as bridges between personal healing and collective change. By integrating breath, creativity, and reflection, these practices support a rewilding of leadership – fostering the capacity to hold paradox, embrace uncertainty, and create spaces for authentic expression and collective transformation.

Somatic Breathing Exercises for Presence and Resilience

Just as breath bridges body and spirit, these somatic practices invite leaders to release systemic constraints and reconnect with their innate resilience.

Walled Woman Breath Release

This exercise serves to reconnect with inner resilience and release systemic constraints.

- Find a comfortable seated position.
- Close eyes and place hands on your heart.
- Inhale deeply for 4 counts, imagining breath filling any "walled" spaces within.
- Exhale for 6 counts, visualizing releasing old patterns and constraints.
- Repeat 7–10 times.
- After completing, journal any insights or emotions that emerge.

Winged Heart Expansion Breath

The exercise cultivates compassion, openness, and personal liberation.

- Stand with feet shoulder-width apart.
- Inhale, raising arms slowly overhead, imagining wings expanding.
- Exhale, bringing arms down and across heart in a gentle embrace.
- Focus on the sensation of internal spaciousness.
- Practice for 5–10 minutes.
- Reflect on feelings of freedom and interconnectedness.

Creative Practices for Personal and Collective Healing

Creativity becomes a powerful portal for healing, transforming personal narratives into collective wisdom and hope.

Metaphorical Art Journaling

This exercise explores personal symbolism to transform our inner landscapes.

- Choose a personal metaphor perhaps from dream (e.g., caged heart, walled woman).
- Create a multi-layered artistic representation.
- Explore this metaphor through history and myth.
- Write a narrative exploring the metaphor's personal and collective meanings.
- Reflect on how the metaphor connects to larger societal experiences.

Reflective Practices for Depth and Awareness

In the quiet spaces of reflection, we discover the profound connection between our inner world and the broader landscape of human potential.

Active Imagination Journaling

The exercise helps to develop intuition and connect with unconscious wisdom.

- Create a quiet, sacred space.
- Choose a dream symbol or recurring image to explore.
- Surrender rational control.
- Imagine yourself in a landscape (e.g., the beach or the forest) with all of its sensory elements. How does it smell? What do you hear? Invite your symbol or image to find you. Be patient. Ask questions and listen for the answers. See what other things unfold in this imaginative space. Think of this as a waking dream. At the end of the session, thank the figures for their guidance and slowly return to the room and open your eyes.
- Write down any thoughts or memorable occurrences.
- Reflect on emerging insights.

Conclusion

The rewilding journey from personal trauma to collective empowerment demonstrates how leadership emerges through our wounds. By embracing vulnerability, creative expression, and depth practices, we transform suffering into catalysts for social change. The Walled Woman's journey – from imprisonment to liberation – mirrors our collective potential to break free from oppression and create more compassionate communities. By honoring personal and collective dimensions of change, we forge a new leadership paradigm that embraces the full spectrum of human experience. In so doing, we can liberate the authentic, wild essence needed to create the more beautiful world our hearts know is possible.

References

Adnams-Jones, S. (2018). *Art-making with refugees and survivors: Creative and transformative responses to trauma after natural disasters, war and other crises.* Jessica Kingsley.

Burvall, A. (2016). *From the lips of Vincent: Life lessons from Van Gogh.* Medium. https://medium.com/@amyburvall/from-the-lips-of-vincent-life-lessons-from-van-gogh-fec043108a44

Dundes, A. (1996). *The walled-up wife: A casebook.* The University of Wisconsin Press.

Epel, N. (1994). *Writers dreaming: 26 Writers talk about their creative process.* Vintage Books.

Grof, S. (2000). *Psychology of the future: Lessons from modern consciousness research (Suny series in transpersonal and humanistic psychology).* State University of New York Press.

Jung, C. G. (2010). *Dreams (From Volumes 4, 8, 12 and 16 of the collected works of C.G. Jung).* Princeton University Press.

Keltner, D. (2023). *Awe: The new science of everyday wonder and how it can transform your life.* Penguin Press.

Kline, J. (2023). *Nonrational logic in contemporary society: A depth psychology perspective on magical thinking, conspiracy theories, and folk devils among us.* Routledge.

McNiff, S. (2015). *Imagination in action: Secrets for unleashing creative expression.* Shambhala Publications.

Paris, G. (2011) *Heartbreak: New approaches to healing-recovering from lost love and mourning.* Mill City Press.

Rilke, R. M. (2019). *In praise of mortality: Selections from Rainer Maria Rilke's Duino Elegies and Sonnets to Orpheus* (J. Macy & A. Barrows, Trans.). Echo Point.

Slater, G. A. (1996). *Surrendering to psyche: Depth psychology, sacrifice, and culture* (Order No. 3002405). Available from ProQuest Dissertations & Theses Global: The Humanities and Social Sciences Collection.

Woodcock, J. (2018). *Cultural dreams: Windows to the future*. Self-published.

Part 2

Poetic Response – RECENTER: 5 Reasons to Spin the Wheel

Danny Smith

One.
Freedom tastes sour in this hour
Because I still care,
And ache to be near what drains my power.

Kissed by a soft blink,
I come-to,
My heart pumps,
I remain,
Free.

Two.
Over here is funny like that.
You can wed your mind and soul, bleed wide open,
And still have time for coffee.

Three.
Crashing
Into the same wall
That's kept you small and frozen,
That's cradled you in times of raging seas.

Scaling
This stone wall, taller than Everest,
Seeing what you'll see,
Fleeing safety for depth.

Over the wall,
Both feet planted or clumsy landing,
Still standing outside
Your caution,
Outside your hesitance,
Outside of reason.

The reason to breakthrough is that it's time.

Four.
It's hard to walk away, but there's nothing left to do.
Except, hold open your eyes
and breathe.

Endings end.
And beginnings begin.
And stories are retold.

No walking necessary.

Five.
Only you can run
the full mile with tender soles
despite rocky roads.

Part 3

Rewild

> The Edenic return we unconsciously long for and so desperately need
> is a resurrection to the truth of our own wildness. (Williams, 2020)

Cultivating a "wild mind" was described by depth psychologist and wilderness guide Bill Plotkin (2013) as having "a whole mind … [having] cultivated and embodied their innate human wholeness." As outlined in his book, *Wild Mind*, Plotkin noted the primary task necessary to turn our society around from life destroying to life enhancing is to reclaim our "original wholeness," our "indigenous human nature granted to us by nature itself." In 2021, 33 researchers from around the world published a paper entitled *Guiding Principles for Rewilding* (Carver et al., 2021) in *Conservation Biology*, wherein, rewilding was described as "the process of rebuilding, following major human disturbance," promoting the idea of a resilient, self-sustaining eco-system. A sense of wholeness and interconnectedness gained from a journey of retreat and recentering is a goal of this book. To rewild, in this sense, signifies a return to an earlier time when imagination, playfulness, and curiosity were part of our youth. To see ourselves within the web of interconnectedness activates a sense of responsibility to ourselves, others, and the planet.

Rewilding is the ultimate movement toward reclaiming wholeness, creativity, and connection to the natural world. Inspired by Brendan E. Williams' and Bill Plotkin's calls to rediscover our "wild mind," Part 3 explores rewilding as a metaphor for reconnecting with our innate human nature and cultivating a leadership paradigm that nurtures resilience, imagination, and systemic awareness. Through themes of ecological interconnectedness, relational leadership, and creative transformation, rewilding invites leaders to embrace the playful, curious, and imaginative aspects of being, fostering a sense of responsibility toward the self, others, and the planet.

References

Carver, S., Convery, I., Hawkins, S., Beyers, R., Eagle, A., Kun, Z., Van Maanen, E., Cao, Y., Fisher, M., Edwards, S. R., Nelson, C., Gann, G. D., Shurter, S., Aguilar, K., Andrade, A., Ripple, W. J., Davis, J., Sinclair, A., Bekoff, M., … Soule, M. (2021). Guiding principles for rewilding. *Conservation Biology*, *45*(6), 1882–1893. https://doi.org/10.1111/cobi.13730

Plotkin, B. (2013). *Wild mind: A field guide to the human psyche*. New World Library.

Williams, B. E. (2020). *Seeds from the wild verge: Myth, nature, and theology in the border stream of Celtic wisdom*. Ancient Oak Ritual Arts.

Chapter 13

Leading from the Ecological Self

Kathryn Goldman Schuyler

Founder, Coherent Change, USA

Abstract

This chapter explores the concept of leading from the ecological self, a perspective that recognizes the fundamental interconnectedness between humans and all living systems. Drawing from deep ecology, systems thinking, Indigenous wisdom traditions, and Buddhist philosophy, the author examines how this expanded sense of self can transform leadership approaches in the face of our current polycrisis. The ecological self, developed by Arne Naess, Joanna Macy, and John Seed, offers a framework for leadership that moves beyond anthropocentric perspectives to embrace stewardship of all life. The chapter identifies five key themes for ecological leadership: consciousness-centered stewardship, re-storying our relationship with Earth, cultivating warmth and love, nourishing planetary resilience, and appreciating beauty through the arts. By integrating contemplative practices, Indigenous knowledge, and a felt sense of interconnection with all beings, leaders can foster the transformative consciousness needed to shift human societies from extractive to regenerative relationships with the Earth. While such ecological leadership may seem distant from current political realities, it represents a vital developmental step forward rather than a return to the past, offering a path toward collective flourishing for all life on Earth.

Keywords: Ecological self; deep ecology; leadership; Indigenous wisdom; planetary resilience; interconnectedness; polycrisis; contemplative practices; regenerative relationships

Artful Leadership: Retreat, Recenter, and Rewild, 175–189
Copyright © 2026 by Kathryn Goldman Schuyler
Published under exclusive licence by Emerald Publishing Limited
doi:10.1108/S2058-880120250000010014

It is the reawakening of the ecological self that can save us and the
life of our planet.

– Joanna Macy (as quoted in Fleming, 2020, p. 43)

Introduction

Human beings often reach out for leadership: guidance, maybe wisdom, about
which path to choose when there is a fork in the road. We all – all beings – need
to know what will keep us alive and what will destroy us. There are examples of
leaders and leading in all species. In our species of human beings, there seems to
be a belief among many that our fellow humans should turn to the largest, most
dominant, or strongest among us. On the other hand, we could seek leaders who
are wise: who aim to take into account as many as possible of the forces that
affect life on this planet and to craft a path that will enable human beings and all
life to thrive. This chapter describes one way of looking at such leadership: *leading from the ecological self.*

In formulating this book, Crumpton wrote in her call:

> A sense of wholeness and interconnectedness gained from a jour-
> ney of retreat and recentering is a goal of this book. To rewild, in
> this sense, signifies a return to an earlier time when imagination,
> playfulness, and curiosity were part of our youth. To see ourselves
> within the web of interconnectedness activates a sense of respon-
> sibility to ourself, others, and the planet.

What I am contributing to formulating by writing this is not (from my perspective) a journey to an earlier time, either in our own lives or in that of human
beings as a species. It is a significant developmental step forward, where we
ground ourselves in what many people have felt nonverbally when very young,
a sense of oneness, wholeness, ease, and naturally being nourished, and unite
that with what maturity can bring: the wisdom of appreciating what it is to be
alive with a human mind and body. Bring these together means that we are able
to communicate using language in ways that let us know what has happened not
only in our own lives and our personal ancestors, but in the lives of many groups
of people, over centuries. It means we know how to use extremely complex tools
that we construct in ways that build additional tools and structures that last far
beyond our own lives.

Connecting with one's ecological self is a way for human beings to sense ourselves as interdependent and interconnected with all forms of life. Developed
initially by Arne Naess, Joanna Macy, and John Seed (Seed et al., 1988), this
perspective shifts the ground from which leaders function, nourishing a spacious,
vital sense of identity and agency. By living from this view, leaders can support
those focused on developing and implementing policies to enable human societies
to shift from an extractive to a generative relationship with the Earth.

This short piece will give readers an understanding of what the ecological self is, how it is essential for leadership at this time, and of practices for living in this way. Before setting out on this journey, I want to more fully presence myself and why I find this so nourishing at this time. As child of 5 or 6, I grew up with a mother who walked around the house singing *Vici d'arte* from Verdi's opera Tosca. This beloved aria tells of a woman who lives for art and love and senses that her life is heading toward pain and suffering as the country where she lives is leaving behind its hopes for democracy. My mother once took me for a walk when there was a huge storm with gale winds. Holding my hand, she urged me to be at ease in continuing to walk because "It's just a little wind, Kath!" All of this combined to make art not something separate, but a core element in how I live: somehow weaving beauty and courage together. She had a large book on the coffee table with the title "God is One." Although we almost never participated in formal religious practice in temples or synagogues, I appreciated the spiritual aspects of life in some visceral way. So years later, it was not surprising that I became interested in Buddhism and found myself walking with my wonderful teacher, Lama Tharchin Rinpoche, on a path through the woods where he taught in the mountains near Santa Cruz, California. I was saying something that I thought of as a huge commitment about "all humans," and he stopped walking, put his hand on my arm, and said "Not all humans, Kathryn! All beings! All beings!" I have never forgotten that. It has become a core part of me to consider our relationship with all beings (humans, animals, plants – all!) and the effects of our actions on all beings. So for me, art, liberation, awareness, and love are all interconnected. And at this time in human history, appreciating how leadership can be colored and nurtured by the ecological self seems essential for a flourishing future for humans, all beings, and the earth.

More and more people are concerned about the state of our home, our Earth, our "relatives" from other species and types of life. In speaking at a global leadership conference where few speak about spirituality in leadership, I saw my theme resonate for some listeners. As I spoke, I saw their eyes light up. They leaned forward, commented, and expressed interest. This gives me hope that the potential I perceive may be real! Welcome to my journey!

The Ecological Self and Leadership Today

The roots of the ecological self grew within deep ecology and systems thinking. Deep ecology is a perspective developed by Norwegian philosopher Arne Naess (1986, 1995, 1996; Diehm & Naess, 2004) who focused ecological thinking on large questions such as how human life has been affecting the planet and the sustaining of life on Earth (Devall & Sessions, 1985). As a key insight, Naess distinguished between the meaning of the term *weltanschauung* in German and the term "worldview" in English, pointing out that one's experience of the world combines words and something more:

> A "view" can be totally rendered in language: "My view of the
> world is so-and-so." But *Anschauung* has to do with what you

feel and see, so the Welt-*anschauung* has to do with the integration of this view with feelings; it is how you *feel* yourself and
how you *feel* the world. And because it has to do with what's
immediate – how you feel the world and how you feel yourself –
the *Weltanschauung* cannot be properly expressed in language.
(Diehm & Naess, 2004, p. 6)

This suggests that a leader in today's world needs to *feel with* all beings, not
merely know something about them and the world. The other core component,
systems thinking, is the capacity to study and understand the interconnected patterns of relationships within social systems and how this impacts change. Leading
thinkers from the 20th century whose influence has continued into the 21st century are Donella Meadows, Peter Senge, and Margaret Wheatley, each of whom
published widely-read books about leading global change toward a sustainable
world (Meadows et al., 1972; Senge, 2006/1990; Wheatley, 2006/1992). This combination of deep ecology and systems thinking is not often brought into leadership development, but I see it as a critical element for the thriving of all.

Everyone alive today faces not only a climate crisis, but a polycrisis: complex,
interacting systems are creating seemingly hopelessly interdependent problems
for life on Earth (Waddock, 2025). Many are convinced that if human beings as a
group do not change direction, we will destroy not only the biodiversity of life on
Earth but possibly the conditions for life as we know it. This recognition leads to
the need for a dramatic change in the type of leaders chosen to take us forward.

The notion of the ecological self is powerfully conveyed by Joanna Macy
(2021) through both the title and content of *World as Lover, World as Self*.
Tibetan Buddhist teachers have long said that the title of a work should convey
its essence fully to those who understand the real meaning: Here, her title clearly
conveys being in the world with no separation between what we conventionally
experience as ourselves and all the beings. Speaking of an ecological self is a secular way to describe what has been sensed by mystics throughout time. We are passionately loving and being loved by the world! I don't conceive of the ecological
self as a "thing," but rather as a way of seeing or experiencing the relationship of
the particular and the multiplicity of living beings. Having experiences that allow
us to sense our ecological self helps us move fluidly back and forth between our
own particular way of being in this world and the sense of the whole. Realizing
the ecological self can be a source of nourishment when we feel too small for this
huge task of shifting our societies from an extractive to a regenerative way of life.

Sources and Development of the Ecological Self

The notion of an ecological self grew from the collaborative work between
Joanna Macy and John Seed in the 1980s and 1990s. They created a community
ritual that they called *Councils of All Beings,* in which those participating represent whichever being calls to them. Having essentially "become" the various
beings, those participating speak with one another about what the earth needs.
One thinks like a mountain, or an eagle, or an ant. This and other rituals are

designed to enable people to fully experience their grief and anger at what human beings are collectively doing to our planet and its inhabitants, so that they may be freed to move from such deep feelings into action. Both Macy and Seed see this as a way to help people in communities transmute repressed feelings of anger and pain into shared and sustained systemic action. These councils were sourced by Naess's writings on deep ecology and other rituals that Macy had created in order to "awaken people's commitment and courage to act for our planet," as well as by Aldo Leopold's notion (from the 1930s and 1940s) of thinking like a mountain (Seed et al., 1988, p. 7).

As an ecological self, one identifies with all living beings, rather than with one's small physical body. This is part of a philosophical weltanschauung, not an isolated concept or recipe for action. To be human, in Naess's view, is to have a distinct perspective from that of other beings: We can understand the interrelations of all species over time (Diehm & Naess, 2004).

> When we realize this, we must put an end to things such as war, the humiliation of the planet. Within the next several hundred years we should begin to feel that these things are childish – not that we are more ethical but, really, to kill things? That is immature. (p. 7)

Infusing a deep sense of interconnection – indeed "interbeing" (to use the term created by the Zen Buddhist teacher Thich Nhat Hanh) – with all beings with such an ethical perspective yields the particular sense of an ecological self, as developed by Naess, Macy, and Seed.

According to Macy (2021), "We are beginning to realize that the world is our body" (p. 142). This can be understood literally: Our ability to breathe clean air depends directly on the "breathing" of trees and the absence of raging wildfires. Macy lives from an "unshakable love for Earth, a profound sense of belonging to our home planet. This living planet is our larger self. By widening our sense of relationship with all of life, we open to what Joanna refers to as the ecological self" (Kaza, 2020, p. 1). People can experience themselves not only as a physical small self with a personal name like Susan or Paul, but can also sense their interconnectedness with all life through highly somatic experiential explorations during workshops. Participants would take an evolutionary journey from the beginning of history to the present time, performing rituals in the mountains or doing role-plays of being nuclear guardians (pp. 122–123). Macy and Seed saw these experiential learning processes as ways to access the ecological self.

In addition to Macy and Seed's rich notions about the ecological self and how to nurture it in ourselves, we can turn to Indigenous traditions for similar perspectives. Roshi Joan Halifax took a "journey through Buddhist practice and tribal wisdom" in *The Fruitful Darkness* (1993). Can we learn to know the Earth both through the analytical mind of science and through our heart-mind, through becoming still and listening? Halifax (1993) quotes a shaman, who says:

> What the people of the city do not realize is that the roots of all living things are tied together. … There is too much cold in the

world now, and it has worked its way into the hearts of all living creatures and into the roots of the grass and the trees. (p. xix)

Reflecting on the nature of the ecological self and ecological thinking, Halifax describes various people's experiences of the inseparability of oneself and the Earth: Black Elk's vision that all things are woven of the same spirit; her friend Chato's description of the mountains where he lives; and the oneness of Ogobara's familiarity with the clifftops of Dogon territory in central Africa. All seem at one with the Earth where they live and walk. "In our bones is the rock itself; In our blood is the river" she writes (Halifax, 1993, p. 150). She continues:

> We share the same body and the same self. Ch'ansha, a ninth-century Chinese Zen monk, said, "The entire universe is your complete body." Shunryu Suzuki Roshi said, Tathagata is the body of the whole earth." Walt Whitman [1855] wrote, "I am large… I contain multitudes." And Thich Nhat Hanh says in the Zen *gatha* he composed to be recited before eating,
>
> In this plate of food,
>
> I see the entire universe
>
> Supporting my existence. (p. 152)

As Halifax (1993) reminds us, Gregory Bateson regarded the notion that the mind is separate from the world as "the great epistemological error of Western civilization" (p. 156). Through Buddhist and other spiritual practices and the perspective of deep ecology, we can experience the ecological self: the self that is not separate from the entire living world.

The Ecological Self and Leading

Today, there are many programs and trainings for leadership, influenced by decades of leadership research and by people's desire to gain roles that are associated with power and monetary rewards. During much of history, leaders have been respected and honored, but today, somehow, they have become both widely discussed and simultaneously disrespected. Top national leaders in many of the wealthiest nations have low "popularity ratings," including the leaders of France, Canada, the UK, Germany, and the United States. An analysis of what is causing this trend would be a different piece than this, so I will simply state my belief that if humanity and the earth are to flourish together, we need leaders who relate not just to people (and probably their own "tribe" of people) as having importance, but all beings and ultimately, all life.

Some intriguing ideas for what is needed in such leaders can be sourced by those knowledgeable about Indigenous traditions (see Chungyalpa et al., 2025; Nelson & Kimmerer, 2023; Spiller et al., 2025). These sources convey a very different feeling for how to search for social solutions. They do not conduct experiments or analyze data; instead, they listen with humility to ancient stories. They seek to sense a path forward in the stories of the ancestors – seeking to reconnect with the images the ancestors used and to again feel connected with the Earth and those other beings seen as "all our relatives." There is an emphasis on women's knowledge and on practices that have allowed Indigenous peoples to live sustainably for hundreds or thousands of years. When I listen through the sense of being an ecological self, these themes come to the foreground for me.

"A Sacred Responsibility to Give Back to the Earth" and Consciousness-Centered Stewardship

Melissa K. Nelson and Robin Wall Kimmerer (2023) raised a fascinating question: Do humans have a sacred role on the Earth? It is evident that increasing numbers of people think of humans mainly as wrecking the Earth, but both of these globally honored professors spoke of humans as having a sacred responsibility to give back to the Earth. Both Kimmerer and Nelson said there is too much emphasis in climate action on THINGS and policies that have to be changed and too little on how we as people need to change ourselves. Both emphasized that there are too many outward solutions, with too little focus on transforming our consciousness. Speaking from the kind of sense of self we are invoking here, Nelson asked:

> How do we fall in love with creation as an embodied being? We are water, we are rivers. How do we relearn and remember the sacred gifts of life? With all the knowledge we have about what is needed, why do we still not change? Why do we work against our best interests?

As described by Spiller et al. (2025), *Consciousness-Centered Stewardship* means focusing on caring for Earth and her biodiversity as Indigenous Peoples have done for centuries. This reverses the trend toward *dominion over* that has been present as a part of colonialism and capitalism. It is a reversal, because the capitalistic mind has long viewed the people who practice such stewardship as *underdeveloped* (Spiller et al., 2025). Such an ethic of care is characterized by the Māori term *Kaitiakitanga*, which refers to a "long-term intergenerational obligation to protect, maintain, and enhance the spiritual and material wellbeing of precious resources that have been handed down by ancestors and will be passed on to future generations" (Nicholson et al., 2015, p. 6). Māori enterprise is expected to be aligned in purpose with the needs of the whole community, in contrast to capitalist beliefs that all must serve the accumulation of capital. All is grounded in a connected view of life and well-being of the whole.

A Need for Re-Storying

Nelson and Kimmerer (2023) spoke about story and *re-storying*: Not restoring, but re-storying! I have found that across all the scholars who have Indigenous roots, whether in the United States, Canada, New Zealand, or Australia – all seem to tell stories and learn from stories and see life through the stories that people tell one another. As Archibald (2008) explained, Indigenous stories come from the elders, and it takes many years, typically decades, for learners to appreciate the many levels of meaning within them. The way settlers and public school curricula have used them does not convey their place in teaching within Indigenous cultures. From what I hear and read, the core seems to be in connecting with the intentions and wisdom of the elders, and rarely in the words or text itself. They see settler or colonist societies as telling the wrong stories – stories about endless taking and material wealth. They urge us to re-focus our stories on our sacred role and responsibilities, on the intersection of wisdom and knowledge. Nelson suggested that climate change can be experienced as a gift of Mother Earth, who is responding to the actions of a small group of humans – the colonizers – who created the Anthropocene era (the geological epoch dating from the commencement of significant human impact on Earth's geology and ecosystems). Archibald said that we are seeing the impacts of the exploitative ways of the settlers, the colonizers, who acted with the arrogance of scien*cism*, rather than from deep wisdom *nourished by science.*

Such re-storying is expressed in Chellie Spiller's (2021) exploration of "I AM" consciousness across various Indigenous traditions. This is a way of understanding the inseparability of oneself and all life, all beings, which she discusses in the context of Irish, Māori, and African wisdom traditions. To me, this seems like other wording for the ecological self! To the Māori, *"Ko te awa ko au, ko au te awa – The river is me, I am the river,"* even legally, as a river in New Zealand has been viewed as having the same rights as a person (Spiller, 2021, p. 2). There is "human kinship with all of creation whereby everything is connected as a totality" (Spiller, 2021, p. 2). Similar traditions can be seen among the Xhosa, Hadza, and Maasai peoples, and in Irish poetry from between 400 and 700 BC. Such re-storying can help us let go of old stories that separate us from one another and the Earth, that teach our children that coldly manipulating tools is what makes humanity great, rather than our innate heartfelt interconnectedness with life forces.

Warmth, Connectedness, and Love

When I read or listen to stories with Indigenous roots, I sense a weltanschauung that is distinctly different from what is taught in schools and universities and imbibed from popular culture. For example, in the conversation between two esteemed scholars with Native American roots, the scholars closed with expressions of love for one another in this very public setting. Each expressed great warmth and appreciation for the fullness of the other – the richness of mind, heart, and spirit – and how honored they felt to walk together within academia and on the Earth. This is not what is normally seen in academia today – or in politics.

A similar connection with love comes from Otto Scharmer's (2023) discussion of his relationship with noted systems thinker Edgar Schein, an MIT professor, a founder of the field of Organization Development who always aimed to place people in charge of their own change processes. As Scharmer described what he learned from Schein, it was how to create a learning relationship that inverted the more typical relationship between teacher and learner. Instead of relying on the teacher as expert, they have both created processes "based on what learners know without realizing it, a learning structure in which the educator coaches the learner on how to access those deeper layers of knowing" (Scharmer, 2023, p. 3). Scharmer described what he learned as well as "accessing your love" (Scharmer, 2023, p. 3).

Christiana Figueres was the UN Executive Secretary of the Framework Convention on Climate Change (UNFCCC) when the Paris Agreement was reached in 2015. She is not only a noted international leader, but also a longtime student of Zen Buddhist teacher Thich Nhat Hanh et al., and she took a leading role in a major online course that was developed based on his book *Zen and the Art of Saving the Plane*t (2021). I mention this, because what was perhaps most powerful in her talks was her openness in talking about her personal struggles at the time she was leading these climate accords: her longtime marriage was falling apart, yet she wished to continue as leader and be publicly strong. The way that she conveyed her love for the Earth and her sense of the interconnectedness of life was extremely powerful.

Nourishing Planetary Resilience

Leaders are selected by the people to be governed in democracies, and more typically, gain power through strength and maneuvering. In no case are they chosen for their stewardship of the entire Earth and her biodiversity. Yet that is what many of us see as needed today.

An intriguing project lead by Dekila Chungyalpa at the University of Wisconsin, known as LOKA can offer insight into this type of leadership. The term LOKA comes from a Sanskrit word that "refers to 'our world' as the basis for all life. ... Each Loka or world is in a sense many worlds, overlapping and embedded within each other. Evocatively, the word Loka also means 'vision,' the act of seeing that not only beholds a world but brings it into being" (Center for Healthy Minds, n.d.). The initiative, supported by His Holiness the Dalai Lama, brings scientific and spiritual leaders together to develop strategies for a resilient world. They have determined, based on conversations among faith leaders of many traditions and scientists, that "inner, community, and planetary resilience are interdependent" and accomplishing any one of these requires working on all three (Chungyalpa et al., 2025, p. 5). Drawing upon traditional Tibetan Buddhist wisdom traditions and Indigenous Traditional Knowledge from North and Central America (also known as Turtle Island), they are exploring what practices can make a difference. Based on these two knowledge systems, they have concluded "that interdependence is the unifying principle for building inner, community, and planetary resilience, which is reinforced by science at all levels" (Chungyalpa et al., 2025, p. 9). In this perspective, we look to leaders who appreciate all of their relations – their interconnectedness with all creation. "Reconnecting with one another, and with the land and water through culturally rooted practices is critically important for Indigenous peoples and communities," and also maintaining ties with ancestors (Chungyalpa et al., 2025, p. 10).

Appreciation for Beauty Through the Arts

Finally, if we seek ways that such leadership intersects with the arts, an example came to me immediately from the students of Thich Nhat Hanh, who have become teachers in the Plum Village tradition. They created a course that has now been offered online several times, based on his book *Zen and the Art of Saving the Planet* (Nhat Hanh et al., 2021). It gathered approximately 500 people from around the world to move through a curriculum of learning, reflection, and small group conversation to support people in developing a sense of personal purpose in service of the Earth. Why I mention it here is because of all online gatherings I have experienced – a great many – only this one is notable for its beauty and artistic quality. It opens with a short video showing nature around the world overlain with music that I believe was composed by one of the teachers. So, in addition to the value of the many and varied teachers, including (as mentioned) Christine Figueres who led the negotiations for the Paris Climate Accords, it brought in an emotional power that came from this beautifully-crafted opening video, thus being intrinsically an exemplar of artful leadership.

From Ideas to Being: Visions of Life That Make Ecologically Awake Leadership Less Far-fetched

Considering the polycrisis in which we find ourselves today, this is a moment in time when the need for cross-sector innovation coming from an awareness of societal wholeness is not matched by the level of development of the leadership in most countries and most sectors. Scharmer (2022) sees collective sense-making as having four stages: (a) denial, (b), distancing, (c) depression, and finally (d) deep sensing and co-creativity. He believes that today most leaders are in what he describes as the first two levels of collective sense-making and decision-making (denial and distancing), leaving large numbers of the population in the third stage (depression). A hope (which perhaps is realistic) is to move into the fourth stage of "Deep sensing and Co-creativity": managing to stay present, be with the struggles and pain, and then let go of attachment to old ways enough for new possibilities to emerge (Scharmer, 2022).

Such a level 4.0 system is where eco-awareness flourishes. As in Waddock's (2025) writings, a level-4 system is grounded in the intention for wellbeing among all: There is respect for the value of all beings, which means of all ages, stages of development, and cultures – so that all are educated in a whole-systems perspective, have sufficient economic means to thrive, have comparable access to healthcare, and can participate in governance in meaningful ways.

Finally, from the perspective of Māori cosmology, the universe is evolving and this evolution is inspired by a welling up of emotion. Life spirals from potential to consciousness to manifestation and then back again into potential (Nicholson et al., 2015). This force or vibration of potential is called *hihiri*, and it can become manifested through intention. Intention "orchestrates and organizes life-energies into new forms and expression," and then attention and awareness support this in becoming manifest. Intention, attention, and awareness are processes that we human can influence through training our minds, as is taught in traditional wisdom practices from both Indigenous peoples and Tibetan Buddhism. In other words, although this way of being, living, and leading from the ecological self seems far-fetched from the vantage point of the 2025 political situation in the world, there are long streams of thought that attest to the power of such forces for change and life.

All of this depends on the collective will, and the cultivation of healthy collective will has not been focused upon by contemporary societies. If cultivated at all, it is stirred up through forces in popular culture that encourage fear and hostility-based emotions, rather than a feeling for the common good. There are few if any channels for contemplating and nourishing a healthy collective will grounded in a sensing of mutual reciprocity, awareness of interconnectedness, and love – grounded in the ecological self. Fortunately for human beings, other species, and the Earth, such an awakening is merely difficult and not impossible.

Reflections and Implications for Practice

Given how much potential there is for leading in ways that recognize the interdependence of humans on all forms of life and the importance of giving back to the Earth, creating a path forward in this direction feels to me like a sacred duty – a charge our generation has received that is both a gift and a challenge. This option has always been a potential, but its necessity seems more evident because of the power humans have been using to destroy species and influence the conditions for life.

Sandra Waddock (2025) addresses this challenge often in her writings on systems change in the face of the polycrisis. Like the Indigenous authors, she writes of the need for new stories, which she refers to as *Eco-Social Narratives for Awakening an Era of Transformative Change* (Waddock, 2025). The story or narrative that I can see is one in which potential leaders cultivate their heart-minds (because what we perceive in the West as "mind" is often merely the brain, without the heart) through a combination of training, practice, and good common sense, and also learn the socio-technical skills of engineering and management in order to innovate in today's large complex systems. This does not guarantee anything, but might provide a population that values the Earth and has the skills and resources to work collaboratively across all of the many boundaries we humans draw around ourselves (such as race, nationality, and class).

Recent research suggests that intentional mind training can transform behavior so it aligns with core values (Dahl et al., 2020 as cited in Chungyalpa et al., 2025). If we wish to participate in such a process ourselves, one path is to begin with inner work, such as recognizing the interdependence of all elements within us and our connectedness with others and life. This may involve various specific meditation practices, some of which are being taught by Thich Nhat Hanh's community of teachers, others by Tibetan teachers such as Mingyur Rinpoche, and many by Indigenous teachers around the world (for example, see Halifax, 1993; Macy, 2021; Kaza, 2020; Nicholson et al., 2015). It may mean combining these with artistic practices such as calligraphy (Tanahashi, 2016), walking in nature, or immersing oneself in the wildness of life (Norris, 2025). Chungyalpa et al. (2025) describe what they see as the three pathways to such deep resilience. My own research has shown that simply making time to sit quietly or take a walk often leads people to feel more connected with the original purpose that led them into their area of work (Goldman Schuyler et al., 2017, 2018). Our research also suggested that such simple processes influenced participants to feel more connected with nature; we did not mention this as a goal or intention, it simply happened (Koskela & Goldman Schuyler, 2016).

In closing, as an example, here is one process that I found deeply meaningful related to living and leading from our ecological selves. Walk through it in your mind with me! Pause, and sense you are breathing as you sit and read. Let yourself become aware of yourself sitting and breathing –and of the space and beings around you...

In the tradition of Thich Nhat Hanh et al., in his text *Zen and the Art of Saving the Planet* (2021), he guides the reader through the following pathway of contemplation:

1. You are the Earth; the Earth is you. This is what is meant by the term interbeing. We are not separate from each other and the environment: we inter-are.
2. Live in feelings, speaking from feelings and the heart – not from concepts or theories.
3. Embody the four core insights of the Diamond Sutra:
    *   There is no self, as we and everybody and everything are all composed of Earth, water, air, fire, and space – the five elements;
    *   therefore, there is no worthwhile distinction between a human being and other beings; and
    *   actually – why distinguish between living and nonliving beings – all are composed of the same elements; so
    *   is there really any meaning to a lifespan, if our awareness is on these elements of which we are all composed?

Everything is composed of water, earth, air, fire, and space, coming together in different ways. This dissolves the experience of my "self" as being more solid and real than these component elements. They began to become foreground, alongside my sense of "Kathryn" as a being persisting over time. I seemed to sense this Kathryn-being as composed of elements, with space, and somehow inexplicably keeping itself together sufficiently to experience itself, myself, as "me" and to be perceived by others as Kathryn – yet the reality, almost a cosmic joke, is this dance of elements.

When I had this powerful experience, at the same time it felt light and even funny. It became harder to take myself and my irritations too seriously. It seems a bit like wave-particle duality in physics, where a subatomic behavior may be described either as wave behavior or particle behavior. I can experience myself as me, Kathryn, one being, and I can sense myself almost like a cloud of elements somehow cohering sufficiently to seem to be what we all accept as a person.

> From there, I can look at dogs, other people, and other living beings in the same way.

And then, consider rocks, trees, the bay, and perhaps my husband in a similar way.

I find this notion that all living beings are composed of the five elements helps me sense myself as interpenetrated by nature, flowing with life, dancing.

When I read in Okumura's (2018) *The mountains and waters sutra: A practitioner's guide to Dōgen's "Sansuikyō"* that "Sansuikyō means 'Mountains and waters are sutra'" (p. 15), I had a sudden sense of "How amazing!" Here was the missing piece. This major Zen teaching wasn't a sutra *about* mountains and waters, but one written *from* them – written from being one with what lives, with the Earth, the waters. This is the most profoundly clear expression of the ecological self I've encountered. I felt it when sitting with it, without needing to understand cognitively. *The mountains and waters are sutra*; my "self" is not this small physical being and this personal history – it is being one with the forces of life and Earth and water, the scale of life beyond the human.

"Being confined to words and phrases are not the words of liberation. There is something free from all of these views" (Dōgen, 1240, p. 3). I couldn't "understand" the words, yet I had a felt sense that they described my path. And if "I" am all beings throughout time and space – the ecological self – I am indeed not only "seeing into mind and seeing into essence" which is "the activity of people outside the way" (p. 3). Therefore, just sit. Sitting may be seated or walking, since mountains are always walking. One is with whatever is: mountains, waters, thoughts, outrage, flowing, stillness.

Conclusion

The purpose of this chapter is to explore what it might mean to lead from the ecological self and how this could help shift humanity from using up the Earth to treasuring it and understanding ourselves as one among many forms of life, evolving together.

The concept, developed initially by Naess and his colleagues (Seed et al., 1988), could transform leadership. The ecological self is larger than our small, personal selves, and is our sense of interconnectedness and interdependence with all forms of life. From this, we sense our "sacred duty" to sustain and nourish life. This kind of sense of the self incorporates appreciation for the arts and is nourished by the arts.

Themes related to leading from the ecological self include:

- "A Sacred Responsibility to Give Back to the Earth" and Consciousness-Centered Stewardship;
- A Need for Re-Storying;
- Warmth, Connectedness, and Love;
- Nourishing Planetary Resilience; and
- Appreciation for Beauty Through the Arts.

While it doesn't appear at this moment in time that humanity is heading toward such leadership, we really do not know. Both social science-based wisdom practices like presencing and ancient Indigenous wisdom practices suggest that we can, through deep listening to the sacred, find our will and our way.

References

Archibald, J. (2008). *Indigenous storywork: Educating the heart, mind, body, and spirit*. UBC Press.
Center for Healthy Minds. (n.d.). *The Loka initiative*. University of Wisconsin Madison. https://centerhealthyminds.org/programs/loka-initiative
Chungyalpa, D., Gauthier, P. E., Goldman, R. I., Vikas, M., & Wilson-Mendenhall, C. (2025). A framework for deep resilience in the Anthropocene. *Humanist Management Journal, 10*(1), 49–64. https://doi.org/10.1007/s41463-024-00195-7
Dahl, C. J., Wilson-Mendenhall, C., & Davidson, R. (2020). The plasticity of well-being: A training-based framework for the cultivation of human flourishing. *Proceedings of the National Academy of Sciences, 117*(51), 32197–32206. https://doi.org/10.1073/pnas.2014859117
Devall, B., & Sessions, G. (1985). *Deep ecology: Living as if nature mattered*. Peregrine Smith Books.
Diehm, C., & Naess, A. (2004). "Here I stand": An interview with Arne Naess. *Environmental Philosophy, 1*(2), 6–19. https://doi.org/10.5840/envirophil2004122
Dōgen, E. (1240). *Mountains and waters sutra* (K. Tanahaki, Trans.). [Provided by Upaya Zen Center for Rohatsu 2021 Online Retreat]. https://www.upaya.org/uploads/pdfs/MountainsRiversSutra.pdf
Fleming, P. (2020). The work takes root in the UK. In S. Kaza (Ed.), *A wild love for the world: Joanna Macy and the work of our time* (pp. 38–48). Shambala.
Goldman Schuyler, K., Skjei, S., Sanzgiri, J., & Koskela, V. (2017). "Moments of waking up": A doorway to mindfulness and presence. *Journal of Management Inquiry, 26*(1), 86–100. https://doi.org/10.1177/1056492616665171
Goldman Schuyler, K., Taylor, M. O., & Wolberger, O. M. (2018). Bringing mindfulness and joy to work: Action research on organizational change. In J. Neal (Ed.), *Handbook of personal and organizational transformation* (pp. 1193–1217). Springer. https://doi.org/10.1002/jls.21661
Halifax, J. (1993). *The fruitful darkness: Reconnecting with the body of the Earth*. HarperCollins.
Kaza, S. (Ed.). (2020). *A wild love for the world: Joanna Macy and the work of our time*. Shambala.
Koskela, V., & Goldman Schuyler, K. (2016). Experiences of presence as a key factor towards sustainability leadership. *Journal of Leadership Studies, 9*(4), 54–59. https://doi.org/10.1002/jls.21427
Macy, J. (2021). *World as lover, world as self* (30th Anniversary Ed.). Parallax Press.
Meadows, D. H., Meadows, D. L., Randers, J., & Behrens, W. W. (1972). *The limits to growth: A report for the Club of Rome's project on the predicament of mankind*. Universe Books.
Naess, A. (1986). Self-realization: An ecological approach to being in the world. In J. Seed, J. Macy, P. Fleming, & A. Naess (Eds.), *Thinking like a mountain: Towards a council of all beings* (pp. 19–31). New Society Publishers. https://doi.org/10.1007/978-1-4020-4519-6_128

Naess, A. (1995). Industrial society, postmodernity and ecological sustainability. *Humboldt Journal of Social Relations*, *21*(1), 130–146. https://doi.org/10.1007/978-1-4020-4519-6_138

Naess, A. (1996). Living a life that reflects evolutionary insight. *Conservation Biology*, *10*(6), 1557–1559. https://doi.org/10.1046/j.1523-1739.1996.10061557.x

Nelson, M. K., & Kimmerer, R. (2023, October 5). Sacred activism [Video, Conference Presentation]. Climate Convergence, Pachamama Alliance. https://vimeo.com/showcase/climate-convergence

Nhat Hanh, T., Khong, C., & Dedication, T. (2021). *Zen and the art of saving the planet*. Harper-Collins.

Nicholson, A., Spiller, C., & Hēnare, M. (2015). Arohia te rangi o te hihiri: Heeding the melody of pure and potent energy. In C. Spiller & R. Wolfgramm (Eds.), *Indigenous spiritualties at work: Transforming the spirit of enterprise* (pp. 273–298). Information Age Publishing.

Norris, J. (2025). Original nature: Awakening world-changing leadership in the wild. *Humanist Management Journal*, *10*(1), 31–47. https://doi.org/10.1007/s41463-024-00194-8

Okumura, S. (2018). *The mountains and waters sutra: A practitioner's guide to Dōgen's "Sansuikyo"*. Wisdom Publications.

Scharmer, C. O. (2023). In memory of Ed Schein: From accessing your ignorance to accessing your love. *Journal of Awareness-Based Systems Change*, *3*(1), 9–16. https://doi.org/10.47061/jasc.v3i1.6272

Scharmer, C. O. (2022, September 6). Protect the flame: Circles of radical presence in times of collapse. *Field of the Future Blog, Medium*. https://medium.com/presencing-institute-blog/protect-the-flame-49f1ac2480ac

Seed, J., Macy, J., Fleming, P., & Naess, A. (1988). *Thinking like a mountain: Towards a council of all beings*. New Society Publishers.

Senge, P. (1990/2006). *The fifth discipline: The art and practice of the learning organization*. Doubleday.

Spiller, C. (2021). 'I AM': Indigenous consciousness for authenticity and leadership. *Leadership*, *17*(4), 491–496. https://doi.org/10.1177/1742715021999590

Spiller, C., Nicholson, A. & Spiller, R. (2025). Consciousness-centered stewardship: An indigenous standpoint. *Humanist Management Journal*, *10*, 65–76. https://doi.org/10.1007/s41463-024-00202-x.

Tanahashi, K. (2016). *Heart of the brush: The splendor of East Asian calligraphy*. Shambhala.

Waddock, S. (2025). Eco-social narratives for awakening an era of transformative change. *Humanist Management Journal*, *10*(1), 11–29. https://doi.org/10.1007/s41463-024-00201-y

Wheatley, M. (1992/2006). *Leadership and the new science: Discovering order in a chaotic world*. Berrett-Koehler.

Whitman, W. (1855). *Song of Myself 51*. https://poets.org/poem/song-myself-51

Chapter 14

Rewilding Leadership: Lessons from the Wolf

Julian Norris

University of Calgary, Canada

Abstract

This chapter explores the concept of rewilding through the lens of the Yellowstone wolf reintroduction, offering profound insights into complexity leadership, ecosystem dynamics, and systemic change. By examining the transformative impact of wolves on the Yellowstone ecosystem, it is demonstrated how complex living systems self-organize, adapt, and generate emergent properties. Seven key patterns of ecosystem engineering are revealed: predation, disturbance, exchange, stabilization, energy transfer, connection, and diffusion – and their relevance to leadership practices. The narrative bridges ecological science and leadership theory, arguing that effective systemic intervention requires understanding relational dynamics rather than imposing rigid control. It emphasizes the importance of creating conditions for emergence, learning from natural systems, and developing a consciousness that recognizes interconnectedness. Ultimately, leaders are called to "rewild" their psyches, reconnecting with the natural world and adopting a more holistic, adaptive approach to leadership and system transformation.

Keywords: Rewilding; ecosystem engineering; complexity leadership; systems thinking; ecological restoration; wolf reintroduction; Yellowstone national park; network dynamics; emergence

Introduction

To be wild, according to desert author, Terry Tempest Williams (2016), is "to be whole. To be complete. Wildness reminds us what it means to be human, what

Artful Leadership: Retreat, Recenter, and Rewild, 191–205
Copyright © 2026 by Julian Norris
Published under exclusive licence by Emerald Publishing Limited
doi:10.1108/S2058-880120250000010015

we are connected to rather than what we are separate from." But this view of wildness as wholeness is far from universal; the term has more commonly been used as a placeholder for everything that the settled world is not. Wild places are uninhabited or uncultivated, wild animals untamed, wild plants undomesticated, wild people uncivilized and their behavior unpredictable or unconstrained.

Wild derives from the Germanic *wald* meaning forest. We might imagine that it was originally synonymous with home. But to the Romans, whose northward imperial expansion was definitively terminated in those same forests, "untamed nature was portrayed as a resistant, antipodal enemy of Roman civilization" (Östenberg, 2018). Like America's Wild West, the northern Wald was an unsettled – and unsettling – frontier that lay beyond colonial control.

Rewilding is a broad concept with both methodological and philosophical implications. As a *method*, it offers policies and practices for rebuilding ecosystems that have been significantly altered by anthropogenic influence. Such solutions can include minimizing human activity, reintroducing keystone species, or restoring natural processes within a particular landscape with the goal of revitalizing self-regulating ecological relationships and recovering ecosystem functionality.

As a philosophy, rewilding challenges human-centric environmental management and the idea that nature needs constant human intervention. It suggests that wildness represents much more than a set of ecosystem functions and services; rather it points to the self-organizing, creative energy inherent in all living systems. According to George Monbiot (2014), whose writing and films have helped to popularize the concept, rewilding is not about returning to some romanticized or nostalgic view of the past, whether ecological or cultural. Rather it is about enhancing the complexity and abundance of existing ecosystems while creating new opportunities for human engagement with wild processes. Monbiot argued that rewilding should therefore be seen as additive rather than substitutive, it is about creating new opportunities alongside existing land uses, not necessarily replacing all human activity.

Who's Afraid of the Big Bad Wolf?

It does not get much wilder than a wolf.

Wolves have lurked at the imaginal edges of the human story for generations. Even in landscapes that have not felt the footfall of a wild wolf for centuries, they continue to exert an archetypal potency for modern people. Their memory lives in us through myth, parable, and folk memory. Romantic images swirl together with the fearful tales modernity continues to tell its children; bad wolves blowing down lazily constructed homes or masquerading as sick relatives to ravish innocent maidens; sheep-snatching night monsters, werewolves, and false prophets with an unholy lust for slaughter. They are there at the beginning, Romulus and Remus the founders of the Roman Empire suckled as babes by a she-wolf. And at the end, whether as Fenrir, the Norse wolf, whose unbinding signifies the apocalypse or in Isaiah's vision of a peaceable kingdom where the wolf grazes beside the lamb. Occasionally tamed by prophets and saints, but always ravenous, wantonly savage, slavering, lurking at the forest's edge to deceive the unwary villager.

The Mayflower departed England in 1620 carrying stories of diabolical wolves and leaving behind a land where the wolf had been intentionally driven to extinction. The *New World* was altogether different. Here the wolf ran free and was invariably respected as a relative by First Peoples. One Nunamiut elder (as cited in Lopez, 1978) described this sense of kinship beautifully:

> "The wolf" [the old man said] is my fellow hunter. We speak the same language, have the same needs. We follow our brother, the raven because he leads us to caribou. If we falter, we die. We learn from each other. We are both animals in need of life.

According to Anishinaabe leader John Johnson Sr (as cited in Keuthan, 2022), "the wolf and first man were once brothers. They were companions...they must look out for each other." Many peoples, including the Cheyenne, Lakota, Blackfoot, Assiniboine, Arikara, Arapaho, Osage, Shoshone, and Pawnee, viewed wolves as teachers and role models (Fogg et al., 2015) and there is a strong body of evidence to suggest that the relationship between wolves and human beings involved cooperation and co-evolution across the North American continent (Schleidt & Shalter, 2003).

But that kinship and need for life were not recognized by the newcomers. By the time Yellowstone was created in 1872 as the world's first national park, bounties and poison bait had been used to silence wolves across their historic range. The park's creation took place under the shadow of the massive North American ethnic and ecological cleansing project that saw Indigenous peoples, along with the bison and the wolf, slaughtered and driven to the edge of extinction in a violent wave of colonial expansion and settlement. Unsurprisingly, a wolf control campaign was quickly initiated in the park, and by 1926, the last wolves in Yellowstone were exterminated.

Their voices would remain silent for another seventy years.

To the settler mindset, it made perfect sense to eradicate wolves. They were dangerous and unpredictable. They ate desirable *game* animals like elk. They *terrorized* farmers and *slaughtered* their livestock. Killing wolves, it was argued, would preserve the natural resources and beauty of the park and lead to happier hunters, outfitters, tourists, and local ranchers. There appeared to be little downside. But it is never possible to control a complex living system. Eliminating wolves led to a host of unintended and unwanted consequences and the rangers charged with protecting and preserving the park inadvertently throttled its vitality and choked its resilience. The elk and coyote populations exploded while other animals – from beavers to songbirds – began to decline. Within a decade, scientists were raising the alarm about overgrazing within the park.

Often, it's not until we get rid of something that we discover its true importance.

In 1966, biologist Robert Paine demonstrated that removing a single predator species, sea stars, from intertidal ecosystems caused dramatic *decreases* in local biodiversity. It turned out the sea stars had been preventing prey species from over-exploiting the available resources. This process, whereby a small number of apex predators positively impact an entire ecosystem, came to be known as a *trophic cascade* (Wootton, 1994) and at whatever scale researchers examined natural phenomena – from the microscopic to the planetary – they found much greater complexity, coherence and connectivity than previously imagined. Such findings had significant implications for how to intervene wisely in wild landscapes. Phenomena like forest fire and predators turned out to play vital roles in maintaining the health of ecosystems. The delicate – often invisible – relationships between the discrete parts of an ecosystem were central to understanding ecological integrity and change.

The mindset that had viewed Yellowstone as a landscape that could be carefully controlled like a Victorian estate or a large farm began to shift. By the mid-1960s, the bison in the park which had been managed as a captive herd were released and allowed to self-regulate. A diverse range of voices, ecologists, scientists, poets and philosophers, began to challenge and reframe the very notion of how *wildness* was understood within Western culture. And, a range of human rights, sovereignty, and cultural renaissance movements resulted in the growing inclusion of traditional ecological knowledge systems of Indigenous people that brought a sophisticated understanding of systems ecology and trophic cascades (Pierotti & Wildcat, 2000). For centuries, the mindset of modernity had viewed the *wild* as something chaotic, disorderly, and unproductive that must be dominated and forced into submission. Increasingly, and this story is far from over, *wildness* pointed to graceful patterns of deeper underlying order and the capacity for generative self-organization. And within this cultural shift, a growing consensus called for wolves to be returned from exile to once again play their critical role in Yellowstone.

To *rewild* the park.

You likely know the story. In the mid-1990s, 31 wolves were trapped in the Canadian Rockies and then re-released into Yellowstone. They quickly established themselves and their impact was dramatic. They began to hunt elk in large numbers, around 20 elk per wolf per year. They bred quickly, eventually stabilizing at around 90 wolves dwelling in less than a dozen distinct family packs. The elk population thinned and the remaining elk used the landscape differently. There was widespread regeneration of shrubs, willow, aspen trees, and berry bushes and this in turn impacted numerous other species. Beavers returned to the rivers feeding on the willow, building dams which created rich wetland habitats for moose, otters, water birds, insects, and amphibians. Trees regrew along the edges of rivers which stabilized the banks and provided shade for fish to spawn. Grizzly bears ate the berries and followed the wolf packs to feed on the elk – and increasingly bison – carcasses alongside wolverines, eagles, and other opportunists. Growing numbers of songbirds found food and shelter in the underbrush. The wolves killed most of the coyotes, driving the remainder to the high country, which in turn seems to have increased the antelope and fox populations. And so on. This story is still unfolding and much remains unknown and hotly debated. But one thing everybody agrees on: A handful of wolves, simply by being themselves, fundamentally shifted the web of relationships within the park thereby impacting the entire ecosystem – increasing its diversity, complexity, and resilience.

It is a compelling story (Smith & Ferguson, 2012) that stands alone as a contemporary case study of the perils and possibilities inherent when we intervene in complex living systems. It is a rich story with many entry points, players, and perspectives. Causal chains, cross-scale dynamics, trophic cascades, phase transition, tipping points, feedback loops, boundaries, strange attractors, unintended consequences, and emergent outcomes all have walk on parts in this story. There's some exaggeration, hyperbole, wishful thinking, and a few romantic projections mixed in there too. Some researchers (Fleming, 2019) argued there is insufficient research data to validate the widely shared conclusions related to trophic cascades that have become so popular. The story itself has become a kind of *myth* – one that has escaped the park boundaries and the confines of academic journals. Carried by the winds of YouTube (Sustainable Human, 2014), it has found its way into the imaginations of millions for whom it is a story of insight, healing, and possibility. Rewilding our way to a regenerative future with cute wolf puppies. Such sentiment has helped generate popular support for a number of European rewilding initiatives with mixed results. Some have been successful. In other cases, the ecological benefits have been tempered by conflict with farmers and local communities. A meta-review of such projects by Gerber et al. (2024) found that ecosystem-level benefits from such rewilding projects require a careful management regime to address the potential unintended consequences. According to the International Union for Conservation of Nature (2021), "misuse of the increasingly popular rewilding concept risks alienating communities, harming existing biodiversity."

It's clearly a complex story, and for those of us interested in leadership, systems change, and organizational network theory there are a couple of vantage points to view it from. What the *wolves* did and what the *rewilders* did.

What the Wolves Did

A small group of intelligent social carnivores, with no strategic plan or defined leader, had a transformative ecosystem-level impact in less than a decade. They did a few, very simple, wolf things. They hunted elk. They chased off the coyotes and made life harder for the mountain lions. They reproduced. And when their family pack got to a certain size, they split off and created new ones. The main impact was on the elk who modified their behavior. For one thing, they no longer ate all the young poplar shoots growing along the rivers. If you are an elk, you don't want to get trapped against a river by a wolf pack, it significantly constrains your chances of escape. This *first-order* effect led to a cascade of *second-order* effects that emerged in the relationships between species that had no direct contact with the wolves such as beavers, songbirds, and fish. And those changes in relational dynamics between systems agents led to a set of *third-order* effects – new *bottom-up* systems properties ranging from hydrological impacts to structural vegetation changes. The impacts of such non-consumptive effects seem like magic when you watch the YouTube video (Sustainable Human, 2014), but it's just the way nature works.

Ecologists have a term to describe this kind of impact; *ecosystems engineering* (Jones et al., 1997). Ecosystems engineers are species whose activities lead to the creation of new micro-habitats within an ecosystem. They complexify the world around them by creating spaces for species that might otherwise not exist. Some of them, like beavers, wolves, and bison, change the environment by transforming the relationships and materials within. Others, like trees, coral, and kelp, do it by transforming *themselves*. Wilby (2002) warned against trivializing the concept, reminding us that all organisms impact their environment to some degree. Nevertheless, the term remains in widespread use, and, according to Romero et al. (2015) "ecosystem engineering is increasingly recognized as a relevant ecological driver of diversity and community composition."

I offer a note of caution around the term *engineer*. After all, an engineered solution is the exact opposite of an ecological emergence. The difference between engineers who built the Hoover Dam and beavers along the Yellowstone River is not simply one of scale; their impact is *categorically* different. But the concept has been a valuable placeholder for describing distinct patterns of ecosystem influence and it offers a useful way for leaders to think about working in situations of high complexity. Ray Anderson (Anderson & White, 2011), founder of *Interface*, famously observed that "everything you need to know about running a business, you can learn from the forest." Understanding the dynamics of the wild world has much to offer anyone interested in leadership, complexity, and systems change. I suggest there are at least seven distinct patterns of ecosystem engineering that merit deeper consideration.

Patterns of Predation

It's what wolves are born to do. They kill, they feast on the dead, and they instill the fear of death in the living. These things act as a behavioral modifier and restraint on the otherwise uncontrolled population growth of elk. When the wolves showed up in Yellowstone, the rules of the game changed. When other boundary conditions allow, ungulates that don't get preyed on or hunted will grow in numbers and exploit the available resources to the best of their ability. They will shape the environment and often destroy complexity-generating foliage such as young trees and shrubs. Co-evolutionary patterns of predation are important negative feedback loops that constrain over-exploitation and exponential population growth and they are found across the wild world.

Each wolf and wolfpack has agency and makes decisions locally. Replicated at scale, the wolf and wolfpack drive whole systems properties. It's important to remember that elk have agency too. They are not just passive-wolf snacks. I once watched a lone cow elk face down three wolves that were blocking her route through a mountain meadow. Her bravery and power were humbling to watch and the wolves wisely backed down. The wolves drive patterns of adaptive response amongst the elk who learn to live in human settlements where the wolves are more reluctant to hunt them.

The fear of death can make quick learners of us all.

Patterns of Disturbance

Left undisturbed, certain forest ecosystems sequester energy unevenly, shut out the light from the forest floor, monopolize resources, and inhibit diversity. It takes a mighty force to get them to share. Often that force is elemental, fire, wind, and flood. But elephants will do the same thing on a more localized scale. They knock over trees, clear pathways, and break things open allowing energy to be redistributed and creating patches within which new forms of diversity can flourish.

Such patterns of disturbance are common and critical. Herds of bison will graze and trample an area intensively for a couple of days and then move on. It breaks up the soil and allows for a more diverse array of plants and grasses to grow. Regenerative ranchers have learned to mimic this pattern to mitigate the otherwise inevitable erosion of complexity that takes place when you place herds of ungulates into pastures with rigid boundaries. The bison will also create wallows, they take baths on the land leaving dusty indentations behind which then become important seasonal micro-habitats for other species. You can still find old wallows on the east slopes of the Rocky Mountains that remain generative micro-habitats more than a century since bison were eradicated from the landscape.

Patterns of Exchange

Nothing in the natural world does only one thing. Large animals don't just disturb landscapes. They leave something of themselves behind, their bones, dung, and fur, that creates opportunities for others to inhabit the landscape more successfully. Bison dung becomes a habitat for insects that in turn provide food for birds. That same dung, when dried, provided prairie-dwelling hunters with the fuel needed to flourish and keep warm. And it wasn't just humans they kept warm. Next to musk oxen, bison have amongst the warmest known inner fur. It comes out in clumps at the end of the winter and blows around the landscape. Birds weave it into their nests and this turns out to be important for the survival and reproductive success of smaller-bodied and above-ground nesting species (Coppedge, 2009). Cows don't do the same thing. The way cattle raised under typical industrial feedlot systems survive cold winters is by having a thick layer of fat and a hot-burning metabolism that is kept stoked with energy-rich, water-hungry monocrops. The second- and third-order effects of sustaining large numbers of cattle in this way lead to an *erosion* of ecological complexity and biodiversity under most conventional management regimes.

Patterns of Stabilization

Who doesn't love a good watering hole? Beavers dam flowing water creating pools and wetlands that in turn allow multiple other species to live, interact, and flourish. When they were extracted at a continental scale to provide the raw materials for the British hat industry, their absence precipitated an ecological aftershock that reverberates to this day. There are many other species that slow down and stabilize energy flows within ecosystems and create generative new habitats resulting in greater diversity and flourishing. Some, like beaver and moss, act as hydrological *buffers* to the volatility of water flow. Biotic soil crusts create rich micro-climates in arid landscapes that prevent the soil being blown away by the wind, allowing other species to gain a foothold. Similarly, delicate flowers like the alpine dryas will find a foothold in the alluvial deposits at the base of glaciers and along mountain rivers. Over time, they form a rich mat from their own decaying bodies that trap other nutrients and create a micro-nursery for tree seedlings to establish themselves (Giupponi & Leoni, 2020). Such patterns of accumulative stabilization are similarly found with sea grasses and mangrove trees which construct vast carbon-rich sediment banks beneath their roots, gradually building up coastlines while simultaneously protecting them from erosion through their dense network of stabilizing roots and trapped sediment.

Patterns of Energy Transfer and Transformation

Species like salmon and caribou move vast amounts of energy within and between ecosystems making it available for a diverse range of other species. When salmon return to their birthplaces in the coastal temperate rainforest to spawn, they are completing a cycle that can see them bring the energy of the Pacific Ocean depths thousands of kilometers inland to the mountainous headwaters of great rivers. Along the way they have helped to birth and sustain entire ecologies, economies, and cultures. Even after their death, their decomposing bodies, dragged far from the river by bears and made available through the critical mediating influence of fungal networks (Larocque, 2022), provide critical nutrients for forest and riparian ecosystems. Everywhere you look, energy is being moved, stored, released, competed for, shared, and transformed to be made available for other life.

Patterns of Connection

Some species create entire worlds of opportunity for others by connecting things together, linking up, cross-pollinating, or moving DNA around. Sometimes it's obvious. Liana vines in rainforests create arboreal pathways that other species can use to travel between trees. Much less easy to see, but far more significant in terms of ecological impact and global reach, are the networks of mycelial filament that link every part of a forest together and enable it to grow. One cubic inch of soil can contain *miles* of mycelia which fundamentally shapes the dynamics of forest ecosystems in multiple ways. Mycelia helps to cycle and distribute nutrients. Mycelia engineers soil structure by binding particles together into aggregate thereby increasing soil stability, water retention, and aeration. Mycelia forms symbiotic relationships with other plants, helping to transfer critical nutrients and timely information within a forest community. And mycelia helps decompose plant compounds thereby releasing stored nutrients back into the ecosystem and creating new habitats for other organisms.

Patterns of Diffusion

Symbiosis, parasitic interactions that co-evolve into mutually beneficial relationships, is a widespread pattern. As the philosopher Peter Kropotkin (1902) famously noted, nature cooperates just as much as it competes. Many plant species rely on birds and insects to pollinate and spread their seeds, offering nourishment in return. And sometimes that can have landscape-level impacts. An oak tree produces about two thousand acorns a year. But only about one in ten thousand acorns actually becomes an oak tree! Every acorn has the *potential* to become an oak, the pattern is genetically encoded in their DNA and under the right circumstances they will unfold and develop according to these original instructions. Most never get the chance, young oaks cannot grow in the shade of their parents. But given the opportunity, jays will transport and store large numbers of the acorns to eat later. The birds bury the acorns in the loose soil of open areas at the woodland's scrubby fringe. Other animals will do this, but jays seem to have a special relationship with oak trees (Gómez, 2003). Jays will even dig up new oak seedlings, eat the remaining acorn, and then replant the sapling, a process which many young trees survive. This remarkable and critical relationship between bird and tree was responsible for the rapid dispersal of oak forests across Europe as the last ice age receded. And in case it doesn't go without saying, the jays weren't *trying* to plant forests; they were simply creating food caches for themselves in ways that led to systemic effects.

Predation, disturbance, exchange, stabilization, energy transfer and transformation, connection, and diffusion: seven simple patterns that enable agents to shape and influence entire ecosystems. Disrupt or remove one pattern from the landscape and the system dynamics change. Add it back in and the agents self-organize in ways that lead to new systems-wide outcomes. There's a lot to learn here, if we understand leadership to be fundamentally a process of social influence (Deng et al., 2023), these principles hold relevance for anyone seeking to influence a network or social field. Study the pattern language and you will not only have a better understanding of the dynamics but hold the keys for changing or stabilizing virtually any kind of complex living system at virtually any scale.

But it's less than half the story.

What the "Rewilders" Did

As we have seen, species like wolves have an outsized impact within an ecosystem. The behaviors of such ecosystem *engineers* lead to patterns of increasing complexity, diversity, resilience, and adaptation. But in this story, they couldn't do it on their own. Their wolf skills were being deployed in service of the aspirations of others. The very same agency, the National Park Service, that had so successfully killed them off was now responsible for their reintroduction.

These rewilding technicians had the mandate to manage Yellowstone Park and address the consequences of out-of-control elk populations. For decades this involved firstly encouraging the elk population, then trying to cull the herds themselves, and then being forced to stop by politically-organized hunters.

For reasons that we've touched on, the decision was made that the best way to restore the Park involved wolves. The National Parks Service was simply restoring a preexisting negative feedback loop into a bounded system in order to address the downsides of a positive feedback loop. *That* was the leadership move. They built understanding of the system dynamics, ran and evaluated experiments, generated learning, and increased the flow of high-quality information. They created the conditions for beneficial patterns of emergence to take place. The National Parks Service successfully re-introduced wild wolves into the Park and monitored the impacts.

The Parks staff were clearly operating at a meta-level from the wolves. And, at the same time, they too were being deployed as another layer of network agents to do what park rangers do. Catch and radio-collar wolves, follow them around, count elk, measure just about anything measurable, write reports, make presentations, and deal with unanticipated social and ecological consequences. They had to learn a few new skills, but they turned out to be just as efficient at reintroducing wolves as they had been at eradicating them. Some of the skills, wolf trapping, patrolling the backcountry, and following the chain of command, were *identical.*

They were simply repurposed by the next level of complexity leaders!

As systems scholar Donella Meadows (1997) reminded us, shifting *purpose* can be a deep and potent systems leverage tool. Changing the purpose of Yellowstone Park, however, was a lengthy and intricate journey. From the recommendations of wolf hunter turned environmentalist Aldo Leopold in the 1940s until Clinton's Secretary of the Interior Bruce Babbitt signed the Record of Decision in 1994, it required an enormously complex, multi-faceted, and multi-stakeholder process. Many individuals, organizations, and networks played important leadership roles. The National Parks Service, the US Fish and Wildlife Service, various state-level wildlife agencies, academics, politicians, writers, environmental groups, communities, and culture shapers played a role. We could point to many significant actors, but no single individual *did* it, and indeed those who played significant roles were doing completely different things. Biologists who deepened our collective understanding of ecosystems through their research. Journalists who translated their findings into compelling stories. Activists who applied pressure. Agency officials who prepared scenarios and facilitated unprecedented levels of community engagement. Richard Nixon who, as president, championed the 1973 Endangered Species Act that passed with unanimous Senate and near-unanimous (355-4) Congressional support. All the people who actually wrote the Act, and those who crafted the earlier acts on which it was built. A 50-year process of influencing the paradigms, processes, policies, practices, power structures, and institutions of a complex, pluralistic society. And that process didn't simply end with the arrival of the wolves. A judge ordered the removal of the Yellowstone wolves in 1997. That decision was itself reversed in 2000. The wolves never got the memo about the Yellowstone Park boundary and made their way into its tri-state neighbors: Wyoming, Idaho, and Montana. Cow country!

I think you get the idea. There are a lot of moving pieces here and it's exhausting just thinking about it. But if we step back for a moment, we can see the *rewilders* employing the principles of ecosystem engineering but with a critical difference. Their behavior, unlike the wolves, was shaped by intentionality, self-awareness, meta-contextual reference, deliberate learning, and a clearly defined underlying purpose. They used deliberate interventions intended to impact the relational dynamics of a complex system in ways that led to new systems states, properties, and outcomes. Ecosystem engineers are *unconscious* network agents while systems leaders aspire to *conscious* network agency. As leaders, every one of us is an agent in a complex living system whether we are aware of it or not. We continually exert our agency and influence in contexts that we don't real-ize are complex or in ways that have complex consequences that are largely invisible to us. We don't *become* complexity leaders; we already *are* complexity leaders! But for the most part, we don't realize it. What we become is more conscious. It's why practices and relationships that help us become less subject to our biases, that help us understand the way we perceive, make meaning, and cultivate self-awareness or reflexive capability are so important for anyone seek-ing to influence systems.

Rewilding Practices

After many years teaching systems and complexity principles to leaders of all kinds, the hardest thing is seldom learning *new* principles and practices. It's letting go of *old* patterns of control, reactivity, and linearity. The foundational attrib-utes required for complexity leadership are developed and deepened through a range of *transformative learning practices*. Describing such practices is obviously beyond the scope of this paper, but I offer the following two activities as ways to explore the practical lessons offered by rewilding:

Pattern Mapping Activity

For many years, it appears that those responsible for managing Yellowstone Park were unable to fully perceive the complex ecological relationships at play. The following activity offers a way to look at a particular organizational or systems challenge through an ecological lens and perhaps find new opportunities for crea-tive action.

- On a large sheet of paper, draw a cross-scale map of your organizational eco-system with at least three nested levels (e.g. team/division/organization, local/regional/national, service provider/stakeholders/disruptive technology land-scape). Represent key systems agents and dynamics along with the relation-ships between them.
- Articulate a clear orienting question around a desired system property. For example, if you are currently using the number of customer complaints as a service performance metric in a healthcare system you might ask something like "what would be happening in our system if the rate of customer com-plaints were to drop by 50%?"

- Identify how the presence or absence of each ecosystem engineering pattern might be helping to generate your *current* systems state:
  o *Predation* (e.g. competition, market protection, constraints, talent poaching)
  o *Disturbance* (e.g. creative disruption, innovation, external pressure)
  o *Exchange* (e.g. resource sharing, collaboration, story-telling)
  o *Stabilization* (e.g. organizational structures, scaling, planned redundancy)
  o *Energy Transfer* (e.g. resource flows, funding relationships, energy "leaks")
  o *Connection* (e.g. key partnerships and alliances, information flows, networks of networks)
  o *Diffusion* (e.g. ambassador networks, early adopter programs, demonstration projects)
- Use different colors and symbols to represent the different patterns
- Pay attention to their presence both *within* and *between* levels
- Identify potential places for "rewilding" interventions. Pay particular attention to small actions that can create new *relationships*. Where might amplifying or dampening a pattern lead to potentially desirable second- and third-order effects? Which patterns could you actually influence?

Reflective Activity: Nature as Teacher

This exercise explores how we become better students of the natural world and shift our attention from the obvious structural elements of a living system to the relational dynamics that generate its properties. It can be done solo or with a whole team.

- Find a natural area with diverse ecological elements – ideally with varying terrain, plant communities, and evidence of ecological processes. It doesn't have to be large but it should have a wild character; the edge of a pond or river, a small area of woodland, or hedgerow, an uncultivated or overgrown "patch" would all be suitable.
- Take a moment to center yourself and "tune in" to the place – its sounds, smells, textures, and contours. Consciously open your senses and "beginner mind." Take a moment, especially in an area that you already know well, to awaken your curiosity and sense of wonder.
- Spend some time to slowly wander and observe. Stop often. Shift perspectives and levels. Get close to the ground. A magnifying glass and notebook will be helpful. As you wander:
  o Notice patterns of *predation*: Who eats what? Where is competition happening? How does predation shape behaviors and adaptations? Which species thrive despite constraints?
  o Notice patterns of *disturbance*: What disruptions exist? How has life responded? Which species capitalize on disturbance? What needs disturbance?
  o Notice patterns of *exchange*: What mutual benefits exist? Where is symbiosis evident? What invisible exchanges might occur? How might competition serve collaboration?

- o Notice patterns of *stabilization*: What creates resilience? What niches exist? Where do you observe regulation processes? Which elements buffer against change?
- o Notice patterns of *energy transfer*: How does energy flow through the system? Where are resources concentrated? What pathways exist? How does information travel?
- o Notice patterns of *connection*: What relationships link elements? Which species interdepend? How does connectivity create resilience? What serves as bridges between parts?
- o Notice patterns of *diffusion*: How do patterns spread? What transports seeds or genes? Which "keystone" species have rippling influence? How are successful adaptations replicated?

At the end, you can take some time to journal and reflect on what you notice. Alternatively, you could use a state-shifting practice such as stream-of-consciousness writing to integrate your learning. This involves writing continuously for 4 minutes in response to a prompt. Write the prompt at the top of the page and don't analyze or overthink the process; just keep writing and come back to the prompt. Examples might include:

- Sitting here I need to remember…
- This place reminds me that our team must…
- I can see how disturbance has enabled…
- I'm curious about…

Final Words

In this chapter, I have proposed that there are valuable lessons to be learned from the practice of rewilding. It offers a compelling case study in complexity leadership and network influence. Rewilding succeeds not by micromanaging nature but by restoring the foundational conditions and relationship that allow ecosystems to self-regulate. It rests on a profound trust in the deep evolutionary intelligence of living systems. It underscores the importance of setting the conditions for emergence and creative experimentation rather than trying to control outcomes or impose rigid solutions. It reminds us that any intervention can only ever be as good as our diagnosis which rests, in turn, on the accuracy of our maps. If our leadership practice reflects an overly mechanistic and incomplete view of reality, we not only compromise its efficacy but are likely to be dismayed by its unanticipated consequences. Above all, rewilding invites us to become serious students of nature and apply the lessons across our practice domain.

In closing, let me invite a final consideration. *The world needs leaders who have rewilded their own psyches!* The modern era has left far too many of us spatially, emotionally, and even linguistically separate from the natural world and our utter dependence on the rest of life. Nature has become a concept, somewhere we go when we are not engaged in our real lives. Something fundamentally *other*. And we end up living, leading, and creating from a dangerous place of isolation, severance, and illusion. To rewild the psyche is to awaken from the trance of such illusions and re-incorporate our consciousness within the broader fabric of creation. I am not alone in the conviction that a relational mindset of deep connectedness offers the only viable foundation for long-term human and planetary flourishing. And whatever community, country, or corporation has claimed our allegiance, and whatever transactional or competitive goals we serve, such flourishing must surely be the core mission to which our leadership is dedicated in these times.

For in the end, perhaps the greatest lesson offered by the wolves is a reminder of our *own* deep humanity and wild potential. An invitation to see ourselves as a planetary caretaker species with the capacity for maintaining and regenerating the kind of healthy social and ecological systems we'd most want to leave for our descendants. And thus, to carry what mythologist Martin Shaw (2011) called "the vast intelligence of the wolf right into the center of the human community."

References

Anderson, R. C., & White, R. (2011). *Business lessons from a radical industrialist: How a CEO doubled earnings, inspired employees and created innovation from one simple idea.* St. Martin's Griffin.

Coppedge, B. D. (2009). Patterns of bison hair use in nests of tallgrass prairie birds. *The Prairie Naturalist, 41*(3), 110–115.

Deng, C., Gulseren, D., Isola, C., Grocutt, K., & Turner, N. (2023). Transformational leadership effectiveness: An evidence-based primer. *Human Resource Development International, 26*(5), 627–641. https://doi.org/10.1080/13678868.2022.2135938

Fleming, P. J. S. (2019). They might be right, but Beschta et al. (2018) give no strong evidence that "trophic cascades shape recovery of young aspen in Yellowstone National Park": A fundamental critique of methods. *Forest Ecology and Management, 454,* 117283. https://doi.org/10.1016/j.foreco.2019.04.011

Fogg, B. R., Howe, N., & Pierotti, R. (2015). Relationships between indigenous American peoples and wolves 1: Wolves as teachers and guides. *Journal of Ethnobiology, 35*(2), 262–285. https://doi.org/10.2993/etbi-35-02-262-285.1

Gerber, N., Riesch, F., Bojarska, K., Zetsche, M., Rohwer, N. K., Signer, J., & Balkenhol, N. (2024). Do recolonising wolves trigger non-consumptive effects in European ecosystems? A review of evidence. *Wildlife Biology, 2024*(6), e01229. https://doi.org/10.1002/wlb3.01229

Giupponi, L., & Leoni, V. (2020). Alpine pioneer plants in soil bioengineering for slope stabilization and restoration: Results of a preliminary analysis of seed germination and future perspectives. *Sustainability, 12*(17), 7190. https://doi.org/10.3390/su12177190

Gómez, J. M. (2003). Spatial patterns in long-distance dispersal of Quercus ilex acorns by jays in a heterogeneous landscape. *Ecography, 26*(5), 573–584. https://doi.org/10.1034/j.1600-0587.2003.03586.x

International Union for Conservation of Nature. (2021). Issues brief: The benefits and risks of rewilding. https://iucn.org/sites/default/files/2022-04/rewilding_issues_brief_final.pdf

Jones, C. G., Lawton, J. H., & Shachak, M. (1997). Positive and negative effects of organisms as physical ecosystem engineers. *Ecology, 78*(7), 1946–1957. https://doi.org/10.1890/0012-9658(1997)078[1946:PANEOO]2.0.CO;2

Keuthan, A. (2022) Wolf and first man: An Anishinaabe story of companionship and protection amid the growing threats of poachers and habitat loss. https://nativeland. info/uncategorized/wolf-and-first-man-an-anishinaabe-story-of-companionship-and-protection-amid-the-growing-threats-of-poachers-and-habitat-loss/

Kropotkin, P. (1902). *Mutual aid: A factor in evolution*. McClure Phillips & Co.

Larocque, A. T. (2022). *Fish, forests, fungi: Soils in the 'salmon forests' of British Columbia* [Doctoral Dissertation]. University of British Columbia. https://open.library.ubc. ca/collections/ubctheses/24/items/1.0413041

Lopez, B. (1978). *Of wolves and men*. Simon & Schuster.

Meadows, D. (1997). Places to intervene in a system. *Whole Earth, 91*(1), 78–84. https:// wholeearth.info/p/whole-earth-winter-1997

Monbiot, G. (2014). *Feral: Rewilding the land, the sea, and human life*. University of Chicago Press.

Östenberg, I. (2018). Defeated by the forest, the pass, the wind: Nature as an enemy of Rome. In J. H. Clark & B. Turner (Eds.), *Brill's companion to military defeat in ancient Mediterranean society* (pp. 240–261). Brill.

Paine, R. T. (1966). Food web complexity and species diversity. *The American Naturalist, 100*(910), 65–75. http://www.jstor.org/stable/2459379 https://doi.org/10.1086/282400

Pierotti, R., & Wildcat, D. (2000). Traditional ecological knowledge: the third alternative (commentary). *Ecological Applications, 10*(5), 1333–1340. https://doi.org/ 10.1890/1051-0761(2000)010[1333:TEKTTA]2.0.CO;2

Romero, G. Q., Gonçalves-Souza, T., Vieira, C., & Koricheva, J. (2015). Ecosystem engineering effects on species diversity across ecosystems: A Meta-analysis. *Biological Reviews, 90*(3), 877–890. https://doi.org 10.1111/brv.12138

Schleidt, W. M., & Shalter, M. D. (2003). Coevolution of humans and canids: An alternative view of dog domestication: Homo Homini Lupus? *Evolution and Cognition, 9*(1), 57–72.

Shaw, M. (2011). *A branch from the lightning tree: Ecstatic myth and the grace in wildness*. White Cloud Press.

Smith, D., & Ferguson, G. (2012). *Decade of the wolf: Returning the wild to Yellowstone*. Rowman & Littlefield.

Sustainable Human. (2014). How wolves change rivers [Video]. YouTube. https://www. youtube.com/watch?v=ysa5OBhXz-Q&t=4s

Wilby, A. (2002). Ecosystem engineering: A trivialized concept? *Trends in Ecology & Evolution, 17*(7), 307. https://doi.org/10.1016/S0169-5347(02)02511-9

Williams, T. T. (2016). *The hour of land: A personal topography of America's national parks*. Sarah Crichton Books.

Wootton, J. T. (1994). The nature and consequences of indirect effects in ecological communities. *Annual Review of Ecology and Systematics, 25*, 443–466. https://doi.org/ 10.1146/annurev.es.25.110194.002303

Chapter 15

Rewilding the Soul, Resouling the Wild: Toward a Reclaimed Metaphysical Relationality

Brendan Ellis Williams

University of St. Andrews, Scotland

Abstract

This chapter explores the fundamental divide between Western dualistic, reductionistic worldviews and relational, animistic ontologies, arguing for the reclamation of "metaphysical relationality." The Cartesian split between mind (*res cogitans*) and matter (*res extensa*) has led to an exploitative relationship with the natural world and contributed to contemporary ecological crises and the development of habitual, corrosive socio-cultural patterns. As an alternative, "*res anima*" is proposed as a unitary multiplicity that recognizes all beings as conscious agents within an interconnected web of relationships. Effective leadership, particularly in addressing environmental concerns, must arise from this shift in metaphysical understanding. Drawing on diverse philosophical and theological traditions, practical contemplative exercises are presented to facilitate this "spiritual rewilding," including ritual offerings to the land, *natura divina* (contemplative engagement with natural beings), and open-awareness meditation. This chapter frames these practices as steps toward realizing what philosopher Josiah Royce called the "Beloved Community," reconceived as an animistic *communitas* that honors the consciousness and agency of all beings.

Keywords: Worldview; relationality; metaphysics; relational leadership; animism; beloved community; ecology; rewilding; culture; contemplation

Artful Leadership: Retreat, Recenter, and Rewild, 207–223
Copyright © 2026 by Brendan Ellis Williams
Published under exclusive licence by Emerald Publishing Limited
doi:10.1108/S2058-880120250000010016

Res Anima

From Duality to Unitary Multiplicity

The vast majority of what is typically called *Western* thought and endeavor is, at a deep structural level, rooted in a fundamentally world-negating and individualistic ethos. Judeo-Christian metaphysical assumptions constitute a partial explanation for this, as does the contrived Cartesian split between mind or consciousness (*res cogitans*) and unconscious matter (*res extensa*), along with the elevation of the human agent to a singularly unique metaphysical position. This modern Western outlook stands in stark contrast to the world-embracing and relational (and often animistic) worldviews that have otherwise been normative throughout human history, including in Europe and those regions that are now considered part of the *West*. Whatever their location and cultural specificity, indigenous worldviews (in the broadest sense of that designation) tend to be animistic, which is to say, to imbue all things with animacy, and to assume that matter and the whole of manifest or incarnate beingness itself is in a very real sense *alive*, and, in various ways or to varying degrees, *conscious*. For our present purposes, the most crucial dimension of this kind of worldview is that it is consciously relational in the way it conceptualizes the world, formulates human ethics, renders ritual practice within the human community, manifests and articulates authority, and, by extension, leadership. This means authority and leadership not only within the human community, but within the localized family of being or *web of relationality* at large, since the human community is merely one subset of the *communitas* of Nature as a whole, and this *communion* includes *all* persons (many of whom contemporary Western materialism would reduce to the ontic status of *mere things*: lifeless objects or purely unconscious phenomena, akin to *nonplayer characters* appearing in the game-field of subjective human experience).

But even in the thoroughly Christianized thought of medieval Europe with its excessive anthropocentrism, neither reductionism nor the notion of the *mechanical universe* were represented. It was not until the beginning of the scientific revolution, and Descartes' published work more specifically, that such notions emerged. In the medieval European mind, neither the cosmos nor the human person was generally conceptualized in a dualistic fashion, but rather in a triune fashion. This is in large part attributable to the inheritance of a deep-rooted Hellenistic philosophical and theological tradition of inquiry and discourse (about which Paul of Tarsus and other New Testament authors were clearly informed to some degree, cf., for example, 1 Thessalonians 5:23 and 1 Corinthians 2:12–15) that suggested not a binary, overtly reductionistic outlook on experience and the cosmos, but rather a trinary approach to conceptualizing both divinity and the human person – a model which was pregnant still with the dynamic possibility of a genuinely immanent presence of *anima*. (A similar approach is found in a host of Indo-Tibetan philosophical and religious traditions, for instance in the trinitarian models evinced throughout Hinduism, in the threefold micro- and macrocosms of Mahāyāna Buddhism, and in the nondual expressions of Vajrayāna: Dzogchen and Mahāmudrā.)

Notwithstanding, the Christianization of so-called *pagan* or pre-Christian European worldviews set in motion a host of problematic ideological developments that eventually shaped the worldview and theories of Descartes, Newton, and others considered part of the scientific revolution. As Lynn White (1967) summarized: "By destroying pagan animism, Christianity made it possible to exploit nature in a mood of indifference to the feelings of natural objects." That exploitation is precisely representative of the ideological shift from a world filled with countless other-than-human *persons* to a world of mere *insensible objects*. This began with a Judeo-Christian anthropocentric monotheism that, as White noted, overcame and eventually replaced the indigenous, animistic and polytheistic worldviews of Europe, taking the sacred out of Nature and relegating it to an essentially unknowable transcendent object. The pattern found its final and most complete expression in the emergence of Cartesian dualism and the advent of both the reductionistic materialism and the maximal anthropocentrism that eventually became synonymous with Western science and rationality, as understood within the specific constraints of modernity.

In this shift was lost, among other things, the inherently animistic tendency to see an impulse toward relationality as a supernal *telos* in and of itself, an ever present and irreducible reference point, a kind of figurative *axis mundi* holding up the whole cosmos of human thought and action, a *sine qua non* of incarnate beingness and therefore of all worthy intellective and spiritual pursuits. As Hallowell (1960) noted in his groundbreaking study of Ojibwa (Anishinaabe) ontology, we can say of animistic cultures generally: that the relational activities of all *persons* (human and other-than-human alike) constitute the crux of the worldview inhabited by such cultures. In what I am here terming *metaphysical relationality,* which is in essence a more formal and precise descriptor of what is generally called *animism*, all beings are understood as persons and all persons are understood as agentic. Reciprocal honor and mutually supportive action among beings are paramount in cultural contexts that express a worldview of metaphysical relationality because the notion of shared destiny acts as the practical backbone of such a worldview. I would argue that relationality in this form (or at this depth) has much to offer human communities, regardless of cultural particularities. One of the many gifts modern industrialized societies in specific could glean as a result of reclaiming genuine metaphysical relationality is a correction of the inherently de-personalizing, exploitative, and domineering manner in which such societies have generally treated the natural world around them, yielding increasingly obvious catastrophic consequences.

The relational (animistic) approach stands entirely in contrast to what Feuerbach (1989) called the "absolute intolerance" (p. 114) of Judeo-Christian monotheism: at base an exclusionary orientation toward the world which casts aside the sacred commitment of interspecial reciprocity in favor of an unbounded anthropocentrism, a hyper-limiting conceptualization of divinity and the sacred, and a yet more overtly radical and corrosive reduction: the restriction of ultimate metaphysical value to a single human group (i.e., those who happen to have been born into or joined a given religio-cultural faction). We can similarly characterize the hard dualism of the Cartesian model as a sort of *absolute intolerance*, in that it arbitrarily (and violently) rends the cosmos into living and dead domains, and places the human agent, along with God and the angelic hierarchies, in the unique position of the living, leaving the rest of creation or manifest beingness resigned to the metaphysical trash-heap of the dead.

Until this demon of reductionistic intolerance, which lies coiled at the root of all Western thought and endeavor, is exorcised, it will continue to haunt us thoroughly from its shadowy realm in the unconscious, from where it has long dictated, however subtly, the manner in which we conceive of ourselves and all our collective and individual aims. I would be remiss not to emphasize, however, that the needful manner of exorcism is not to be found in mere deconstruction of Western religious systems or dogmas; that work, though significant, has already been thoroughly accomplished by scholarship, from a practically endless variety of angles: philosophical, historical, socio-cultural, etc. Rather, what is most needful now is *reclamation* to fill the void of what has already been deconstructed: namely, reclamation of a worldview that is deeply relational and expansive enough to account for the true diversity, multiplicity, and innate interdependence not only of human experience, but of all conscious agents – indeed, of Life itself – and is therefore morally astute enough to (re-)formulate a sound ethic vis-à-vis all beings or *persons*. I would posit that only from such a rich and nourishing soil-bed can something like a truly sensible and life-giving cultural construction grow. And, by extension, only under those conditions can a genuinely transformational and life-giving form of leadership take birth. Since worldview underlies and shapes all human endeavor, whether consciously or unconsciously, genuinely transformational leadership must involve itself in the analysis, intentional curation, and/or transmutation of worldview elements: determinative parts or dimensions of a given worldview structure.

The reclamation of a worldview founded in metaphysical relationality could be conceived of as a *spiritual rewilding*: both a *rewilding of the soul* and a *resouling of the wild*. That is, I refer here to a *spiritual rewilding* in two distinct but interrelated ways: firstly, in that the individual *psykhé* or *anima* is, in the aforesaid worldview transmutation or *conversion*, restored to a conscious state of interdependent interconnection with the larger family of beingness, with the endlessly diverse and mysterious *wilderness* of Life at large (viz., a *rewilding of the soul*); and, secondly, the cosmos or expanse of manifest beingness is once again perceived and experienced by the human locus of consciousness as utterly alive: a matrix of conscious agents to be related to, rather than a plane of inanimate matter to be manipulated at will and ultimately dominated (viz., a *resouling of the wild*).

To adopt – or rather, *reclaim* – a worldview hinged on the wholing, expansive principle (and experience) of metaphysical relationality is what we could term a *metánoia* (a *turning* or *conversion of mind*) toward the principle of *res anima*. Rather than the dividing, reductionistic principle of Cartesian dualism enshrined in the *res cogitans-res extensa* binary, *res anima* affirms that all *stuff* is *spirit stuff*, all particularities are ensouled and sacred in themselves, not merely by virtue of an underlying metaphysical unity they each innately share in, but additionally by virtue of their particularity, their uniqueness of ontic expression. In this framework, *cogitans* and *extensa* are unified, since the totality of the "expanse" (*extensa*) of manifest reality is seen as arising from – and as always already imbued with – the "stuff of mind" (*res cogitans*), the sacred aliveness or ensouled nature of all that appears.

In and Toward, Not Over and Against

The two types of mutually opposing worldviews laid out here – a strongly dualistic, world-negating view on the one hand, and a fundamentally nondual, relational view on the other – naturally produce very different cultural constructions, styles of critical analysis, and socially sanctioned endeavors. They also tend to produce oppositely situated aims. In a religious context, the former inevitably engenders what I have come to call a *metaphysical escape paradigm*: a metaphysical construction that foundationally rejects the world (e.g., as inherently corrupted, evil, or innately and irrevocably imbued with undesirable suffering) and seeks to remove the mind or soul (*psykhē, anima*) in some supposedly permanent way from the fabric of beingness or manifest reality.

We must begin the process of worldview transformation by fully accounting for the degree to which these deep-seated, underlying metaphysical assumptions have shaped – *and continue to shape* – our worldview and endeavors, even if, at the conscious level, we have separated ourselves from the religious systems that originally transmitted said assumptions and made ourselves into *secular* people. The world-negating, anthropocentric metaphysical assumptions in question continue to determine the nature of our science and scholarship.

World-negating paradigms necessarily render nonrelational teleologies (e.g., the human person alone *ascends*, whether in a religious or materialistic *mythos*). Teleologies arising from a world-embracing, relational paradigm will seek not a way *out* (i.e., to escape life), but a profound and meaningful way *in*. This is to say that a relational worldview seeks always to move more fully and profoundly *toward* rather than *away from* Life in its totality; it seeks to move ever more deeply into the vast expanse of interbeing, which is in essence a unity that is marked precisely by its particularities. Mary Oliver (2016) gestured toward this paradigm when, reflecting on the transition of death, she wrote: "May I stay forever in the stream" (p. 4). Such a profound assent to Life is part of the necessary ground for engendering cultural and religious systems that pursue the ultimate welfare of every being, of the *whole*, rather than just the immediate subjective agent (i.e., the human intellect which inherits and co-constructs a given view).

Relational Leadership and Metaphysical Relationality

Whether in a religious or secular context, leadership intended to be transformational with reference to the most pressing issues presently faced by the human species (and, by extension, all earthly species) must arise from and take part in precisely this fundamental shift of worldview. This proposal of *conversion* and *reclamation* might also provide an additional valence of meaning to the concept of relational leadership. As explained by Mary Uhl-Bien (2006), this relatively recent category in leadership theory has been utilized primarily to describe two modes of observation and analysis: (a) "an entity perspective that focuses on identifying attributes of individuals as they engage in interpersonal relationships," and (b) "a relational perspective that views leadership as a process of social construction through which certain understandings of leadership come about and are given privileged ontology." It is the second expression of relational leadership that I am concerned with in the context of the present work. Holmberg (2000) described this relational approach as "an opportunity to focus on processes in which both the actor and the world around him or her are created in ways that either expand or contract the space of possible action." What I am advocating for is precisely this kind of conscious, co-creative shift of process, but at the most foundational level of worldview structure. The means of doing so should be conceptualized as both systemic (especially with regard to discourse, communal ritual, and other reinforcing socio-cultural patterns) and experiential (i.e., as necessitating an integral shift of mentality, which over time expresses the transformative actuality of the shift in question through direct, felt, immediate perception). The latter will be explored briefly at the end of this article.

The needful (and unavoidable) "process of social construction" referred to by Uhl-Bien (2006) is something to be optimally navigated through intentionally shaped instructive and formational models that invite communities and individuals, in a fully transparent and participatory manner, into practices, modes of discourse, and learning that consciously shift the foundational terms and assumptions constituting their prior inherited (in the present case, *reductionistic*) worldviews. The question of worldview is not something that has hitherto been substantially examined in leadership studies, and I would argue that, without seriously assessing this underlying foundation out of which all leadership is necessarily and inexorably shaped, no fully lucid accounting of leadership – past, present, or future – can be given. By *worldview* here I mean to indicate a conscious and unconscious, conditioned set of fundamental assumptions, perceptive orientations, and interpretive lenses that determine one's mental framing, understanding, and experience of the world and one's role within it.

As Valk et al. (2011), have rightly pointed out, a concrete framing and analysis of worldview is something that requires an interdisciplinary approach. In the context of religious studies, the examination of worldview is explicitly foundational to the entire field of inquiry. I would argue, however, that worldview and the particularities of its structure in a given cultural environment are equally fundamental to any field that aims to more deeply understand and improve socio-cultural systems and dynamics. But what seems ultimately most significant in the context of leadership is not to merely analyze and account for worldview as a *prior* and an often overlooked, determinative factor in human dynamics – that is certainly needful, but is only the first step. What seems most crucial is to *operationalize* that critical apparatus into a consciously relational, strategic set of actionable techniques to alter the inherited worldview frame that has rendered the lethal socio-cultural problems that an endeavor like relational leadership should wish to help correct – and to do this by carefully and intentionally replacing or transmuting determinative elements within that inherited worldview frame.

More specifically, relational leadership – and leadership in general – cannot be soundly conceived or adequately undertaken apart from both a careful examination of worldview and a relational methodology to *turn* or alter, where necessary, a given worldview structure *toward actualizing the highest possible good for the greatest number of entities*. Since worldview determines human outlook and behavior, it follows that it must necessarily inhibit or suppress some aims of a given human pursuit, while nurturing or advancing others. Thus, if we understand the stakes and take seriously the problems facing us, we will have to begin to look toward worldview *conversion* and *curation* – not in a manipulative manner, but in a manner that is fully consensual and transparently participatory, that partakes of an organic wholing process experienced by each participant through established techniques and practices. Leaders, then, must above all endeavor to equip individuals with precisely such tools or *spiritual technologies*.

This of course implies not only analysis, but *practicum*. As endeavors originally grown from the soil-bed of reductionistic Western thought and discourse, critical fields and apparatuses – whether leadership studies or any other – must find a way to move beyond the boundaries of the worldview frame that has birthed and hitherto contained them – beyond the metaphysics of exclusion and duality, into a metaphysics of inclusion and multiplicity – and to become active agents of that most needful *metánoia*.

Communitas as "Beloved Community"

"Beloved Community" As Animistic Ontology

In various progressive Christian contexts, and particularly in the Episcopal Church in the United States, the moniker *Beloved Community* has recently been employed as an alternative designation for the *Kingdom of God*, or, *Kingdom of Heaven*. The phrase Beloved Community was in fact coined around the turn of the 20th century by the American idealist philosopher, Josiah Royce and was later popularized to some degree by Martin Luther King, Jr. and Thích Nhất Hanh. As Royce (Parker & Pratt, 2022) articulated it, the ideal of the Beloved Community is, in broad summary, a continuously widening sphere of relational embrace that takes a kind of supernal *loyalty* to and for all beings or persons as its central guiding ideal – what Royce called *loyalty to loyalty*: "In practice, the formula of loyalty to loyalty demands that one's moral and intellectual sphere become ever broader."

In my own estimation, this ultimately implies an embrace of *all entities* as conscious participants in a metaphysically unified *communitas* (in both of the primary senses in which this term has been employed by anthropologists, namely, to designate the *spirit* of a given community, and to signify a communal context in which all persons are treated as equal, as well as in its metaphysical sense as a *communion* of fundamentally spiritual agents). As previously noted, *persons* here refers to *all beings*, or all conscious agents, since all beings are, properly speaking, *persons*, and other-than-human persons enjoy the same ontological status as human ones.

Royce (Parker & Pratt, 2022), a student of Buddhist thought, seems to have intended Beloved Community to imply a shared project of mutual unfoldment toward the individual and collective realization of both relative and absolute truths. (With regard to the latter, Royce was an objective idealist, so here we must speak in terms of the *Ground of Being* or an absolute, primordial consciousness to which all pursuit of truth ultimately refers.) In this capacity, the model can facilitate and encompass, in a panentheistic fashion, a nondual, simultaneous, and equal embrace of both the unitary and the particular. The *Ideal Beloved Community*, as Royce referred to it, can also be understood as gesturing toward an eschatological vision in which all beings are finally brought to perfect freedom and illumination – what in Christian theology would be called *deification* (*théōsis*), not merely as a project of the individual, but in reference to a *participatory* eschatology aimed at *apokatástasis*: the ultimate wholing or unification of all things. In Mahāyāna Buddhist terms, this could be readily described as the ultimate realization of the mission of the *bodhisattva*, when at last all beings are enlightened and no obfuscated or deluded instantiations of consciousness any longer labor under the core delusion of duality, and thus beings no longer *wander* in the endless suffering and confusion of *samsāra*.

Pushed to its fullest logical extent, the Ideal Beloved Community, as *communitas*, signifies the totality of the relational matrix or the *great family of being*. It is precisely from this position or worldview orientation that relational leadership can potentially move into its own proper fullness as well: by orienting itself from within a felt and consciously inhabited landscape of reciprocal interspecial relationality.

Resurrecting Great Pan

A friend recently shared with me what is apparently a colloquial truism in the field of architecture: that in each challenge or question there is always one *right* answer and an indefinite number of *best* answers, and the latter is always the more difficult to access. It is the former, however, that essentially underlies our whole approach to life and critical analysis in Western societies. We tend to assume or pursue a singular, *correct* answer to everything we are faced with, while in reality Nature as a whole, apart from the human egoic construct, expresses herself much more through flow, novelty, and multiplicity. As Heraclitus is said to have put it: *Panta rhei*: All flows.

We might call to mind here Newton's vision of sitting on the seashore, imagining before him all the seemingly infinite varieties of Nature, and affirming to himself, in a moment of truly remarkable anthropocentric hubris, that *all* the manifold expressions of Nature will someday be known, fully grokked, perfectly quantified and explained by the rational faculties of the human mind – each mechanistic entity with its own *right* answer, the all-encompassing rational explanation of its existence and the key to all its hidden dimensions just waiting to be perfectly and inevitably grasped by human agents.

Relatedly, White (1967) also points to a misguided teleology endemic to Western thinking, and again attributes this to a Judeo-Christian worldview long embraced by the West: "Our daily habits of action, for example, are dominated by an implicit faith in perpetual progress which was unknown either to Greco-Roman antiquity or to the Orient. It is rooted in, and is indefensible apart from, Judeo-Christian teleology" (p. 1205). This myth of endless progress can be rightly characterized as a process of *man made God*: the human agent elevated to cosmic center.

When Plutarch's (1st century B.C./1936) *On the Failure of Oracles* hauntingly declared, "Great Pan is dead!" (p. 419), the *mythos* of an ensouled cosmos populated by a vast multiplicity of immanent divine powers and guided by responsibility to a reciprocity that honored and upheld a collective *telos* was symbolically severed. As James Hillman (1989) summarized, "nature had [then] become deprived of its creative voice....What had had soul, lost it: or lost was the psychic connection with nature....Nature no longer spoke to us – or we could no longer hear" (p. 97). The inevitable long-range outcome of this severance, Hillman continued, is that Nature can then be "controlled by the will of the new God, man, modeled in the image of Prometheus or Hercules, creating from it and polluting in it without a troubled conscience."

John Moriarty (2007), an historian of Western ideas, has rightly pointed out that the will to reduction, excessive quantification, and domination has long found a ready justification, if not a precedent, in our chosen religious texts, for example, the mandate to *subdue* and *have dominion over* everything on the Earth, found in the Book of Genesis (Genesis 1:26–28; cf. also Moriarty, 2007). Hence, mechanistic material science must dissect (and subjugate or kill) in order to unveil a single "correct" answer about life, and can only imagine dominion and negation as the needful means to attaining that answer, thus creating a paradigm of division, or, *diábolos* (*to throw apart, divide*) as opposed to a path of wholeness, or, *symbolos* (*to cast together, unite*). One could easily lament that Goethe's model of scientific inquiry was not more widely considered in the eighteenth century and beyond, with its holistic and fundamentally relational task of observation in *authentic wholeness*, toward knowledge of *diversity in unity* through conscious – perhaps meditative – participation (cf. Barfield, 1988, pp. 137–141).

It is hardly surprising that much if not all of our contemporary technology is built on the premise of seeking one *correct*, quantifiable, and optimally efficient answer to every question, task, or challenge that might present itself to the human agent. Artificial intelligence and its attendant eschatology of a digital *singularity*, as promoted by technologists like Ray Kurzweil, is perhaps the most charged and salient example for our time (cf. *The Singularity is Nearer*, 2024). We find ourselves now facing the very bizarre possibility that the legacy of hard dualism that has to this point thoroughly determined the course of Western socio-cultural development, strategy, and organization – and, increasingly, by virtue of colonialism and economic globalism, the course of those same things in cultural contexts throughout much of the rest of the world – could become permanently instantiated in a vast, systemic artificial structure of decision-making that we increasingly surrender our own will and agency to. What a supreme irony it would be to in the end surrender our agency to a construct of our own making – a god of our own design, as it were – which, at its foundation, is little more than a disembodied instantiation of the root cause of many of our most destructive tendencies.

But it is still possible to build a worldview, an ethics, an aesthetic, a ritual, and communal life out of the *perfection of imperfection*, the dynamism of organic potential, rather than the presumptive ability to quantify – and, attendantly, rule over or dominate – everything we come into contact with. That would be a collective first step back into the visionary light of *communitas*, of the Beloved Community as I understand it. The Japanese principle of *wabi-sabi* provides both a practical example and a metaphor for how a cultural group might consciously honor, hold in awareness, and align with the irreducibly open and dynamic nature of Life through an integrated, nondualistic process of socio-cultural construction aimed at wholeness. A foundational *conversion* (*metánoia*) of this kind would be tantamount to resurrecting great Pan: in Hillman's terms, a casting off of the Herculean ideal and a reclamation of the Panic (animistic) ideal, in which the human agent once more intuitively understands him- or herself within the context of a vast web of relationality, one node of being in a *Phýsis* that once more lives and speaks. And this neither requires nor implies anachronistic fantasy of any kind.

The reductionistic, alienated way of thinking, perceiving, and being that has characterized the Western cultural experiment to this point (along with the vast majority of its projects) has clearly led us to where we now collectively find ourselves as a species: at the proverbial precipice, holding the very real possibility that our shared human legacy on this planet might, in the final estimation, turn out to be one of confusion, folly, and destruction. As I write this, the world appears to be on the brink of thermonuclear war, with the International Science and Security Board, via the *Bulletin of the Atomic Scientists* (2025), proclaiming that the world is now "the closest to global catastrophe it has ever been." The nonprofit group of global scientists and leaders has characterized the present year as "a moment of historic danger," setting the famous *Doomsday Clock* at ninety seconds to midnight, the closest to midnight (i.e., totalizing catastrophic destruction) it has ever been set at, citing not only "ominous trends" in global politics and increased militarism, but also the previous calendar year being, globally, the "hottest year on record," as well as the rapid, unchecked development of highly disruptive technologies, such as artificial intelligence (Science and Security Board, 2025). The crucial choice of our age can therefore be nothing less than a paradigmatic one – in other words, one of worldview.

How do we lead – and articulate models of leadership – in a manner that fundamentally problematizes, undermines, and eventually reverses the course of the reductionistic waters we have hitherto been swimming in, while at the same time building (or reclaiming) a genuinely life-giving, relational worldview that has the capacity to carry us – and all beings – toward wisdom, mutual wholeness, greater flourishing, and ever deeper, more transformational encounters with beauty and ultimacy?

This question necessarily guides us to the matter of *praxis*. With the aim of helping to inspire a foundational shift toward an integrated metaphysics of relationality, what follows are a few provisional suggestions for how we might begin to practically approach that needful worldview conversion – both in ourselves as individuals and in the relational contexts we inhabit – to attempt to co-create, in conscious interbeing, something akin to the Beloved Community as I have summarily (re-)defined it in this chapter.

Practicum: Some Tools of Transmutation

It is a perennial truism that human beings need effectual, actionable *techniques* (from the Greek, *tékhnē*) in order to legitimately and sustainably transform our minds. *Tékhnē* refers to an art, craft, technique, or skill set. For our purposes here, we could conceive of a legitimately fruitful *tékhnē* as an anti-mechanistic, anti-reductional methodology, representing an entry into a constellation of practical skills that can equip us to intuit and directly experience the connections inherent to a maximally relational metaphysics. These techniques should equip us for lucid seeing, for wisdom, and perhaps ultimately for illumination or deification (*théōsis*). It is only with minds genuinely transformed toward greater wholeness and conscious interbeing that we can hope to aid in healthfully transforming the world around us. In theological terms, this transformation – both inner and outer – must come in the manner of a *participatory eschatology*: a realized Beloved Community that we as conscious agents co-create in and with the particularities (individual souls, *loci* of consciousness) of the vast web of beingness. We cannot realize anything close to the ideal of the Beloved Community if we, each and all, do not pursue and *actualize* this kind of totalizing transmutation, beginning with its interior components.

I will use a poetic offering of Gary Snyder's as a framework for very briefly suggesting some possible practices and modes of contemplative reflection pertaining to the proposed mode of worldview conversion. *Conversion* here, in addition to the Greek word it translates in Christian scripture, *metánoia*, as described above, could also call to mind for us the Latin phrase used by Benedictines: *conversatio morum, conversion of life*. This indicates the integral depth of alchemical transmutation required to truly move into the psychic or spiritual landscape of metaphysical relationality. Snyder (1974) writes: "To climb these coming crests/one word to you, to/you and your children://*stay together/learn the flowers/go light*" (p. 86).

Stay Together

In the context of metaphysical relationality or *res anima*, *stay together* implies more than simply togetherness in human community; it also means sustained togetherness in and with the entire family of being. This finds ready expression in participation in the agentic web of a particular localized landscape – wherever one happens to find oneself in a natural setting.

The preliminary practice of approaching the Land and all entities in a given landscape *as if* they were ensouled, or, real conscious agents, is a good way to begin to cultivate a gradual, authentic return to this primal, foundationally intuitive way of beholding the world and situating ourselves within it. Even if it seems quite foreign at first, making a small effort regularly in this kind of practice can go a long way toward a gradual but sustained, reclamatory shift of perception.

I strongly recommend reinforcing this with the practice of making offerings on the Land: leaving natural gifts for the other-than-human spirits or consciousnesses who inhabit the place where you live. In many animistic traditions, simple rituals of this kind are a standard daily practice, because it is understood that they help to maintain good, harmonious, and reciprocal contact with our other-than-human relations, and this in turn keeps us all – human and other-than-human alike – on the same proverbial page, moving together in the direction of flourishing.

I approach this in my own daily practice in three ways:

1. Through maintaining permanent outdoor shrines where I regularly make offerings of prayer, song, flowers, tea, etc.
2. Through making offerings (e.g., of dried tea leaves or tobacco, which I always carry with me) on any landscape I happen to visit, to make a relational connection with the spirits of that place, celebrate their beauty, and pay them appropriate homage.
3. Less frequently, particularly when I encounter a landscape that I feel a deep instinctual bond with, I will make a small, circular gathering of stones and decorate it or place inside it things like flowers and other brightly colored natural curios found in the landscape (each of which I've first asked permission to gather as offerings), then offer some prayer and song to the spirits of that place.

I aim to regularly give something of aesthetic value to the localized environments in which I find myself, to leave in each place a bit more beauty. This has always seemed to me like a good approach to life in general, and it is certainly good animistic devotional practice. To bring more beauty and blessing into the vast ocean of being is a simple but worthy aim, and one which gradually reconditions the mind to a different way of understanding the cosmos. Partly this means awakening to a cosmos filled with an immeasurable number of conscious persons. As Joseph Campbell and Moyers (1998) once observed: "You can address anything as a 'thou' and you can feel the change in your psychology as you do it. The ego that sees a 'thou' is not the same ego that sees an 'it.' Your whole psychology changes when you address things as an 'it.'"

Learn the Flowers

Another practice I recommend experimenting with is something that has occasionally been labeled, *natura divina,* after the ancient Benedictine practice of carefully and contemplatively reading sacred text known as, *lectio divina. Natura divina* involves the practitioner in approaching the natural world around him or her as a kind of sacred *text,* and the same general steps anciently employed in *lectio divina* are adapted to the practice of very closely engaging things in the natural environment that might draw the attention of the practitioner. This is my own version of the practice:

Step One: *auditio* (*listening*) and *lectio* (*reading*): Allow intuition and the larger intelligence of the environment to guide you in being drawn in or selected by a being in the landscape around you. It is important that you allow another (nonhuman) person in the landscape to choose you, rather than you choosing someone. This *someone* might be a particular tree or plant, for instance, or a creek, a mushroom, a bit of lichen, or a bird. Once you have been chosen or *drawn in*, move toward that being and move as closely with your body as you can. Hone in on a small portion of the entity that has drawn your attention and look, feel, smell, and engage with it very acutely with all the senses you can reasonably (and safely) apply in this instance. Focus with the totality of sensory power you possess and *read* the being before you as carefully and as closely as possible – *not analytically*, but with a totally open, clear mind and a receptive heart. As Mary Oliver (2016) observed, "attention is the beginning of devotion" (p. 4). It is also the beginning of wisdom.

Step Two: *meditatio* (*meditation*): Engage the intellective mind now and reflect for a few minutes on what this being might have to *say* to you. Obviously, one is not expecting human language to emerge from the entity in question, but we are referencing here a much subtler, metaphoric speech. What might this sacred being have to offer you in this moment, particularly by way of wisdom and insight? Once you have a sense of something worthy of reflection, take a moment to distill that down to one, two, or three words, a bit like a *mantra*. Sit quietly for a time now and slowly repeat that word or short phrase quietly in the heart. If you like, you can link its inward repetition to the rising and falling of the breath. Breathe slowly and deeply, relax, and let the whole of your being sink into the repetition of this sacred word or phrase and the essence of the transmission it signifies.

Step Three: *oratio* (*speech*): Briefly formulate a few words in your mind that you would like to offer to this living being who has drawn you into a deep connection, in gratitude for his or her presence, invitation, sharing, and transmission of insight. Quietly, but aloud, offer this extemporaneous prayer of thanks and praise from the heart to the being you've been communing with.

Step Four: *contemplatio* (*contemplation*): In this final stage of the practice, which is the most open, fully receptive, unprogrammed portion, allow the mind to completely relax and disengage. Do not pay attention to thoughts but simply let them arise and pass away in their own organic rhythm. As St. Benedict (530 c./2001) implored at the start of his Rule, "listen with the ear of your heart." You have allowed yourself to be drawn in by this beautiful being, you have received a gift, you have offered thanks in return for that gift, and now it is time to simply sit in quietude, in natural *communitas*. Do not contrive anything, visualize anything, or follow ideational threads. This is the time to simply *be*, in the totalizing presence of pure awareness.

Go Light

The final practice I will offer here is related to the last stage of the previous practice, but in this case it is to be cultivated on its own, without all the other steps involved in *natura divina*. I will be a bit more fulsome here in describing this particular approach of entrance into the state of *pure contemplation* or perfectly open awareness.

Sit in a comfortable place, in a relaxed but upright posture, and begin to breathe slowly and deeply, with each in-breath drawing the air all the way down below the navel, so that the stomach naturally expands gently on each inhalation. Elongate the exhalation, so that it is a bit longer and more drawn out than the inhalation.

Allow the mind to rest in total relaxed alertness, with the eyes opened gently and their focus softened, gazing at empty space. Let your mind be wide open, spacious as the sky, in total embrace of all that exists in this and every world, rejecting nothing and clinging to nothing. Don't grasp at anything that might arise in thought, feeling, or perception, and don't push anything away, either. As an old Tibetan phrase would have it: *Rest just so*. Let awareness behold itself, in silence and wonder.

In this practice we totally relax into embracing all that is, here and now, *exactly as it is*: not wishing to change something or reform ourselves or the external world in any way, but, just for this time, in the sanctioned space of contemplation, abandoning all striving, all notions of what should or shouldn't be. The inner commentary is released and allowed to unravel, so the practitioner may experience a truly natural state of being, without the overlay of mental noise that normally accompanies, perturbs, and distorts the raw perception of awareness.

Such contemplation marks the advent of genuine equanimity, and true equanimity is a sign of developing wisdom, of insight into the nature of things. It allows natural healing to find a course, often in ways we aren't conscious of. It restores and replenishes the human vessel for the work of compassionate transformation – for the life, blessing, wholeness, and liberation of every being.

References

Barfield, O. (1988). *Saving the appearances: A study in idolatry*. Harcourt Brace.
Benedict, S. (2001). The rule of Benedict: Prologue. In L. J. Doyle (Trans.), *Saint Benedict's rule for monasteries*. Order of Saint Benedict, Liturgical Press (Original work published 530 c.). https://archive.osb.org/rb/text/rbejms1.html#pro

Campbell, J., & Moyers, B. (1988). *Episode 3: Joseph Campbell and the power of myth* [TV mini-series]. https://billmoyers.com/content/ep-3-joseph-campbell-and-the-power-of-myth-the-first-storytellers-audio/

Feuerbach, L. (1989). *The essence of Christianity* (G. Eliot, Trans.). Prometheus Books.

Hallowell, A. I. (1960). Ojibwa ontology, behavior, and world view. In S. Diamond (Ed.), *Culture in history: Essays in honor of Paul Radin* (pp. 20–21). Columbia University Press.

Hillman, J. (1989). *A blue fire*. Harper & Row.

Holmberg, R. (2000). Organizational learning and participation: Some critical reflections from a relational perspective. *European Journal of Work and Organizational Psychology*, *9*(2), 181. https://doi.org/10.1080/135943200397932

Kurzweil, R. (2024). *The singularity is nearer*. Viking.

Moriarty, J. (2007). Seeking to walk beautifully on the Earth. [Sound Recording]. *One evening in Eden*. The Lilliput Press.

Oliver, M. (2016). *Upstream: Collected essays*. Penguin Press.

Parker, K., & Pratt, S. (2022, Spring). *Josiah Royce, The Stanford Encyclopedia of Philosophy* (E. N. Zalta, ed.). https://plato.stanford.edu/archives/spr2022/entries/royce/

Plutarch. (1936). *Moralia Vol. V*. (F. C. Babbitt, Trans.). Loeb Classical Library. (Original work published 1st B.C.)

Uhl-Bien, M. (2006). Relational leadership theory: Exploring the social processes of leadership and organizing. *The Leadership Quarterly*, *17*(6), 654–676. https://doi.org/10.1016/j.leaqua.2006.10.007

Science and Security Board, Bulletin of the Atomic Scientists (2025). 2025 doomsday clock statement (J. Mecklin, Ed.). https://thebulletin.org/doomsday-clock/current-time/

Snyder, G. (1974). *Turtle island*. New Directions.

Valk, J., Belding, S., Crumpton, A. Harter, N., & Reams, J. (2011). Worldviews and leadership: Thinking and acting the bigger Picture. *Journal of Leadership Studies*, *5*(2), 54–63. https://doi.org/10.1002/jls.20218

White, L. (1967). The historical roots of our ecologic crisis. *Science*, *55*(3767), 1205. https://doi.org/10.1126/science.155.3767.1203

Part 3

Poetic Response – REWILD: Woodspell

Danny Smith

Deep in the woods, a poet prays
To overhear the wild winds' ways,
To dance like trees on gentle days,
And wear on her sleeve the black sun's rays.
Nearby her third eye, the taut thread frays
Unveiling a portal, an entryway:

The enchanted woods look the same
As the forest she came from,
Where she hides from sin and is made to pretend
That the savage within is shameful.
But this version – unprocessed, ungoverned, uncharted –
Where the guarded parts of mind and heart roam free,
Realizes a primordial dream.

Our poet, barefoot, moves with certainty.
Certainly, this familiar wood will greet her warmly…
The clear skies turn stormy and the wind turns violent;
The thunder is silent but looming. Frightening.
And there's lightning striking the grounds.
Still, somehow she's at ease.

A Great Oak tree stands tall in the middle of it all,
The air smells of close rainfall,
But the wildlife don't scatter.
As a matter of fact, the untamed terrain is home
To unknown poems of strange life forms
That circumvent norms and uniformity.
Normally, normalcy blends in.

Our poet, now drenched, strides forward
With strength against forceful winds,
Determined to slow her roll
And break the hold civility has on expression.
The second she reads the grooves of the tree,
Its canopy blinks and drinks up the rain.

What remains was pre-written.

She's given a vision of a wild world where
Pain is painful
And tears are salty
And love wounds
And you can't get it wrong as long as you live.

Deep in the woods, beyond the tension,
is a suspension of comprehension,
And even more important,
The desire to make meaning is dismantled;
And chaos is handled by letting it resolve
free from a goal of peace, or taming the beast
to appease human needs.

Our poet, redeemed, notes:
"What an interesting way to spell/resist/."

Index

www.ingramcontent.com/pod-product-compliance
Lightning Source LLC
Chambersburg PA
CBHW060240220326
41598CB00027B/3994

9 781805 925002